Politics, Inequality and the Australian Welfare State After Liberalisation

Politics, Inequality and the Australian Welfare State After Liberalisation

Ben Spies-Butcher

ANTHEM PRESS

Anthem Press
An imprint of Wimbledon Publishing Company
www.anthempress.com

This edition first published in UK and USA 2025
by ANTHEM PRESS
75–76 Blackfriars Road, London SE1 8HA, UK
or PO Box 9779, London SW19 7ZG, UK
and
244 Madison Ave #116, New York, NY 10016, USA

First published in the UK and USA by Anthem Press in 2023

British Library Cataloguing-in-Publication Data
A catalogue record for this book is available from the British Library.

Library of Congress Control Number: 2025931874
A catalog record for this book has been requested.

ISBN-13: 978-1-83999-532-3 (Pbk)
ISBN-10: 1-83999-532-7 (Pbk)

Cover Credit: Crowd rally image by Sharon Hickey and courtesy of the New
South Wales Nurses and Midwives' Association

This title is also available as an e-book.

CONTENTS

TABLES AND FIGURES

Table

Figures

ACKNOWLEDGEMENTS

Books are never truly sole authored. That is particularly the case for this book, which is built around collaborative research and lessons learned through collective action.

The key concepts developed in the book were built together with my colleague Adam Stebbing and my friend and comrade Gareth Bryant. Thank you also to co-directors at the Australian Basic Income Lab – Troy Henderson and Elise Klein.

The ideas, cases and questions reflect the influence of two groups of intellectuals centred around Macquarie Sociology's critical theory and economic sociology and the radical insights of Political Economy at Sydney University. I owe a great debt to my colleagues at both and to the students at Macquarie University.

A particular thank you to many generous teachers and mentors, including Frank Stilwell, Gabrielle Meagher, Shaun Wilson, Pauline Johnson, Michael Fine, Ariadne Vromen, Susan St John, Michael Pusey, Ian Marsh and Anna Howe, all of whom directly informed aspects of this book through collaborations on earlier articles or commenting on drafts.

A big thank you to Jebaslin Hephzibah, Gomathy Ilammathe and Anthem Press for being so patient with this project.

I also owe an intellectual debt to those I've worked with in campaigns and policy discussions outside the academy, through Shelter, the Anti-Poverty Centre, the Edmund Rice Centre, ReconciliACTION, Council on the Ageing, Just Reinvest, Unions NSW, the Nurses and Midwives Association, the Centre for Policy Development, the Search Foundation, REDWatch, the Fabian Society and many more. Thank you to Michael Whaites and the Nurses' union for the use of the cover image.

Many of these conversations inside and outside the academy overlap friendships from politics, primarily through the Greens, but also with those in other parties with common goals. I cannot imagine this book without learning what I have from these comrades. A particular thank you to Damiya

Hayden and Mark Riboldi, with whom I discussed much of the content of the book.

Finally, to my family. My parents, Julie Spies and John Butcher, who taught me the importance of community and solidarity, and a healthy disrespect for experts alongside a passion for knowledge. And to my partner Sylvie Ellsmore. So much of what I have written we have done together and learned together. Thank you especially for patiently reading and editing the final drafts.

PRELUDE

On the 2nd of April 2019 Australia's Treasurer, Josh Frydenberg, rose in Federal Parliament to declare 'the Budget is back in the black and Australia is back on track' (Frydenberg 2019). It captured a strange obsession with economic accounting categories, which have taken on a mystical role in the Australian imagination, enamoured with the magic of the Budget Bottomline.

For years fiscal discipline has captivated Australia's political leaders. Each Labor government comes to office pledging not to spend more, either through deficits or taxes. Each Coalition government decries debt and deficit, instead creating Commissions of Audit to slash and burn an unaffordable welfare state.

The constant drum of fiscal responsibility lies at the heart of Australia's experience of neoliberalism. Not only have Australian governments accepted the need for balanced budgets (even if they struggle in practice to achieve them), they have also largely accepted a cap on taxation. The fiscal trade off that marked the long boom after the Second World War, where taxes rose to fund more generous social provision, has eroded. Instead, targeting, user payments and privatisation have sought to ration public dollars by integrating social policy into the market.

Frydenburg's celebrations proved pre-emptive. The forecast surplus never appeared. The projections were already looking wobbly by the end of 2019. In 2020, they were blown apart. As Covid-19 swept through China and Europe, long forgotten health regulations suddenly came into force, and the rules of fiscal discipline disappeared.

As Australia, and the world, briefly switched from prioritising budgets to prioritising health, economic rules, too, appeared to melt. Public spending rose as interest rates fell. Poverty and homelessness fell even as the economy contracted. The abstract numbers of conventional economic coverage were briefly replaced by the immediacy of social needs and the essential workers providing care.

Then almost as suddenly, austerity returned. Programs ended. Poverty and homelessness increased. After a brief crisis of faith, fiscal discipline was restored, loudly supported by both sides of politics. The Reserve Bank reneged on its promise to get wages moving, and began increasing interest rates. The world made by liberalisation remained.

Hopes that Covid-19 would break the hold of neoliberalism have receded. Instead, it was a new Labor government, again committed to fiscal rectitude, that delivered a surplus, bolstered by surging profits and prices, as real wages fell.

However, the remarkable experience of the pandemic tells us something of the possibilities of Australia's liberalised welfare state. It suggests fiscal discipline is as much a political as an economic reality. It revealed how much we continue to rely on each other, rather than on abstract markets. That even in the most difficult times we can afford a more equal world.

Fiscal rules dissolved in quite specific ways. 'Off-budget' spending across the Organization for Economic Cooperation and Development (OECD) matched traditional budget spending. Fiscal support seemed targeted to preventing a collapse of house prices as much as helping people manage lockdown. Payments looked strangely like a basic income.

How do we understand the policy and politics of our (post-)liberalised world? Looking back to how Australia negotiated neoliberalism – and more specifically, the processes of liberalisation – we can see how the politics of the welfare state was reconstructed. That shift does not necessarily follow the contours of conventional stories, which tell, either, of the death of equality or the triumph of productivity. Instead, liberalisation has changed how public and private finance are contested and, potentially, how more equitable policies can still emerge.

Australia's obsession with constraining state spending can give the appearance of a small state. Yet, a closer look reveals a slight of hand. The state has not been shrinking, instead liberalisation has seen the *measures* of public finance constrained.

In the face of strong democratic demands to maintain social protection, a *dual* welfare, delivered through the tax system, has grown. Hidden from conventional spending measures, dual welfare sees the state distributing resources and creating incentives, just as it does with conventional spending. Hidden from proper oversight, the dual welfare state supports a broad constituency of beneficiaries. However, these better-off citizens are separated out from those receiving more explicit and stigmatised forms of support.

More egalitarian measures have also advanced, but again in forms that hide their fiscal scale. Progressive reformers often converted dual welfare to fund new programs and structured spending as 'investment'. These *hybrid* strategies expand the state's capacity to insulate people from risk, while also mimicking elements of market competition. By mimicking the market, fiscal power can expand with less resistance, militating the constraints of austerity. And by appealing to the supposed 'neutrality' of economic reason and accounting categories, hybrid policies can at once assert universal needs and challenge the biases of market economics. However, these less visible strategies also tended to erode the social support needed to challenge market rule.

Both dual welfare and hybrid welfare reflect the technocratic nature of Australia's 'economic rationalism', yet their differences suggest a deeper politics. Egalitarian policies consistently advanced alongside political claims to recognise common social needs and to have those needs universally met. Only once political claims were established were hybrid strategies effective at overcoming fiscal constraints. Dual welfare tended to win out, under both Labor and Coalition governments, when needs were not recognised, or not deemed universal. Dual policies were then sustained by growing private interests.

The organisation of politics has changed alongside the tools of policymaking. While the welfare state developed through struggles in the industrial economy, increasingly social policy is contested within the welfare state itself. Basic social needs for homes, health and care increasingly underpin growing financial markets and the emerging 'asset economy' funded by dual welfare. Those involved in the work of care and education have proven the most effective allies of equality by building alliances to assert social rights. Battles over equality and profit are increasingly struggles over and within social policy, fought between an ethic of care and the logic of finance.

Rather than simply reversing liberalisation, it is by recognising this shift in politics and looking within the relations of care that a different and more equal welfare state is most likely to emerge.

Chapter 1

POLITICS RECONSTRUCTED

The welfare state is not what it was. Decades of liberalisation have transformed how governments provide social policy and how citizens experience social protection. Services that were once the sole domain of public sector workers are now run by non-profit, even for-profit, firms. Payments that were once straightforward to access and understand are increasingly conditional and stingy, or require expert advice to invest in complex financial products. Even within the public sector, new public management and competition policy have created markets within the state, transforming the public sector into something that looks much more like the private sector.

Yet for all this transformation, predictions of a crisis of the welfare state have proven premature. Across the OECD, and particularly in Australia, the welfare state is on the march. The growth is both quantitative and qualitative. Through the height of neoliberalism social spending grew, and even before Covid-19, had moved closer to the OECD average (OECD 2022c). Areas of social need, such as child, disability and elder care, are supported in ways they were not before. And even though inequality overall has increased, social spending has also become more redistributive, doing more to ease inequalities than in the past (Whiteford 2017).

Much of this change is structural. As populations age there is more need for pensions and healthcare, two of the biggest components of the welfare state. As family structures change and women enter paid work in greater numbers, demands for paid care expand and parenting payments increase. Welfare states redistribute more when our initial market incomes are less equal, as happens when labour and capital markets are deregulated. However, deliberate policy also played a role. New programs have been introduced, and existing spending increased under both Labor and Coalition governments.

This book attempts to understand the varied politics of liberalisation in Australia and understand how to change it. Of course, we can exaggerate difference. Australia never developed a comprehensive welfare state equivalent to those in Europe, or even the UK. We have always had sizeable private sectors in health, education and care and relatively low social benefits. Social policy and the politics of welfare have changed since the 1980s, however less dramatically than many imagine. Liberalisation has not meant the end of the state, but the expansion of markets alongside welfare.

The analysis in this book follows an earlier political economy tradition that understands the welfare state as a form of social compromise between capitalism and democracy (O'Connor 2017; Offe 2018; Streeck 2014; Esping-Andersen 2015). From this perspective, liberalisation is generally understood as a winding back of that compromise. Liberalisation was driven by a political project, neoliberalism, to limit democratic state action. It imposed hard limits, or fiscal constraints, on the economic size of the state (see Streeck 2014, 72–77), and delegated economic decisions from democratic politics to technical experts (Mattei 2022). I suggest this is an important, but partial, understanding. Alongside the imposition of fiscal constraints on welfare expansion, people have continued to resist the insecurities and inequalities produced by market economies, and this social resistance continues to shape policy outcomes.

While pressures of fiscal constraint and social resistance are common across the OECD, Australia's response is somewhat distinct. Our welfare state has more thoroughly embraced the logic of competition. Unlike much of Europe 'social' questions are invariably referred to the 'Productivity' Commission. And unlike the more overt politics of the New Right in the United States and the United Kingdom this has not been simply 'anti-state', rather Australia is, to use Michael Pusey's famous phrase, 'economically rationalist' (1991). Liberalisation has been far more technocratic than overtly political.

Technocracy, of course, is often a tactic of those opposed to the democratisation of the economy (Mattei 2022). Australia's technocratic politics has driven unpopular privatisation and marketisation (McKenna 2000). But as austerity has confronted political pressure, it has also proved fertile ground for novel policy innovations. Caught between economic pressures to constrain state finances and democratic pressures to insulate people from inequality and insecurity Australia has favoured technical solutions.

Technocratic policy entails new forms of statecraft that shift how and where social policy is contested. Rather than only viewing neoliberalism advancing against a previous order, this book understands liberalisation as a process that reworks the terrain on which politics is contested, producing new patterns of insecurity, inequality and social protection.

Rarely is the state wound back. It is instead rolled out (Peck and Tickell 2002) and reorganised to imitate and enforce market structures. 'Choice' and 'self-reliance' advance through the expansion of *hidden* (Howard 1999, Morel et al. 2019) or *dual* (Stebbing and Spies-Butcher 2010) welfare. Fiscal support expands to assist largely middle-class households manage social risk through private providers. However, constructed primarily through concessional tax arrangements and regulatory impositions, the 'public' nature of finance is obscured and democratic scrutiny that might contest the distribution of benefits avoided.

Liberalisation has also seen *hybrid* policies that appear to extend social protection while mimicking elements of market competition (Spies-Butcher and Bryant 2024). *Hybrid* policies respond to democratic pressures, but avoid fiscal constraints by constructing public action in forms that mimic private markets, challenging and reorganising the boundaries of public and private finance in the process. Hybridity has the potential to make hidden welfare visible and dual welfare universal.

Australia's focus on technocratic governance and its role in pioneering many elements of Third Way governance have seen it develop a reputation for innovative and 'evidence-based', 'hybrid' policies (see esp. Fabian and Breunig 2018). Indeed, many of the policies examined here have been examined as exemplars of combining states and markets. I build on this literature. However, my analysis is also distinct in two respects. First, while most of the hybrid policy examples I examine are technically efficient, my focus is on the political circumstances and strategies that saw these models advance, while in similar policy domains much less egalitarian forms of dual welfare flourished.

Second, and relatedly, I understand hybridity as a solution to a political, as much as an economic, problem. Hybridity is born from the relationship between public accounting, social need and fiscal constraint that creates pressures for novel policy models. The blurring of boundaries between public and private finance are not simply technical solutions, rather hybridity creates political opportunities to reduce the inertia of austerity, which constrains social spending.

The most egalitarian features of recent social policy were won as political demands, even if their form reflects new modes of liberalised statecraft. The least egalitarian policies have not involved a withdrawal of the state either, but a remaking of state power in less visible and less egalitarian forms, allowing more visible public spending to be stigmatised.

The core of the book is a set of case studies selected to reflect what I see as the most important processes of liberalisation and to highlight differences in how these processes proceed in practice. By analysing how payments are targeted, services marketised and welfare financialised, it aims to understand opportunities to reshape outcomes.

The case studies aim to explain how sometimes means-testing creates poverty and stigma, as with JobSeeker, while at other times payments genuinely reduce poverty and create security, as with the aged pension; or why the marketisation of early education and care saw the rise and fall of ABC Learning, while a similarly marketised health insurance system, Medicare, is held up as an exemplar of public provision.

Across the examples explored in this book several common patterns emerge. Social protection only expands where organised social pressure makes social needs visible, forcing governments to protect citizens from these risks. Egalitarian policies overcame resistance from an increasingly pro-competition state through hybridity. Hybridity promotes competition alongside social protection, and appears to limit increases in state finance while simultaneously expanding the capacity of the state to protect citizens from risk. And egalitarian policies prove durable when they foster large constituencies and frame provision around universal needs.

The importance of organised political pressure appeals to universal values and building broad constituencies all echo earlier welfare state success (Esping-Andersen 1990; Baldwin 1990; Jacques and Noel 2018). However, the locus and dynamics of those movements have changed. Where social policy victories in the post–War Keynesian welfare state were largely the result of industrial struggle by (mostly male) workers, increasingly egalitarian success is the result of alliances built by the (primarily women) workers and citizens most directly engaged in care and welfare provision. Where welfare states were built using Keynesian tools that managed demand by separating public and private finance, liberalisation has increasingly given rise to hybrid models that subvert the discipline of austerity by socialising risk beyond the boundaries implied by measures of public finance. By understanding these dynamics I hope to not only explain Australian patterns of liberalisation but also inform strategies to change them.

From Keynesian Welfare to Neoliberal Austerity

Examining processes of change implicitly sets up a comparison between a previous order and the new order. Following broader social policy scholarship I understand this as a shift from a post–War Keynesian welfare state, which took the form of the 'wage earner' model in Australia (Castles 1985), and the emergence since the 1980s of neoliberalism (see Ramia 2020; Cahill and Konings 2017; Jessop 2018). Comparative scholarship sees this shift reflecting a change in the political dynamics of the welfare state (see Wren 2013; Thelen 2014). Powerful unions and social democratic parties initially drove an expansion of social spending (Korpi 2006). More recently business interests mobilised to tighten fiscal constraints and resist attempts to use social policy to respond to new democratic demands. Fiscal constraint creates a politics of 'permanent' (Pierson 1998) or 'enduring' (Jessop 2015) austerity.

The initial post-War years saw significant welfare state expansion in many countries alongside the growing intellectual and bureaucratic dominance of Keynesian economics. In Australia the Wartime Labor government created the powerful Ministry of Post-War Reconstruction to plan for a post-War economy. While the implementation of the plan was mixed, Labor expanded federal powers over key areas of the welfare state and implemented several important reforms, like the unemployment benefit, pharmaceutical benefits scheme and maternity payments (Watts 1980).

Post-War efforts to develop a formal welfare state were only modestly successful, and noticeably less successful than in Britain or northern Europe. However, Australia proved more open to Keynesian macroeconomic management (Smyth 1994), which sat comfortably alongside its existing 'national building' traditions (see MacIntyre 2015). Australia committed to achieving full employment in 1945 (Watts 1980, 177), and broadly retained this commitment until at least the mid-1970s.

Full employment was advanced through a model of industry protectionism, public works and migration restrictions. Workers' incomes rose through the ongoing, and increasingly dominant, role of centralised wage arbitration, where courts set wages, in part, by considering social needs. This combination of commitments, discussed further in the next chapter, became known as the 'Australian Settlement' (Kelly 2008) and provided the main features of Francis Castles' wage earners' welfare state (1985).

The limited welfare state that did develop reflected a 'wage earner' logic. Policy models that entrenched inequalities in other countries instead facilitated egalitarianism, at least amongst white, male wage earners, here. Australia used wage arbitration to build benefits into wages through occupational welfare that other countries fund through social welfare. Australia's flat-rate benefits were limited compared to more generous social insurance, but also more universal because they did not require past contributions (see Watts 1980; Castles 1985). Capital controls, state planning, public works and decent wages ensured most workers could gain secure tenure through home ownership, which lowered living costs and protected them from poverty in retirement (Castles 1997a). Even so this was no Eden, as the landmark Henderson Inquiry laid bare in the 1970s, levels of Indigenous, child and aged poverty were significant (Henderson 1975).

The lack of formal welfare state development provided space for private alternatives. After the High Court struck down Labor's attempts to nationalise healthcare, the Coalition introduced a scheme to support non-profit, private health insurance (Mendelson 1999). Australia's school education system developed a much larger role for non-public (especially Catholic) schools than in most comparable countries (see Thompson et al. 2019). Aged care, while limited, was largely provided by religious and benevolent organisations. Regulation was used to mitigate inequality in each of these areas, but governments also routinely offered financial support through the tax system (fiscal welfare), a mechanism that is radically less visible, accountable or equitable than government payments (see Titmuss 1965). Limited welfare state expansion produced modest public services where many people, especially single parents and First Nations people, remained excluded.

The regulatory commitments of this model came under increasing strain from the 1970s and by the late 1990s were largely dismantled. Changes to the global economic order, particularly the deregulation of exchange rates and the changing role of the international financial institutions, left Australia's model of protectionism vulnerable (Kelly 2008). Australia's reliance on imported capital and persistent current account deficits were seen as a source of economic vulnerability. The 'twin deficits theory' posited that these problems were made worse by government deficits (see Brittle 2009, 1–3), fostering the Australian variant of fiscal austerity.

Without the overt anti-statist rhetoric of Margaret Thatcher or Ronald Reagan, the nature of such policy change in Australia was potentially less clear. It gained coherence and visibility in part through the work of Michael Pusey, whose term, 'economic rationalism' (1991, 1993) evokes the reforms examined here as 'liberalisation'. Pusey's analysis emphasised the ideational and economic origins of reform, and the central role of state bureaucracies, especially the economic agencies like Treasury and Finance, in managing change.

Australia's economic rationalism was driven by a particularly 'pro-competition' state. In contrast to the historical emphasis on fostering solidarity, policymakers now assume fostering competition is self-evidently beneficial (see Productivity Commission 2016). The salience of competition and fiscal constraint as policy goals reinforce the power of economic arguments and economic agencies, while competition itself fosters individualism and rationalisation. However, in Australia this has not been as closely connected to attacking the redistributive role of the state. Within social policy this combination often meant extending competition and the logic of market exchange *alongside* the logic of redistribution via the state.

Liberalisation itself involved a reworking of the way states govern. Keynesian welfare states were largely built on a separation of 'public' and 'private' finance (Spies-Butcher and Bryant 2024). Public budgeting was organised to facilitate macroeconomic management, allowing governments to more easily identify the net stimulatory (or contractionary) impact of fiscal policy by tracing the movement of money across private and public sectors. In Australia, other elements of the wage-earner model complemented the macroeconomic focus of public budgeting. Arbitration played a macroeconomic as well as social function (Beggs 2015), and as did a variety of other price setting institutions (like the many collective purchase arrangements implemented by farmers).

The separation of public and private finance was not simply a technical device; it facilitated a political strategy, albeit one more successful in northern Europe. Each sphere became imbued with a different organisational logic. Public finance was understood to reflect social goals, determined via democratic processes. Private finance served competitive goals, determined by market prices (see Spies-Butcher and Bryant 2024). These distinct logics mirror Polanyi's (1957) distinction between state distribution and market contract as forms of economic integration.

Following Polanyi (Adereth 2020), welfare state theorists saw private finance organising the production and distribution of 'genuine commodities' according to market contract, while public finance organised the social reproduction of workers and their families according to state distribution. As Stephanie Mudge (2018) argues, the rise of the welfare state mirrors a shift in the organising strategies of left parties, which increasingly reflected the dominance of 'economic technicians' who sought to manage the state for social democratic ends.

Unsurprisingly, the separation and reorganisation of public and private finance created a strong correlation between the size of public spending (especially social spending) and social outcomes, like lower inequality and poverty. While public ownership remained an important goal, political mobilisation was increasingly focused on public finance, especially in social democracies.

Unions and left parties mobilised to advance social rights by expanding the fiscal size of the state. As Esping-Andersen (1990) demonstrated, this produced a clear relationship between the scale of social spending and organisation of the welfare state (and broader economy). Australia's wage-earner model focused on achieving social outcomes by 'other means'. Rather than primarily expanding state finance it also used state power to regulate market prices. This different starting point, as much as Labor political dominance in the 1980s and 1990s, helps explain the emphasis on hybridity.

Liberalisation, in this sense, focuses on constraining the overt fiscal reach of the state and extending the reach of competition. Within the welfare state, where overt retrenchment has proven politically difficult (Pierson 1998; Streeck and Thelen 2005), liberalisation reworked the boundaries of public and private finance. Competition Policy and central banking reforms reduced the ability for states to take advantage of their sovereign powers (see Lemoine 2017). Efficiencies created by socialising costs and integrating planning were now deemed unfair competition, and public providers were forced to pay market rates, often from market providers (Ranald 1995).

Public budgets themselves were remade, constructing social spending and public entitlements as state liabilities, to be managed down (Baker et al. 2020). Many of these changes were asymmetric, imposing the constraints of private finance without any of the potential freedoms (see Ellwood and Newberry 2007). As the private 'asset economy' leveraged debt to make capital gains (Adkins et al. 2020), public finance sought surpluses.

To access the benefits of private finance, states were required to exercise their powers in ways that benefited private providers. Public Private Partnerships and corportised entities can access finance in ways that are limited or prevented by rules governing public debt (see Watson 2003, 3). Tax concessions make fiscal support invisible in public budgets (Howard 1999). These actions occupy an ambiguous position. They clearly require state action, and often relied on the state's fiscal power, but they appear in public budgeting documents as private finance.

Politically, liberalised accounting rules facilitated a slight of hand, where the state's powers to shape the economy grew, but democratic control of its influence diminished. The 'hidden' welfare state allowed a massive 'risk shift' (Hacker 2019), as states limited their liabilities by making it more difficult for citizens to access public provision, while extending greater, but less visible, support to less equitable private alternatives. Australia's existing reliance on private providers across the welfare state already reflected this 'dual welfare' logic, and liberalisation encouraged its expansion (Stebbing and Spies-Butcher 2010).

The same ambiguities between the boundaries of public and private finance potentially created opportunities for welfare advocates. Where democratic pressure to expand social protection was especially strong, a different set of policy tools developed. New accounting methods exposed hidden welfare and gendered inequalities, allowing the normative principle of social need, always powerful in Australian welfare, to extend into new domains. The dominance of economic rationalism frustrated efforts at more traditional forms of social democracy. Instead, 'hybrid' models emerged that mimicked elements of market competition, while leveraging the state's unique sovereign role to set incentives, compel insurance and issue credit, socialising risk without seeming to expand public finance.

Liberalisation, Dual Welfare and Hybridity in Australia

Liberalisation describes a set of reforms linked to prioritising the coordinating role of prices and competition within the economy. Unlike many definitions of neoliberalism, which emphasise its role as a project for asserting class power (Harvey 2007, Cahill and Konings 2017), liberalisation focuses on policy instruments, reflecting both the more technocratic model adopted in Australia and allowing an analytic distinction between political forces and policy models. Liberalisation reflects Pusey's definition of economic rationalism as a 'doctrine which says that markets and prices are the *only reliable* means of setting value on anything' (1993, 14).

Applied to the welfare state liberalisation focuses on policy reforms that integrate prices and competition into social policy, centring the market as the primary mechanism for organising economic activity. In Polanyi's (1957) terms, liberalisation extends the logic of market integration. But within the welfare state, it explicitly does so via state power. The use of state mechanisms to mimic the market infers not only technocratic governance but the potential for hybridity. Where liberalisation acts to constrain public finance, hybridity involves the state acting in ways that mimic market models, but socialise risk.

The use of prices and markets to organise social policy has not necessarily required rejecting social equality as a legitimate political aim. The focus on competition created space for new forms of statecraft, often developed by economists, that sought to reconcile competing objectives. After situating the conceptual approach in the next chapter, the second section of the book is organised around what I take to be the three most significant processes of liberalisation within welfare:

- *Targeting* of social benefits, which involves limiting access to payments through conditionality. It often involves surveillance of benefit recipients and potentially penalties for certain forms of behaviour. Conditionality of social payments alongside deregulation of market incomes prioritises market distribution.
- *Marketisation* of social services, which involves the application of competition and price mechanisms within social services. The state generally remains a central player in these markets, both as funder of services and regulator of provision (Le Grand 1997; Barr 2001). However, services are reorganised to promote consumer/client choice, facilitating the entry of private firms.
- *Financialisation* of social insurance, which involves linking citizens' future access to social goods and income to financial markets, such as via superannuation and housing markets. 'Asset-based welfare' is the cornerstone of financialisation (Bryant et al. 2024), but it also includes the application of financial forms of calculation to social provision more generally (Bryan and Rafferty 2014).

I explore each process through exemplars that reflect different institutional logics. The choice of case studies reflects the conceptual framework outlined in the next chapter, which emphasises different political logics (how policies reflect need and merit) and economic logics (how policies structure finance and provision). Even so, it is important the cases reflect broader dynamics, which are more likely to be evident within larger programs, which engage larger constituencies and require significant resources.

Case selection also reflects the institutionalist method applied through the book. Comparison ideally involves differentiation within otherwise similar cases. Here I am interested in the scope to pursue political alternatives within what seem similar processes of restructuring. Thus, within each of the three processes I have sought cases that appear to follow different principles. Following Titmuss (1965, 17–18), I distinguish between the logic of 'dualism' where the principle of need is combined with that of achievement or status and the logic of universalism, which emphasises need alone. Table 1.1 provides an outline of the cases selected.

To examine processes of targeting I focus on two aspects of the benefits system: payments to families and payments to the unemployed. These two payment systems share much in common. Both are flat-rate, means-tested and funded from general revenue, following the policy template of the older wage-earner model. However, the politics of the two programs, at least ostensibly, appear quite different.

The unemployment benefit, JobSeeker, has been subject to an archetypical process of residualisation. Wedge politics (Wilson and Turnbull 2001) has targeted visible and marginalised minorities with new forms of conditionality and then extended conditionality to others. Family benefits, while far from generous, were significantly increased and made more inclusive due to feminist organising. Economic rationalists used means-tests to apply fiscal constraint; however, feminists resisted targeting, making pro-competition appeals to work incentives.

I analyse marketisation through changes to early education and care (EEC) and healthcare provision. Both are sizeable schemes that often feature in election campaigns. EEC is also an obvious form of marketisation. Since the late 1980s public funding has been restructured from funding for services into payments to parents, who spend their subsidies in a diverse market including non-profit and for-profit providers. Drawing on feminist scholarship, I

Table 1.1 Case studies.

Process of Liberalisation	Logic of Universalism	Logic of Dualism
Targeting	Family benefits	Unemployment benefits
Marketisation	Medicare	Early Education and Care
Financialisation	Student loans	Retirement incomes

explore how marketisation generates uneven and expensive services, reflecting the logic of 'two-tiered' markets (Gingrich 2011).

I focus on Medicare, the most iconic element of 'public' provision, as an example of expanding universalism (see Boxall and Gillespie 2013). However, Medicare is also marketised, and was from its inception a compromise between a system of private subsidy and nationalisation. As an insurance scheme, it facilitates private medical practice and operates alongside a sizeable, publicly subsidised private insurance market supporting private hospital provision (Spies-Butcher 2024). While the system is dualised, it is clear the public component dominates. Indeed, Medicare's marketised structure appears to have facilitated the relative expansion of public provision, avoiding fiscal and constitutional constraints while applying monopsony power to discipline private providers.

Finally, the book explores processes of financialisation. Australia's wage-earner model was especially susceptible to finance-based inequalities. Long before the rise of neoliberalism, asset-based welfare was built into the core of Australian welfare through its emphasis on home ownership (Yates and Bradbury 2010). However, the introduction of compulsory superannuation, based on a defined contribution, market investment model, has made finance king. These changes to retirement incomes reflect the influence of generational accounting, an important technical neoliberal innovation used to reinforce fiscal constraints by projecting spending into the future (Spies-Butcher and Stebbing 2019), reinforcing a fiscal logic already present in Australia's Treasury since the 1930s (Watts 1980, 180–181).

The reliance on private investment vehicles to fund retirement reinforces another inequalitarian aspect of Australia's welfare system – reliance on tax concessions. Drawing on collaborative work with Adam Stebbing, I explore how the combination of market finance and concessional taxation reflect the most insidious form of liberalisation (see Stebbing and Spies-Butcher 2010). Retirement incomes policy uses the temporal logic of finance to overcome social resistance to retrenchment by gradually phasing out existing forms of social insurance for older generations and integrating younger generations into ever more financialised models of social provision. Superannuation reproduces, even exaggerates, life course market inequalities, while home ownership steadily falls for each new generation (Stebbing and Spies-Butcher 2016).

Alongside the retirement incomes system, I analyse financialisation within higher education, drawing on collaborative work with Gareth Bryant (Spies-Butcher and Bryant 2018; Bryant and Spies-Butcher 2020). Australia pioneered the widespread use of income-contingent loans (ICLs) for university students, a model increasingly adopted internationally (Chapman et al. 2014).

ICLs are a potentially controversial case selection given they were introduced alongside the reintroduction of fees in universities. In this sense, ICLs are clearly a component of liberalisation. Likewise, universities have also been radically marketised through the rapid growth of international, full-fee student income, reliance on other market finance and changes to university governance that move away from democratic control to a model of managerialism (Marginson and Considine 2000). However, unlike changes in superannuation and housing, the implications of ICLs are not obviously inegalitarian.

Universities have expanded alongside ICLs, increasing access for those previously marginalised. While university entrance remains stratified, there is little evidence fees have increased stratification (Chapman 2014, 18–19). The incidence of fees is not straightforwardly regressive, not only because (predominately poorer) non-students do not pay but also because income-contingency ensures higher-income graduates pay more than low-income graduates.

Hybridity helps to explain different experiences of liberalisation. As the regulatory protections of the wage-earner model were unwound, housing, pensions and other areas saw a more pernicious 'dual welfare' model reinforced (Stebbing and Spies-Butcher 2010). Here the state supports both private and public welfare institutions within the same policy domain. Private welfare for housing and super is delivered through the tax system, making it harder to distinguish as 'welfare' and facilitating much less equal distribution. Public welfare, for both public housing and public pensions, is more explicit, making it more susceptible to austerity and residualisation.

Hybridity emerged from stronger forms of political contestation and social resistance. What appears technocratic is shaped by politics and collective interests. In these cases, political mobilisation either made more explicit processes of liberalisation politically costly or created political pressure to expand social protection in new ways. Those social pressures intersected with an increasingly pro-competition bureaucracy to produce new policy models that provided relatively strong social protections for relatively low (apparent) fiscal costs. The results were always less universal than social democratic systems of social insurance, but were efficient in mitigating inequality and effective at building political support.

Reflecting the broader financialisaton of life, both dual and hybrid policy develops by separating out and re-bundling risks and costs within an otherwise similar policy structure. Dual welfare reflects the asymmetric application of market principles within public budgeting, while hybridity often advances by applying symmetry between public and private finance, enabling the state to use its unique sovereign capacities to set incentives, compel insurance and issue credit.

The Politics of Liberalised Welfare in Australia

The final two chapters reflect on the lessons of Australia's experience of liberalisation to identify strategies for the future. Chapter 6 focuses on the policy lessons of hybrid welfare. Chapter 7 looks to political strategies and forces. A key policy lesson is how hybridity applies symmetry against the institutions of dual welfare. By applying financial logics more symmetrically within the public sector, hybrid policies identify how fiscal power has already expanded and facilitates policies based on universal needs.

Tax concessions are equated with social spending, revealing the extent of the state's fiscal power and to disciplining that power via democratic processes. Punitive means-testing is equated to tax rates, which highlights the incentives created by government claims on income and the principle of capacity to pay. Hybrid forms of marketisation use competition to discipline private providers through monopsony power. Constructing state action as insurance helps avoid fiscal and constitutional limits on state power, while socialising risk. Rather than constructing social spending as a liability, hybrid policies recast spending as social investment by identifying the future fiscal benefits of social solidarity.

Each of these cases extends market logics to reveal fiscal power and thus expand democratic control. By equating different forms of state power – tax concessions and spending, tax rates and means-tests – the distinctions between deserved and undeserved forms of support, which underpins the dual welfare state, are challenged. However, these strategies are only effective where norms of adequate provision are already in place. Only when there is a norm that governments should help citizens save for retirement or access healthcare are fiscal resources made available in the first place. And it is according to norms of need and adequacy that state power is then disciplined through democratic contestation – ensuring everyone has an adequate pension or access to needed healthcare.

The equivalence between hybrid social provision and dual welfare is enabled by changes in public budgeting practices. Tax expenditure statements, gender budgeting and effective marginal tax rates represent political strategies advanced by developing new forms of statecraft. The financialisation of the state, however, has expanded the potential scope of these strategies by enabling the state not only to tax and spend but to lend, invest and underwrite. Those powers have advanced as private finance has advanced within social provision – through mortgage-backed securities, social bonds and pension funds – and as states have sought to manage financial crisis. While state action may initially reflect profit imperatives, once enabled these powers become subject to similar democratic contest. Where governments largely bailed out Wall St in 2008, the pandemic saw most governments directly fund households to underwrite liquidity.

As Adam Tooze noted, '2020 was a moment not just of plunder, but of reformist experimentation' (2021, 16). That experimentation can be seen in NSW government efforts to keep investing in its Future Fund, even as its budget went into deficit (Kehoe 2021), and in housing policies from both sides that use 'innovative' models to expand public support without any significant headline budget impact (see ALP 2022a). The fiscal response to Covid highlighted the expansion of hybrid policy-making models, mobilised during a crisis to maintain household liquidity through relatively universal cash payments and interventions to secure mortgage debt (Spies-Butcher 2020a).

The importance of household finance during the crisis points to changing political, as well as policy, dynamics. Household spending underpins our financialised economy and increasingly asset wealth. The streams of income households are obliged to spend to secure their needs are a valuable source of stability in an otherwise volatile economy (see Adkins et al. 2021). We may stop buying cars and fridges, or going out to the theatre, but we rarely stop paying our mortgage or energy bills.

Bryan and Rafferty (2018) argue financialisation has reorganised how we manage our needs, making debt repayment an important potential site of political struggle. Organising citizens to collectively resist debt and rent payments has the potential to place pressure on the asset economy (Adkins et al. 2020). Such struggles would re-politicise elements of the welfare state – especially housing and income support – where hybrid strategies have yet to achieve lasting gains, but where there is significant potential to advance egalitarian policies.

The politics of work and welfare may also be shifting in another, perhaps more important way. Predicting where politics will head is always a risky and speculative activity. But there are potential lessons in our experiences of liberalisation that point to broader strategies for contesting inequality. At the centre of those lessons is a shift in where the politics of welfare happens, not only through the growing role of social finance but also of social provision. Where the welfare state of industrial economies was largely built on the organised power of those involved in commodity production, increasingly social policy is contested *within* the welfare state itself, through a politics that centres the organisation of social reproduction and care.

Feminists and those directly involved in the provision and organisation of care have been central to successful efforts to contest liberalisation. There are good reasons to suspect that will continue, as care becomes more important to employment and finance. It also suggests a different reading of other political trends. Rather than viewing new cleavages based on age, gender and education as undermining the materialist class politics of work, these cleavages can also be seen to mark new material divides produced by the organisation of liberalised welfare. Education is particularly important because it both defines an important element of the older class order, but increasingly reflects gendered and generational changes within work and welfare.

Education is both human capital and social reproduction. As 'capital', education traditionally structures social inequalities, reproducing class hierarchies. It potentially divides workers between a cosmopolitan, 'Brahman left' and workers dependent on older, local industries who view global competition as an existential threat (Piketty 2020). As a form of social reproduction, education can be incorporated into a politics of care that asserts the economic *value* of care, as it has been in struggles over the definitions of early education and care (see Brennan 2009b).

Within the welfare state, education and professional qualifications have been a political strategy to assert control over how social policy is organised and the value afforded those involved in providing it. Unions have contested the value of care labour by both insisting on the value and skill of care labour and linking care to formal training and professional identities. The shifting role of formal education in training the welfare state workforce changes the political implications of education within different generations of worker-citizens.

For those leaving school today, some form of post-secondary education is no longer the preserve of a select minority, but increasingly a mass experience. Within that education system, the strategies of workers within the welfare state have reshaped the workforce as a whole, as their efforts at professionalisation have moved the mass workforces of education and care into the university system. Our connotations of higher education, professional work and class are complicated by the mass workforces of nurses and teachers, a trend set to continue within EEC, disability and aged care.

The employment sectors most closely tied to the welfare state – health, care, education and public administration – rival blue-collar work in size, and are growing more rapidly. We need to reimagine work, not to dismiss the value of manufacturing, construction or finance, but to de-gender this partial view. Looking through the lens of labour (paid and unpaid), the politics of education can look very different.

In the final chapter I explore the successes of welfare state campaigns against liberalisation, and map these against the changing dynamics of politics generally. Welfare state workers have used different strategies to their industrial forebears, reflecting their different position in capitalist economies. Rarely are they able to challenge profitability as directly as energy or transport workers. But they are much better placed to build broad community coalitions, between those providing and receiving care and education, that challenge political legitimacy.

The workers of the welfare state are more likely to be trusted (see Roy Morgan 2021) in a polity where political trust is in short supply. They have direct experience of provision, which can facilitate collective reflection and analysis to identify inequalities and build policy solutions. They are better placed to build an issue-based politics, connected to the financial and time pressures most households face, and to a values framework centred on care. And while union density has declined everywhere, it has been most resilient within the welfare state. Care unions are well placed to combine industrial and political strategies, challenging the asset-price model by confronting wage stagnation as well as socialising risk.

The politics of care has gained growing attention (Folbre 2008; Tronto 1993). Care as a 'frame' for political argument has become key to progressive party strategies (see Lakoff 2014). Care as value is central to struggles for equal pay (England et al. 2002; Brennan 2009b) and for recognition of the skill workers bring in providing, planning and organising social reproduction (Cortis and Meagher 2012). Denying the value of unpaid care labour has become increasingly central to regressive 'welfare reforms', while asserting the value of diverse forms of care and contribution is central to advancing egalitarian visions (Vincent 2023; Klein 2021). Care as a relationship recognises that we all care and are cared for (see Fine 2018) and facilitates coalition building, recognising the expertise of all those involved in care relationships. Care as an ethic provides an innovative means to link struggles over inequality to those of climate justice (Flanagan 2019).

Finally, I argue care as a material relation is now increasingly central to the politics of the welfare state, not because of the 'death of class', but because of the central role social reproduction plays in employment, politics and finance. As the work of care moves into the paid economy it has become the largest and fastest growing segment of the workforce, while the commodification of the spaces and work of care lies at the heart of financialisation. The political economy of the welfare state is therefore increasingly tied to the organisation and financing of the welfare state itself, rather than primarily reflecting struggles originating in the production and sale of physical commodities.

Identifying care as a key site of contest does not suggest any particular outcome. Australia's version of the asset economy, linked to the dual welfare state, creates a much broader political alliance than we might think. Home ownership and superannuation tie the interests of the majority of people to rising asset prices, while fiscal welfare conceals the real inequalities produced. Nor is debt simply the burden of the poor. Instead, middle-class households have driven the explosion of household debt. Rising house prices make debt the key to security of tenure, while a tax system favouring capital gains rewards leverage. It is hard to see any government allowing house prices to collapse, let alone deliberately engineering that outcome. Undoing asset-based welfare is made somewhat easier by socialising the provision and financing of care, and indeed the two can be self-reinforcing. But it will likely require careful navigation.

The enormous fiscal cost of asset-based welfare creates opportunities. Just as converting similar fiscal welfare enabled family payments and Medicare, so there are opportunities to convert fiscal support for super and housing. Undoing the system is complex and risky, but the scale of concessions provides some wiggle room. History suggests conversion works best when changes in tax concessions and new social protections are directly linked, within the same policy domain.

Other principles from hybrid models might also apply. Even in mixed markets, public finance should be based on universal principles and a recognition of the expertise of those closest to provision, not abstract and distant management models. Where we have non-government providers, from EEC providers to universities to super funds, their governance must be democratised, reflecting the expertise of those on different sides of care and education relationships.

Efforts to degender work require changes to degender welfare, not only through paid leave but also through individualising payments. And policy efforts to support house prices should seek to universalise secure tenure, and ensure the benefits of capital gains flow to public finance, either through taxation or ownership. Even incremental change along these lines has the potential to significantly transform liberalisation. Critically reflecting on Australia's experience of liberalisation can help us imagine and advance alternatives.

Chapter 2

LIBERALISATION IN AUSTRALIA

How has liberalisation changed Australia's model of social protection and the politics of equality? Much of the change has simply echoed changes internationally. As markets and money partly displaced states and law in organising economic life, competition and productivity became key watch words for policymakers, even in discussions of social policy. Still, the Australian experience appears distinct. For some it is an exemplar of how liberalisation should be done. Australia moved swiftly from a relatively tightly regulated economy to an increasingly free market model. It broke records for sustained economic growth and won awards for its 'economic management'. It is also distinctive because liberalisation came largely through bipartisan changes led by a Labor government in an explicit alliance with organised labour. That has led to divided views within Australia, but also positioned Australia as a crucial example of the uneven development of neoliberalism, suggesting social democrats not only accommodated but entrenched neoliberalism (Humphrys 2018). This chapter aims to connect an analysis of liberalisation to Australia's institutions and history.

The different accounts of Australian liberalisation reflect unusual combinations and alliances. Rapid reductions in tariffs and privatisations were matched by rising social spending. Labor reformers embraced competition but explicitly rejected the free market think tanks often claimed to be the real driving force of change. Economic success came as much from avoiding crisis as improving productivity, echoing Keynesian efforts at demand management. Of course, Australian novelty can be overplayed. Liberalisation was different everywhere, as it responded to existing institutions, and 'mutated' as reforms moved from place to place. However, the configuration of unusual combinations makes Australia's story a useful one. Australia encountered liberalisation with a history of egalitarianism and labour solidarity that had not yet translated into traditional welfare state structures, with a progressive government chased by the fiscal record of the previous Labor government and strong movements stunned by the seemingly extraconstitutional means for removing it. Those circumstances produced an unusual politics, where the welfare state was reworked in new ways to conceal either its scale or its distributional impact.

The chapter begins by outlining the distinctive model of Antipodean protection developed prior to liberalisation, which often deployed market regulation in place of traditional tax and spend social protection. It then situates the process of economic restructuring against two dominant accounts, which either position Australia's experience as triumphant reform or as a betrayal of egalitarianism. Rather than arguing for one of these accounts, I highlight important limitations in both. Turning to the comparative literature the chapter identifies a number of helpful conceptual tools to make sense of Australian experience, focusing particularly on the 'variegation' and hybridity that emerge in 'actually existing neoliberalism'.

Drawing on these comparative tools the final section of the chapter develops a framework for understanding the case studies. It argues the Keynesian welfare state was built on a particular kind of statecraft, which connected movement claims to specific forms of measurement and policy tools. It was this constellation that shifted social protection from emphasising socialisation to emphasising social spending, and which was then confronted by the fiscal austerity of neoliberalism. Stepping back, political conflicts over welfare can be seen as responding to those fiscal constraints – either attempting to socialise risk outside fiscal limits or conceal the upward redistribution of resources. These strategies, of hybridity and dualism, reflect familiar conflicts between the demands of accumulation and political legitimacy, but, I argue, are increasingly reworked through a new statecraft produced by liberalisation.

Australian Welfare

Internationally, Australia is most often understood as a liberal political economy (Esping-Anderson 1990; Spiker 2012; O'Connor et al. 1999), similar to its Anglo-American allies. While it earlier attracted attention for pioneering democratic and labour reforms, over the twentieth century the dominance of conservative federal governments limited the expansion of taxation and social spending that took place elsewhere. Figure 2.1 compares taxation and social spending as a proportion of GDP across comparable OECD countries. It shows Australia's tax base is modest and its social spending, while closer to the OECD average, relatively low. Australia lacks a contributory social insurance system like those in most European countries, although since the 1980s it has developed a compulsory employer-funded, market-based pension system (superannuation), which complements a means-tested public pension. Like the pension, most social payments are flat-rate and means-tested. Public spending on active labour market programs and higher education are both

50
40
30
20
10
0

USA   Australia   Japan   New   UK   OECD avg   Germany   Italy   Sweden   France   Denmark
                             Zealand

■ Taxation as % of GDP   ▨ Social spending as % of GDP

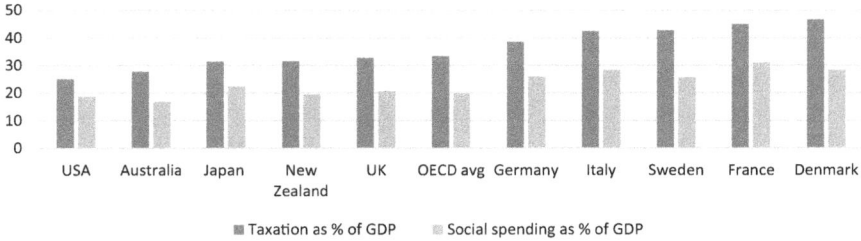

Figure 2.1 Taxation and social spending as proportion of GDP, selected OECD countries, 2019 or closest year. *Source*: OECD Social Spending Database, https://data. oecd.org/socialexp/social-spending.htm. OECD Tax Database, https://www.oecd. org/ctp/tax-policy/tax-database/.

comparatively low, and the private health and school education sectors are relatively large (OECD 2020, 2022c).

The most influential account of a distinctive Australian policy model, at least through the post–War Keynesian period, is Francis Castles' 'wage earner welfare state' (WEWS). Castles argued that Australian social protection developed across the twentieth century by focusing on market regulation. Policy settings aimed to moderate inequalities in market incomes, known as '*pre*-distribution' (Deeming 2014; Wilson 2017), rather than *re*-distributing income through taxation and social spending. The model reflected the early strength of Australia's union movement in the nineteenth century, which facilitated a more active role for organised labour. Early labour movement strength and the early entry of the Labor Party into parliament and government contributed to a period of social experimentation and high real wages, leading many to see Australia as both a 'working man's paradise' (Lane 2009) and a 'social laboratory' (Melleuish 2004). Later, constitutional barriers in the immediate post-War period and a 26-year unbroken period of conservative rule from 1949 saw relatively modest welfare state expansion at a time when many high-income countries established more generous welfare states.

The WEWS model involved strong labour market, industry and migration controls. The foundations of this settlement emerged in the early years after federation at the beginning of the twentieth century, reflecting an alliance of labour unions, reformist 'Deakinite' liberals and domestic industry (Fenna 2012). A complex set of tariffs and industry protection developed alongside strong, racialised migration policies and centralised wage setting. Not all of these policies were distinctive. As Alan Fenna observes, many other Anglo Settler Colonies were protectionist and all were racist, rather it was wage arbitration that set Australia apart (2012).

Arbitration was established in 1904. Two years later the Harvester Judgement formally introduced social considerations into wage setting, determining that workers were entitled to 'live in frugal comfort'. This created a social benchmark for minimum wages distinct from productivity or profitability, albeit only one consistent with a basic reproduction of labour power (McQueen 1983, 146–148). In 1945 arbitration was supplemented by a formal policy commitment to full employment. Keynesian demand management, public works projects and financial repression were actively used to maintain unemployment below 2 per cent for most of the 1950s and 1960s (Cass and Freeland 1994). Arbitration expanded across the period such that by 1980 approximately 80 per cent of the workforce had their conditions directly determined by centralised bargaining through the courts (Castles 2001, 30).

Strong regulation moderated inequalities in market incomes making Australia relatively egalitarian compared to other liberal countries. Financial repression also combined with high wages to support the expansion of mass home ownership from the 1950s. Australia became a model 'homeowning society' (Ronald 2008), with most workers expecting to own their home outright by retirement. Home ownership and full employment intersected with Australia's model of means-tested, flat-rate benefits. Given unemployment was largely frictional, unemployment benefits were effectively categorical and capable of meeting short-term need. High home ownership reduced living costs in retirement, making a low public pension more liveable. Flat-rate benefits were also a higher proportion of a low-income worker's previous wage, ensuring the 'replacement rate' of benefits favoured manual workers (Castles 1985). Importantly, non-contributory benefits also reflected the successful campaigns of women's movements to ensure older women were not excluded (Sawer 2015).

Taken together these features potentially distinguished Antipodean, and particularly Australian, social protection from the rest of the liberal world (Castles and Mitchell 1990). It was not so much that social protection was residualised and the free market prioritised, but rather that access to protection was extended to workers via regulation of employment rather than social spending. Reflecting Richard Titmuss' social division of welfare (1965), Castles suggested that Australia's early development of arbitration meant policy relied more heavily on occupational welfare, provided through employment (Castles 1985).

Arguably, the focus on arbitration engendered tax resistance. Workers prioritised money wages over social spending. Australia instead developed a relatively progressive, but also relatively modest tax base to fund relatively egalitarian, but also modest, flat-rate benefits. High-income professionals, who gained little from these arrangements, won fiscal welfare, that is social support provided via the tax system, with tax concessions for private pension contributions introduced alongside federal income tax during the First World War (see Stebbing 2015, 112–120), and tax concessions than expanding for other areas of social provision (e.g. see Smith 2001).

Accounts of Australia's wage earner focus, as with the broader welfare state literature, centred the role of male workers, obscuring gendered relations of social provision (see O'Connor et al. 1999; Orloff 1996), and the role of colonialism and ongoing appropriation Klein 2023). Arbitration not only created a normative principle for setting wages, it also created normative criteria for family composition (see Smith 2017). The adequacy of wages was explicitly judged against a benchmark of a heterosexual couple with two children and only one market income. Formal gender discrimination was built into wage settings and into pregnancy and marriage bars on woman's employment. In practice, women were presumed to access the benefits of wage earners' welfare via their husbands and were expected to provide considerable unpaid care in return. Unsurprisingly in the 1960s Australia had one of the lowest levels of female labour force participation in the OECD (1992). The labour market as a whole excluded most Indigenous people and other people of colour through overtly discriminatory policy, reinforcing violent appropriation of land and forms of forced labour, including slavery (see Walden 1995; Paisley 2014).

Nonetheless, Castles' description of Australian egalitarianism has proven highly influential. However, most, including Castles, argue it best describes a post-War model that has increasingly eroded (Castles 2001; Esping-Andersen 1999, 88–90; Ramia 2020) under the dual pressures of liberalisation and the service transition. At best the industrial relations institutions that underpinned social protection have been 'hollowed out' (Wilson et al. 2013) or reduced to a focus on the minimum wage (Wilson 2021). Initially this was combined with social policy renovation (Castles 1994), which saw Australia depart from its Antiopodean neighbour, but more recently it is seen to have embraced a more liberalised model (Ramia 2020). In any case, the 'pro-market' politics that emerged in the 1980s substantially shifted Australia's model of social protection.

The Rise of the Market

Advocates for free market reforms emerged in Australia in a surprisingly similar way to the neoliberal heartlands of the United States and the United Kingdom. Australia confronted the same crisis of stagflation that challenged the Keynesian model of economic management everywhere. It had also seen social spending and taxation increase in the 1970s, as the Whitlam government attempted to follow a more traditionally social democratic model. In response, Australia had seen the rise and reinvigoration of free market think tanks. The 1970s saw the beginnings of the free market Centre for Independent Studies (CIS), supported by advice from both the British Institute of Economic Affairs (IEA) and Mont Pelerin Society (Lindsay and Norton 1996, 20), and the radicalisation of the older Institute for Public Affairs (IPA). However, when reform came, it was via a Labor government working with the unions and had less of the overtly anti-statist rhetoric associated with Thatcher or Reagan.

The rise of a 'neoliberal thought collective' (see Mirowski and Plehwe 2015) organised around a number of important think tanks has become central to many accounts of liberalisation. Supported by wealthy backers, think tanks developed a radical critique of the welfare state as a stepping stone to authoritarianism. Think tanks took up these ideas and translated them into more practical, if radical, policy proposals to unwind the institutional protections of post-War welfare states (Kasper 1980; Cahill and Beder 2005). Against the state, they proposed a new, idealistic version of liberalism (Hayek 1949). Think tanks were widely seen as central to driving changes in both Australia's major parties to break down the older protectionist consensus (Marsh 1994), and can sensibly be described as constituting a 'radical neo-liberal political movement' (Cahill 2004). As Michael Pusey put it, Australia's 'structured inequality in interest group representation' (1991, 143) meant think tanks were rarely identified as pro-market (Smith and Marden 2008).

The impact of these ideas and institutions is less straightforward. This neoliberal vision did impact Australian policy, particularly through the Liberal Party. There was an overlap of personnel between think tanks and political offices. At state level, Cahill and Beder (2005) show how think tank publications directly informed the Kennett government privatisation agenda in Victoria. However, it is also easy to overstate their influence. Both think tanks and their opponents have incentives to exaggerate their power. As Stone (1996) and others have shown, there is relatively little evidence of think tanks playing a central role in proposing specific policy measures or ensuring their implementation.

Caution in assessing the influence of think tanks is particularly important given key figures in the Hawke and Keating governments explicitly rejected the positions (and indeed even the role) of free market think tanks. Cahill notes central bureaucratic figures in reform, Michael Keating and Ross Garnaut, explicitly reject the influence of think tanks on policy while Labor politicians openly attacked free market think tanks (2014, 44–52). It was not ideas but interests, Cahill argues, that shaped neoliberalism. Similarly, think tanks were critical of what they saw as the Howard government's 'Big Government Conservatism' (Norton 2006).

Instead, the Labor government governed in concert with the trade union movement. The two organisations entered a formal Accord, mirroring efforts at corporatism by other social democratic parties (Humphrys 2018). The agreement saw unions use their industrial muscle to hold back wage claims as a mechanism to break the wage-price spiral thought to be driving stagflation. In return, unions gained access to government and broader policymaking, including influence over macroeconomic, industry and social policy. Within the union movement, support for the Accord included Communist-led unions who saw the compact as both a defence against the New Right (Bramble and Kuhn 2010) and potentially shifting Australia towards social democracy (Humphyrs 2018). While it became clear the transformation taking place was far from socialist, even several years into the Accord left unions remained committed, supporting *Australia Reconstructed*, a detailed plan for a social democratic turn (ACTU/TDC 1987).

Whether the Accord served to moderate (Quiggin 1998) or implement (Humphries 2018) liberalisation remains hotly contested. Either way, the Accord reflected an important shift in strategy. As Beilhatrz (1994) argues, the experience of the previous Whitlam government caused many radicals to rethink their engagement with both the Labor Party and the state. Having seen Whitlam's government as too moderate, the dismissal caused a change of heart. The Accord facilitated a broader engagement between social movements and the state, both formally through the involvement of union leaders in policymaking but also informally through the entry of movement activists into the bureaucracy. These dynamics, I argue, helped to drive hybridity within social policy, mitigating the inequalities generated by liberalisation, while also weakening movement energy as leaders became incorporated into state structures (see Sawer 2007).

Across approximately three decades from the early 1980s Australia embarked on a sustained period of economic restructuring that, arguably, unwound the foundations of the WEWS. Trade protections were radically reduced, a number of significant public institutions privatised, competition policy and new public management adopted, finance deregulated and wage setting decentralised. Australia was at the forefront of many of these changes. It played a leading role in advocating for lower trade barriers and free trade, and unilaterally lowered protections on its own economy (Pusey 2003, Appendix A). It was viewed internationally as a leader in adopting new public management and new corporate accounting systems (Gregory 1995, 171; Guthrie 1998, 2). And, in 1983, it moved relatively early to a floating exchange rate. Labour markets were also gradually decentralised, first through allowing enterprise-level bargaining and explicit productivity-based wage trade-offs and then through more radical limits on sector-wide bargaining (see Briggs and Buchanan 2000).

While many of the changes were unpopular, most proceeded with bipartisan support. Australia's policy convergence partly reflected and partly anticipated an international crisis in social democracy, which culminated in the collapse of the Soviet Union and embrace of the Third Way (Giddens 2013; Latham 1998), and which was captured intellectually in the assertion of the 'end of history' (Fukuyama 1989) and the 'death of class' (Pakulski and Waters 1996). Partisan conflict did emerge over social policy reforms to implement universal health insurance (Medicare) and employer-funded pensions (superannuation), as well as plans to increase consumption taxation and privatise telecommunications. More recently, industrial relations and climate policy have been (re-) politicised, producing policy instability that is often understood as marking the end of successful 'reform' from the early 2000s (Garnaut 2011, xvi; Parkinson 2021). A new Labor government now sees Accordist-style consensus politics (Grattan 2022) as a renewed solution to stagnating wages and the 'climate wars'.

During the 1990s two influential accounts of liberalisation emerged that have shaped thinking since. The dominant account internationally and amongst policy elites in Australia reflects political journalist Paul Kelly's (2008) influential book *The End of Certainty*. Kelly argued economic reform had swept away a previous 'Australian Settlement', the protectionist institutions Kelly saw as inward looking, 'secure but moribund' (Beilhartz and Cox 2007, 113). Reformers were strong and skilful political leaders responding to a changing world by promoting competition, cosmopolitanism and productivity as a means to raise living standards.

Critics of neoliberalism echo Michael Pusey's initial framing of liberalisation as 'economic rationalism'. Pusey identified technocratic economists in the central agencies of the public sector as the drivers of reform, replacing an older generation of 'nation builders', whose pragmatic and socially connected outlook supported Australia's more inclusive egalitarianism. The 'economic rationalists' favoured the market over the state and community, attacking the welfare state and driving inequality (see Rees 1994; Bryson and Verity 2009).

These accounts each reflect the scale of change and a sense of the Australian 'way' being remade (Cass and Freeland 1994). They both position economic ideas and ways of thinking as central to what reformers were trying to do and to how policy substantively changed. It is perhaps unsurprising, then, that ongoing debates reflect attitudes to liberalisation in general. However, both sides of this debate often rely on claims that are difficult to substantiate in retrospect. While productivity and competition have been central goals of the reformers, and Australia has enjoyed a substantial rise in material living standards, it is far less clear that liberalisation aided productivity. Likewise, while the rise of market models has become central to state governance, it is less clear that liberalisation meant an attack on the scale or egalitarianism of social spending. Taking from each of these accounts can inform an under-standing of Australia's 'actually existing' liberalisation.

The legend and myth of productivity

Productivity lies at the heart of the success story of economic reform. Early advocates of economic restructuring argued protectionism had led to a relative decline in Australian living standards (Kelly 2008). Kelly saw the Settlement as incorporating five key institutional features, similar to Castles WEWS: the racialised and restrictive migration policy of White Australia, industry protection, wage arbitration, state paternalism and Imperial benev-olence. While some took issue with the exact formulation (e.g. Stokes 2004; Brett 2004, 27) his characterisation soon dominated discussions of Australian politics, contrasting an Australia 'protected, closed and nasty' (Beilharz and Cox 2007, 22), with the successful, outward looking and competitive model established by reform.

Change was justified by the seemingly poor economic performance Australia had achieved under the Settlement. Where Australia led the world in per capita incomes in the late nineteenth century, by the 1980s over a dozen countries had overtaken it. As Kelly summarised, Australia had grown rapidly under free trade prior to the Settlement, but stagnated under pro-tection (2008, 13–14). This view was driven by some of the most influential policy minds in economics – such as Ross Garnaut and Fred Gruen (1986), both close to Labor's leadership. The reform agenda, especially reducing tar-iffs and micro-economic reform, was seen as crucial to raising productivity and thus living standards, especially in a globalising economy. The Hilmer Review, which lay the basis for competition policy, positioned 'the challenge of improving productivity' as the primary economic goal (1993, xv).

Initially the success of this model was far from clear. Australia experi-enced a severe recession in the early 1990s, driven in part by tight mone-tary policy designed to address a growing Current Account Deficit (CAD). However, by the early 2000s Australia was gaining a reputation for delivering an 'economic miracle' (Bean 2000; Banks 2003). Productivity and contin-ued economic growth underpinned this story of rising living standards. The Australian Bureau of Statistics (ABS) revealed a surge in productivity over the 1990s, after virtually stagnating in the late 1970s and 1980s. This led the Productivity Commission to develop a powerful account of how economic reform and competition had driven the productivity boom (Parham 2002, 2004). The productivity success story continues to inform much of Australia's policy debate, including the Productivity Commission's own entrée into social policy, extending micro-economic reform to those 'large and growing parts of the economy where goods and services are provided to customers with no or little pricing' (2016, 3).

Australia has become richer since liberalisation (see Daley and Woods 2014). It is less clear this rise in living standards is directly linked to competition-led productivity growth. Productivity itself is a tricky concept. While it has long been central to economic thinking, it is difficult to define and even more difficult to measure (see Wilson 1999, 918–919). Productivity aims to measure outputs relative to inputs. Producing more with less reflects rising efficiency and productivity. It is widely accepted that the post-War boom accompanied a sustained increase in productivity, which came to a somewhat abrupt end across most OECD nations in the mid-1970s and is yet to fully recover (McCombie 1999). Australia's reformers focus attention on productivity, but it is not the only determinant of living standards. Working longer, enjoying rising prices and avoiding crisis all increase incomes.

The productivity story is complicated in two ways. First, Australia's fall down the international league table of GDP per capita is more easily explained by convergence to the mean than underperformance, given Australia's early economic success (Dowrick and Nguyen 1988). As Fenna puts it, 'the condemnation of early protectionism is little more than mythmaking' (2012, 107). This early success also reflects the dispossession and exploitation of Indigenous lands, water and labour, that is, a transfer of resources from Indigenous to the non-Indigenous economies. Many of these stolen resources were over exploited, creating a short-run boom through long-term ecological degradation and human misery.

Second, the productivity surge that seemed to follow liberalisation also appears too brief and poorly timed to make the case. Taking the decision to float the dollar in 1983 as the starting point, multifactor productivity was *lower* in the two decades after reform than before policy shifted from the Settlement (Quiggin 2011; Ferguson 2016). As Quiggin (2006) observes, accounts of the impact of reform are 'story' like, rather than based on rigorous testing. He argues the brief upswing in the 1990s was as likely the result of work intensification during recession as genuine productivity gains. By the early 2000s productivity was again slowing. While some argue this decline is evidence of the need for more reform (Garnaut 2005), productivity growth had already slowed before the implementation of the GST and well before most elements of National Competition Policy had been rolled out (Quiggin 2011, 13).

Rising living standards are better explained through direct reference to sustained economic growth and ongoing resource transfers. In 2017 Australia broke a record previously held by the Netherlands for the longest period of continuous economic growth (O'Brien 2019). Despite the East Asian Crisis, the dot com bubble and the global financial crisis, Australia had not recorded a single quarter of negative GDP growth between 1991 and the shut downs associated with Covid-19. Despite claims of a hard health-economy trade-off (Foster and Frijters 2022), Australia's economic performance through the pandemic has also been impressive. Economic success reflects the good fortune of the mining boom and a rise in commodity prices, alongside Australia's success in avoiding recession.

Over the 2000s rising commodity prices saw export incomes surge without a comparable increase in output. Rising incomes, then, reflected the rising value of existing assets rather than rising productivity (Gregory 2012). Indeed, rising commodity prices made it profitable to mine less accessible deposits, increasing the inputs needed per unit of output and thus reducing productivity. As with the nineteenth century, policy has facilitated resource-led growth by enforcing the ongoing dispossession of Indigenous people – delaying land rights, downgrading native title and resisting Treaty. However, given Australia's dependence on volatile commodity markets the stability of Australia's growth is also remarkable.

Liberalisation is closely tied to Australia's last recession, in the early 1990s, but less clearly responsible for more recent economic success. While Australia's economy as a whole has maintained consistent growth and avoided downturns, this is not true of the state economies taken individually. Australia's very strong form of fiscal equalisation, where GST revenues are used to equalise the fiscal base of each state, significantly redistributes resources, not only from rich to poor but from boom states to underperformers (see Productivity Commission 2018a). Australia's more recent success in avoiding the Great Recession and moderating the impacts of Covid coincided with a significant shift in policy practice and rhetoric back towards Keynesianism (Fenna 2010). In both cases, the stimulus packages were relatively large and redistributive, driven by Treasury (Fenna and d'Hart 2019) and the Reserve Bank (see RBA 2022) – the economic rationalists who previously oversaw liberalisation. Productivity might be at the heart of policy rhetoric, but the main drivers of economic success are less clearly related to competition than to older policy legacies.

The legend and myth of neoliberalism

Criticism of economic restructuring crystallised in the early 1990s around a distinctly Australian critique of liberalisation. Sociologist Michael Pusey had conducted a study of attitudes within the public service to the process of economic reform. He found that abstract, economic knowledge was increasingly privileged, especially within the central economic departments, which themselves were becoming more powerful. Pusey's critique echoed analysis from political economists (see Stilwell 1989), influential within the Australian left, and anticipated an emerging literature that placed Australia (and New Zealand) at the forefront of technocratic innovation in areas like new public management.

Reflecting an emphasis on technocratic governance, Pusey popularised the term 'economic rationalism' to describe what would later be understood as 'neoliberalism'. For Pusey, the Australian Settlement was defined by its social content. The architects of the post-War order, themselves economists, had experience outside the academy and the public service and so understood the importance of social relationships. Economic rationalism ignored this social context, imposing an abstract economic model of market competition everywhere. The analysis was designed to engage the public and successfully gained significant media coverage. However, Pusey's analysis (1991) was also grounded in the critical theory tradition of Jurgen Habermas (see Pusey 2002), which highlighted the expansion of technical rationality over the life world.

Rationalisation advances through both states and markets, as Pusey's title – framed around the role of the state – made clear. In practice, however, the critique of economic rationalism, and later neoliberalism, largely assumed the advance of the market was the result of a retreat of the state. The contention that the state, and the welfare state in particular, was under attack, has been a dominant theme from critics of liberalisation, both in Australia and overseas (see Fenna and Tapper 2012). Nowhere has reality been as clear cut as the imagined shift. In Australia, however, the counter-evidence is particularly stark.

As Fenna and Tapper (2012) have argued, to the extent that there has been an attack on the state in Australia, it is hard to claim it was an attack on the *welfare* state. It is true that total government spending and taxation changed relatively little since the early 1980s, measured as a proportion of GDP. However, *social* spending increased across the period, but particularly through the main period of 'reform' from the 1980s to early 2000s (see Figure 2.2). Social spending increased from 12.1 per cent of GDP in 1985 to 18.2 per cent in 2000 (OECD 2022c). The rate of growth in Australia, 50 per cent in 30 years, was approximately double that experienced across the OECD. Liberalisation saw Australia move from a social spending laggard towards the OECD mean. The gap has re-emerged post-GFC, reflecting both stronger relative growth in Australia and recent policy stasis. As we will see in coming chapters, this almost certainly underestimates the comparative change because the liberalisation saw several significant new initiatives,

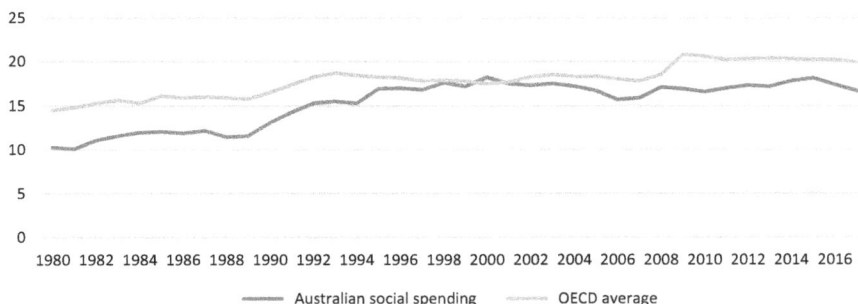

Figure 2.2 Australian social spending and OECD average as a proportion of GDP, 1980–2017. *Source*: OECD Social Spending Database, OECD 2022c.

particularly compulsory superannuation and income contingent loans, which have effects very similar to tax and spend policies, but which are defined as private spending in most social spending statistics.

Not only did social spending rise, and rise more rapidly than else-where, the composition of social spending remains remarkably egalitarian. Australian social policy has always been comparatively 'efficient' at redistrib-uting income. A stronger reliance on progressive income taxes and the wide-spread use of income-tests means relatively more government revenue comes from high-income earners and relatively more goes to low-income earners. Whiteford provides a comprehensive and detailed analysis of the changing dynamics of redistribution. It reveals Australia remains the most intensive redistributor of income (i.e. it redistributes more per dollar of public spend-ing) in the OECD. That redistributive effort increased during the 1980s and 1990s alongside the scale of social spending, although it declined somewhat in the 2000s, largely due to changes in taxation that favoured high-income earn-ers (Whiteford 2013, 40–41). Australia now ranks alongside New Zealand in directing the largest proportion of government payments to the lowest income earners (Causa and Hermansen 2017, 18).

The expansion of egalitarian social spending complicates analysis of lib-eralisation and inequality. While almost all measures indicate an increase in inequality since the 1980s, the broadest measures suggest a more gradual process. Consumption measures suggest low and relatively stable levels of inequality (Productivity Commission 2018b, 65). Here home ownership plays an important role in reducing the impact of rising income inequality. Much higher rates of home ownership amongst retirees, who have lower incomes on average than working-age households, reduce the impact of inequality after accounting for housing costs (*Ibid*, 26; Yates and Bradbury 2010). Home own-ership also complicates analysis of wealth inequality. While a surge of house prices has exaggerated inequalities based on age (and potentially generation), because home ownership amongst older people is relatively egalitarian, it has not necessarily increased overall wealth inequalities as dramatically (Daly and Woods 2014).

The role of social spending and home ownership in mitigating inequalities suggest the ongoing importance of both the old wage-earner model and the renovation of the welfare state. On other measures, however, Australia looks much more like the United States and the liberal world. Andrew Leigh, a Labor MP and member of the international team working with Thomas Piketty to refocus attention on inequality, has shown Australia largely follows the Anglo trend of rising top incomes. The top 1 per cent has increased its share of both income and wealth (Katic and Leigh 2016). The gains are not quite as dramatic as in other liberal countries (Productivity Commission 2018b, 29) but noticeably greater than in most European countries (see Piketty 2014).

Of course, this is a narrow reading of the neoliberalism thesis. Australia's overall rise in inequality alongside an expansion of the redistributive effort of social spending implies a significant increase in inequality of market incomes. From the early 1980s there has clearly been a shift in overall income shares from wages towards profits (La Cava 2019), as well as growing inequalities amongst wage earners (McKenzie 2018).

Some social spending has also become markedly more punitive, especially for those of working age receiving cash payments. Growing numbers in casual work and private rental housing reflects growing economic insecurity, the same trend Jakob Hacker identifies within the United States (2019), and Guy Standing sees creating a 'precariat' (2011).

Rising insecurity suggests the neoliberalism thesis requires clarification, rather than rejection. Liberalisation has not meant the end, or even the decline, of welfare. Rather, the welfare state has been reworked – new market logics have been 'rolled out' as much as old social protections 'rolled back'. Not only do those changes echo experiences elsewhere, they increasingly connect household security to global markets. Drawing on comparative tools can help understand these connections, as well as what is distinctive to Australia's trajectory.

Making and Changing Welfare States

Our understanding of the politics of social policy developed alongside the rise of the welfare state, particularly during the second half of the twentieth century. Political economic explanations focused on class, solidarity and conflict, and sought to explain how welfare states arose. Informed by Marx,

Polanyi and Schumpeter, political economists understood the welfare state as a response to tensions within market capitalism (see Offe 2018; Streeck 2014; Esping-Andersen 2015). Responding to these tensions, however, did not guarantee egalitarian outcomes. Rather, collective power, in the form of industrial organisation and electoral success, fostered different outcomes – or 'worlds of welfare' – in different countries (Esping-Andersen 1999).

Analysing the welfare states that emerged from the post-War period, power resource theorists argued that social democracies had enjoyed significant success in taming capitalism (Korpi 1989; 2006). While the Nordic countries remained capitalist, strong union movements (measured by density and strike activity) and successful social democratic parties (measured by control of executive government) had reshaped the state, expanding taxation and social spending (Esping-Andersen 2015). The welfare states that developed acted to mitigate inequalities and insecurities. Where capitalism led to the commodification of labour, making human life subject to the discipline and insecurities of the market, the welfare state insulated people from market risks, decoupling their ability to sustain themselves from the vagaries of the market, and thus *de*commodifying labour (Esping-Andersen 1990). Welfare states reflected a successful strategy of embedding the economic power of organised labour into the fiscal powers of the state. At the same time, differences in organisation and strategy saw different models of welfare state emerge, from the minimalist protections of the liberal world that acted only as a safety net to the universal entitlements of social democracies.

Since the 1990s welfare-state theorists have wrestled with a different set of problems as the welfare state transformed. This transformation involved both a shift across the OECD from largely industrial to largely service-based economies, known as the service transition (Esping-Andersen 1999; Wren 2013), and liberalisation (Thelen 2014). Those focusing on liberalisation, especially after the fall of the Berlin Wall, shifted attention from explaining welfare state development as a response to social resistance, towards an explanation of how democratic support for existing welfare state institutions promoted continuity and limited radical liberalisation (Pierson 1998). The service transition partly reinforced this understanding, as slower growth rates and rising health and pension costs seemed to confirm the reality of fiscal austerity (Castles 2004). However, the rise of services also paralleled challenges from those outside the male breadwinner model. Unpaid care labour provided within the family moved into the paid economy. Anti-colonial movements and scholars challenged the methodological nationalism of welfare-state scholarship (see Fraser and Jaeggi 2018). These struggles and critiques have increasingly focused attention, not only on the exploitation of wage labour, but of expropriation from those outside the labour markets of the Global North (*Ibid*, Hickel et al. 2021).

Comparative analysts do not deny change; rather, they emphasise continuity within change. The 'institutions of egalitarian capitalism', Kathleen Thelen argues, are not defended through 'stabl(e) reproduction' but by being 'reconfigured' by 'significantly new political support coalitions' (2014, 1–2). They argued it is only by adjusting and updating welfare states to suit new circumstances, not primarily by resisting liberalisation per se, that the purpose and logic of social protection are maintained and even advanced. Welfare states must respond to 'new' risks produced by changes in patterns of employment and the organisation of care (Taylor-Gooby 2004).

Institutionalist analysis explains how states reproduce difference. The structure of interests produced by the industrial welfare states produces similar patterns of care provision in service economies (Wren 2013), while the common experience of liberalisation produces a similar 'variety' of outcomes to initial welfare state formation (Thelen 2014). Australia's strong industrial protections and weak social insurance systems created an unusual starting point for liberalisation. Public spending reflected liberal norms, producing weak constituencies, yet the traditional allies of the welfare state were comparatively strong. Initially, the Accord aimed to convert industrial strength into more conventional social protection, by using social wage increases and industry policy to buffer the impacts of liberalisation (Wright 2014). However, liberalisation also saw the weakening of industrial protections, wage solidarity and unions density, complicating any sustained effort at egalitarianism (see Humphrys 2018).

In the wake of the global financial crisis, welfare states generally appeared increasingly caught in gridlock between strong fiscal pressures to contain social spending and social demands to mitigate rising inequality and insecurity (Streeck and Schäfer 2013). Many jurisdictions have implemented explicit limits on state finance, such as the United States' debt ceiling or borrowing limits in the European Maastricht Treaty. Reliance on international financial markets imposes similar limits on others. Yet, what appeared as stasis can conceal underlying change. Increasingly theorists have rethought how to understand continuity and change, arguing apparently 'incremental processes of change (that) appear to cause gradual institution transformations (can) add up to major historical discontinuities' (Streeck and Thelen 2005, 8).

A set of conceptual tools connects incremental policy change to significant shifts in the logic of state action. Streeck and Thelen (2005) identify several processes whereby liberalisation gradually transformed policy logics by 'layering' new market logics on top of existing social protections, allowing existing systems to 'drift' without being adjusted to new circumstances;

or where policies are not abolished, but rather 'converted' to serve a new purpose. Social policies designed to protect against insecurity, like unemployment benefits, can be gradually reworked to enforce market insecurity, as workfare increasingly demonstrates (Peck 2001; Mcdonald and Marston 2005). Efforts to marketise social services can have quite diverse outcomes, from highly stratifying to facilitating client engagement (Gingrich 2011; Meagher and Goodwin 2015), suggesting markets are also being remade in contradictory ways.

A related literature picks up these complex processes of reworking state and market power. Drawing on Marx and Polanyi, theorists of 'actually existing neoliberalism' critique the dichotomy between (unequal) markets and (equalising) states. 'Actually existing neoliberalism', they claim, involves state action to enforce market norms, often through increased surveillance and punishment (Wacquant 2012; Cahill 2014; Peck, Brenner and Theodore 2018). Examining the detail of neoliberalism in practice highlights how uneven this change has been, as efforts at liberalisation interact with existing institutional and political arrangements. As Jamie Peck (2012, 121) notes, 'Significant opportunities beckon, if markets – in all their hybrid, variegated, and heterogeneous forms – are seriously problematised as objects of study.'

Neoliberalism and the fiscal politics of the state

Fiscal constraint has long been central to capitalism. Liberalisation accompanied a renewed political attack on the size of the state. Liberalisation advanced alongside a tax revolt within parliaments and an intellectual attack on democratic overreach in public debate (Crozier et al. 1975). This reaction partly reflects the successful expansion of welfare states across the twentieth century to mediate the conflicts produced by free markets, allowing the decommodification of labour alongside the continued commodification of goods. The formula was managed through public finance, which was increasingly separated from private finance and managed according to Keynesian macroeconomic principles. The separation of public and private finance not only facilitated economic management, it also clarified political trade-offs between taxation and social spending. Breaking this expansionary model through the 'politics of budgetary surplus', as Scott Brenton (2016) puts it, was therefore central to liberalisation. In Australia, this materialised most explicitly in the backlash against the Whitlam government's fiscal expansion and political concern over debt and deficit.

Understanding the rise of the Keynesian welfare state and the reassertion of austerity through neoliberalism requires a sociology of state finances. Joseph Schumpeter produced one of the first and most influential accounts of fiscal politics within capitalism, which I use to inform an analysis of the politics of liberalisation. He argued taxation and distribution were so central to the development of the modern capitalist state that 'the expression "tax state" might almost be considered a pleonasm' (1991, 110). By making general claims to fiscal resources, rather than specific levies connected to specific purposes, the feudal Prince gradually transformed into the modern state, creating new forms of fiscal politics.

General taxation constructed the state as 'a machine for the common purpose' (1991, 110), whose fiscal claims are made for 'public' purposes. Fiscal claims are made against 'private economic subjects' driven by their personal 'financial interest in production' (1991, 112). Thus, fiscal claims help to constitute public and private economies as distinct spheres, governed by distinct logics. This distinction between the 'public' claims of the tax state on the 'private' resources of individuals underpins a key tension identified by welfare state theorists. Growth depends on profitability to encourage investment within the private sector, while political legitimacy relies on the state's public role advancing the common purpose (see Jessop 2015, 99–100).

The rise of the welfare state helped to mediate these tensions, producing a period of sustained economic growth. Building on the work of Polanyi (2001), many welfare-state theorists understood the welfare state's mediating role in terms of commodification (Adereth 2020). Liassez-faire liberalism had sought to impose market discipline on society. For markets to be 'self-regulating' required not only the use of markets in distribution, but the application of price and competition in production. Land, labour and money needed to become commodities, subject to price competition.

Polanyi argued this involved a 'crude fiction'. People, nature and money are not produced in markets for sale, but are sustained through social and environmental reproduction. As market competition was applied to these 'fictitious commodities' it undermined the conditions for their reproduction, leading society to resist. Polanyi argues this led to a 'double movement' where the state facilitated the application of market competition to 'genuine commodities', but constrained the 'self-regulating market' by ensuring the protection or decommodification of fictitious commodities (Polanyi 2001).

Movement politics was clearly important in building welfare states. The threat of socialism drove Bismark's initial expansion of social protection in Germany. The industrial strength of unions and electoral dominance of left parties correlates with the expansion of social democratic welfare states in Northern Europe. As Claus Offe put it, the welfare state provided a 'peace formula' (Offe 2018) between conflicting social groups by combining profits with rising living standards and social protection.

It was not only political pressure but specific forms of statecraft that drove welfare state expansion. As Stephanie Mudge argues, over the twentieth century left parties turned away from the more overtly political and socialist influence of party activists to instead embrace 'economist theoriticians' who enabled a combination of economic management alongside political consensus building (2018, 6). Drawing on work with Spies-Butcher and Bryant (2024), I argue the incorporation of economic knowledge facilitated a model of statecraft that defined and separated 'public' and 'private' finance and mobilised democratic politics to expand the former.

Economic management advanced alongside new and distinctly 'public' forms of accounting. Public and private sectors developed distinct accounting standards and international governance bodies (Barton 2005). Where private firms were focused on identifying, tracing, and capturing profits by understanding income flows in terms of 'returns' on 'assets' (Barton 2007), the public sector developed cash accounting models that focused more attention on flows of income across and between the 'public' and 'private' sectors (Spies-Butcher and Bryant 2024).

Suzuki (2003) and Rollings (1998) trace how public accounting systems in the United Kingdom were self-consciously designed to reflect the categories of Keynesian macroeconomic management. In both the United States and the United Kingdom, accounting reforms were designed to better track budget impacts on aggregate demand (Rollings 1998, 292–294, Barber 1996, 88). Indeed, this accounting revolution played a central role in constructing the 'macroeconomy' as an object of policymaking (Suzuki 2003). In Australia, Labor's post-War economic planning, including the important 1945 White Paper on full employment, adopted the same economistic Keynesian approach (see MacIntyre 2015).

The separation of public and private finance not only facilitated macro-management, it facilitated the social democratic model of welfare state building. As Richard Titmuss (1965) identifies, the objects of welfare can be advanced through many policy tools. The early strength of unions in Australia saw the rise of arbitration, rather than social spending, as the primary mechanism for providing social protection. In Northern Europe, social democrats tied social protection to the expansion of public money through social spending. Some social democrats saw this incremental use of fiscal power as a gradual pathway to socialism, where the privileges of private property were stripped away 'one by one' (Tilton 1990).

Linking social protection to social spending has two obvious advantages to the earlier emphasis on socialisation of industry. First, it facilitates the economy-wide decommodification of labour, through social insurance, while retaining private control of 'genuine' commodities (in Polanyian terms), allowing social democracy to quantitatively advance within capitalism. Second, it makes explicit the trade-off between 'public' and 'private' money by linking an expansion in the fiscal size of the state via taxation to an expansion of social welfare. The demarcation of public money thus facilitates Offe's 'peace formula', which is mediated by conventional partisan contestation, with social protection and social spending expanding most rapidly where unions and left parties are strongest (Esping-Andersen 1990).

The early success of unions in Australian politics shaped a different path. Rather than prioritising social spending, labour prioritised wages via arbitration. As Keynesian statecraft developed it was most effectively put to work managing full employment, in concert with arbitration and central banking (Beggs 2015). Constitutional constraints and electoral defeats limited Labor's attempts to expand social welfare on anything like the basis seen in Sweden, or even the United Kingdom. When Labor returned to office under Whitlam in 1972 it also returned to welfare state building; however, it faced renewed and increasing fiscal backlash.

The limits on conventional fiscal strategies gave rise to new political tactics. In neither case did politics 'shrink' the state. Instead, the state was reorganised so the categories of state finance increasingly diverged from the reach of state power. Mostly, this saw an expansion of 'hidden' support for privatised or 'dual' welfare systems. However, it also saw the use of similar strategies to expand social protection in 'hybrid' forms that blended forms of market and state regulation.

Hidden Welfare, Social Welfare and Hybrid Welfare

Social policy scholars acknowledge that social protection is not strictly equivalent to social spending nor state 'welfare' limited to public spending. Social spending is taken as a proxy because it has become the primary policy tool for providing inclusive and egalitarian social protection. Particularly in Northern Europe, social democratic welfare is social welfare. Thus, levels of social spending correlate with the organisation of the welfare state. However, states distribute resources in many other ways, and in Australia social protection has also advanced through 'other means' (Castles 1989). Understanding the distinctions within the 'social division of welfare', as Richard Titmuss (1965) called it, can help explain Australia's welfare by 'other means' and reforms associated with liberalisation that can be understood as by-passing the Keynesian logic of expanding democratic control of public money.

Titmuss' examination of the redistributive role of the state is particularly helpful in both explaining the relationship between social spending and equality and for informing the analysis of how liberalisation reshaped welfare state contests. Titmuss rejected the claim that analysis of redistribution should only include taxation and social spending. Redistribution, he argued, did not only involve the state committing resources to cash payments or the provision of services. The state also provided for social needs, and importantly redistributed resources, through concessional tax arrangements, which he dubbed *fiscal* welfare, and through benefits accessed through employment from employers, which he dubbed *occupational* welfare. These policies should be considered redistributive because they involve state decisions and 'they change the pattern of claims on current and future resources' (1965, 17).

The process of redistribution works differently in each case, and is more or less difficult to identify as a result. Social welfare is the most readily identifiable as it involves both the collection of monies and then the distribution of those monies as two separate budgetary events. Fiscal welfare, by contrast, combines the two steps so that, in budgetary terms, they cancel each other out and disappear from budget records. The state first acts to require the payment of tax based on one set of criteria and then through a separate rule, reduces or eliminates that requirement based on a different set of criteria. As others have observed (Smith 2001; Morel et al. 2016; Sinfeld 2018), the outcome is the same in fiscal, distributive and incentive terms as the collection of taxes and then payment of welfare, but organised entirely through the tax system it disappears from public accounts, and from the routine oversight of democratic governance. For most citizens who are neither wealthy nor tax accountants, it appears as if nothing is happening.

Finally, occupational welfare, which is received based on employment status, is managed by private employers, but generally sanctioned or required by the state. Occupational welfare has been an important corollary to arbitration in Australia, with entitlements such as sick leave, superannuation, parental leave and leave loading all emerging through state-sanctioned wage-bargaining processes. The resources controlled through occupational welfare, however, are generally not recorded in public budgeting and instead appear as private transactions. The most obvious example in Australia is superannuation, which is paid by employers to individual employee funds, yet the contributions are compulsory (like a tax) and individuals can only access funds for certain purposes or under certain circumstances (like a social insurance scheme). Occupational welfare involves the state redistributing resources; however, framed as a private transaction it is less visible and less obviously political.

Titmuss' analysis shows how state redistribution is more pervasive, and benefits many more people, than is often acknowledged. However, different forms of welfare tend to follow different distributional, as well as organisational, logics. Fiscal and occupational welfare tend to reinforce and even exaggerate market inequalities because their 'benefits are fundamentally based on the principles of achievement (and) status' (1965, 17–18), as well as need. The expansion of these forms of 'hidden' welfare is a key driver of inequalities through liberalisation internationally and in Australia.

Australia's experience, however, suggests occupational and fiscal welfares have distinct logics from each other. The central role of arbitration has meant many occupational welfare provisions have more in common with social insurance models, particularly when arbitration also compressed wages. Social protections won through arbitration were often subject to explicit social evaluation and were granted in the context of relative full employment. As wage setting was decentralised, so the structure of occupational welfare was reorganised. Less equal wages and labour markets directly translate into less equal occupational welfare.

Even so, the distributive impacts of occupational welfare are distinct from fiscal welfare. Fiscal welfare does not only reinforce the market distribution of income, it often exaggerates market inequalities. Fiscal welfare is usually proportionate to a person's tax liability, which inverts the progressive impact of the income tax scale to provide the largest benefits to high-income earners, not only in absolute terms but in proportionate terms. As with occupational welfare, Australia has a long history of providing tax concessions for privately purchased welfare services, such as private health insurance and private pension schemes (Smith 2001; Stebbing 2015).

The prevalence of fiscal welfare before liberalisation, combined with its hidden fiscal cost and support for private welfare, created conditions for the emergence of a 'dual welfare state' (Stebbing and Spies-Butcher 2010), where two separate welfare systems operate in parallel. Under the dual welfare state, overtly public schemes funded through social welfare become more conditional and residual, targeting only the poor.

Support for middle-class citizens and private welfare providers expands through fiscal welfare. Dual welfare appears to reduce the size of the state by reducing taxation. Unlike tax cuts, however, it extends state control of social provision allowing governments to respond to middle-class demands to manage social risk, and thus build larger and more durable electoral coalitions.

Across the cases examined in the book, there are few examples where the state genuinely shrank or retreated. Instead, liberalisation involved 'roll out' strategies (Peck 2010; Cahill 2010). Policies became more punitive to the poor and more generous to the rich. State spending was redirected from those in need to private providers. And because fiscal welfare appears to shrink state finances, it conforms to the pressures of austerity, even as it creates economic incentives and redistributes resources. Unlike the archetypal model of social democratic welfare, Australia's failure to advance social protection through universal social spending meant less formal retrenchment was required, limiting democratic resistance.

The cases also reveal instances of liberalisation that appear to expand social protection and reduce inequalities. Often these examples see the state and market expanding together in areas where social spending had not fully developed before liberalisation, such as support for families with children, public healthcare and universities. Here, pressure to expand provision confronted fiscal constraints, making traditional social democratic models more difficult. What emerged, I argue, were hybrid policy models that often took advantage of the 'hidden' nature of occupational and fiscal welfare, but applied similar principles to conceal the expanding role of state finance in socialising risk.

Both 'hidden' and 'hybrid' welfare reflect a misalignment between the categories we use to trace and measure 'states' and 'markets' and the patterns of social and economic organisation we use those terms to describe. Liberalisation often advanced new budget and management models within the public sector to overcome democratic resistance and to impose market logics within the state. These reforms – like Truth in Budgeting, Generational Accounting and Liability Budgeting – frequently applied market categories to the state asymmetrically, exaggerating the fiscal costs of egalitarian action, while concealing forms of privatisation. Hybridity often involved applying similar conventions more symmetrically.

Separating 'states' and 'markets' into public and private domains is not straightforward. Modern nation states developed alongside market societies, partly helping to constitute them. However, the emphasis on market 'embeddedness' within sociology potentially leaves the market itself under-theorised, because it focuses attention on what the market is embedded in, leaving out the 'hard core of instantaneous market transactions' (Krippner 2001, 112). Hybridity builds on recent geographical scholarship on the variegated nature of neoliberalism to focus attention on how models of liberalisation and marketisation differ. Not only have states been reorganised to act like markets, what we think of as markets have been reorganised to provide some of the risk pooling we associate with welfare states.

The twentieth century saw social democrats increasingly respond to the crises and conflicts of capitalism through a strategy of welfare state expansion. That expansion involved defining and separating public and private finance, making public finance subject to democratic control, while facilitating continued accumulation in private markets. Through these strategies, particularly through analysis of the most successful Nordic examples, public state finance and private market finance became distinct and coherent conceptual tools. Private finance was both conceptually and empirically the realm of Polanyi's 'self-regulating' market and Schumpeter's 'private economic subjects'. The state's 'public' role was defined in fiscal terms through its claim on resources. The reality never quite matched this analytic ideal, but it served a useful simplification. Liberalisation acts to blur these boundaries.

Liberalisation and 'Hybridity' in Advanced Welfare States

Polanyi is a common intellectual current across related literatures on liberalisation (see Block 2019), and his later work on economic integration offers a useful tool for analysing hybridity within liberalised welfare states. His analysis develops the concept of embeddedness, arguing economic processes are embedded through institutions which give the economy 'unity and stability' (1985 [1957], 7). He identifies three archetypal logics of integration – reciprocity, redistribution and exchange.[1] While each of these processes can reflect individual actions or behaviours, they become logics of economic integration when such processes are supported by institutions – systems of kinship supporting reciprocity, a central state to facilitate redistribution and markets to coordinate exchange.

Polanyi's forms of economic integration are ideal types. All three institutions coexist in actual societies. However, more recent analysis draws on Polanyi to identify forms of hybridity. Hybridity moves beyond co-existence to imply the combination of different forms of economic integration within the same institutions (see Spies-Butcher and Bryant 2018). Thus, institutions can develop that involve both exchange and redistribution, where both logics advance at once, often through a language common to both states and markets – rationalisation. Rather than imagining one logic advancing as the other recedes, hybridity suggests new logics of integration that combine Polanyi's categories in novel ways.

I use hybridity to identify two different logics within liberalisation. First, liberalisation often occurs in relatively straightforward ways, as Polanyi outlines and as theorists of 'actually existing neoliberalism' argue. Here liberalisation involves the extension of processes of commodification, often through reworking existing forms of welfare to enforce market norms. This can be seen in punitive workfare, in the marketisation of early education and care and the enormous inequalities generated by Australia's financialised retirement incomes system. In each of these cases the state remains central, but

---

1 Polanyi originally identifies a forth form of integration, householding, but is later convinced householding is a smaller version of redistribution (Schaniel and Neale 2000, 92).

state power enforces market norms, justified by aiding accumulation and growth, obscuring its role in distributing resources.

Liberalisation advances in part because policy change does not straight-forwardly 'privatise'. 'Hidden' state action manages social risk for the better off via markets, while overt social spending targets the poor, making it easier to stigmatise. In other cases, similar 'hybrid' processes extend social protection. Here the state takes on risks, insulating citizens from the negative consequences of market outcomes, but does so through policy mechanisms that mimic market prices. These 'boundary' conflicts reflect not only the rolling back of democratic norms but also the reworking of social distinctions built into Australia's wage-earner model. Egalitarian politics, then, is not simply a project of reasserting wage earners' welfare but of asserting new models of social protection, often building on the technical neutrality claimed by liberalisation to reveal and challenge gendered and raced inequalities.

In the next section I apply this framework to explore examples of the three dominant modes of liberalisation – targeting, marketisation and financialisation. In each I identify two distinct logics. While fiscal constraints appear to limit state action and create stasis, there are conflicting processes that reorganise welfare to different ends. Taken together, I argue these cases reveal on ongoing distributional politics reconfigured through the process of liberalisation. Responding to liberalisation involves familiar principles of solidarity and democratisation, but adapts those principles to a new context. Adaption not only involves distinct policy models, it likely requires new connections between policy and politics built around the relations of social reproduction.

Chapter 3

RESIDUALISING WELFARE

'Welfare' is most commonly used to describe income support payments. The broader system of taxation and transfer payments is especially important in Australia's model of targeted redistribution. Benefit payments have been significantly restructured since the 1980s, and rising total benefit payments, especially to families with children and older people, have contributed to the increase in total social spending. These changes have not only been driven by demographics but also by deliberate policy decisions. Alternatively, a process of 'welfare reform' has introduced conditionality into income support for the unemployed, seen the erosion of the adequacy of that income support, and shifted many people from more generous and secure payments to the residualised unemployment benefit.

Both these trends – rising spending on families and older people and more conditional and meagre spending on the working-age population – have proven politically resilient. While there are partisan differences in pace and emphasis, these twin trajectories have been broadly advanced under both Labor and Coalition governments and reflect broader international trends (see OECD 2022a; OECD2022b; Knotz 2018).

This chapter explores processes of 'residualisation' as an example of liberalisation within government payment systems. Residualisation restricts the role of social spending to the margins, constructing market incomes, especially labour market income, as the primary means for most people to secure their needs. I argue the examples of family benefits and unemployment benefits provide two models of residualisation that reflect the alternative processes of hybridity and dualism, even though both reinforce the primacy of the market.

The reform of family benefits reflects the mobilisation of feminists, who successfully politicised the needs of families with children to increase benefit rates, and worked inside state bureaucracies to challenge how value was measured and rewards distributed. Those efforts interacted with the rising power of economic rationalists to produce 'affluence testing', combining flat-rate benefits with generous means-testing, that is widely seen as a fiscally efficient 'hybrid' model of benefit support (Stewart and Whiteford 2018). Alternatively, unemployment benefits have become subject to a severe form of paternalism that reinforces divisions between the deserving and undeserving poor.

The chapter focuses primarily on the story of family payments, where a powerful combination of politics and technocratic skill reshaped the benefits system. Feminists drove the expansion of income support by making visible and then reforming a series of distinctions reflecting the market/social categories that underpinned the Keynesian welfare state.

Politically, feminists made successful normative claims for gender equality and against child poverty, strengthened by constructing women as an important electoral constituency. Within the state those claims were advanced through novel accounting strategies, such as gender budgeting and accounting for fiscal welfare, that made visible the asymmetries of state budgeting processes.

Finally, policy reform advances symmetry and universalism by converting social tax expenditures (STEs) into social spending. Once converted, spending is shaped according to more explicitly normative principles of need and market incentives. These changes remain imperfect and subject to subtle forms of austerity, but constitute a clear 'hybrid' dynamic with the potential to expand and redistribute social support.

The chapter ends by contrasting the experience of family payments to changes in unemployment support. While there are commonalities across the payments system, the unemployed have faced a disturbingly harsh and punitive model of reform. The transformation also follows a distinctive logic, predicated on distinctions between deserving and undeserving summed up in the term 'wedge politics' (Wilson and Turnbull 2001). Conditionality advances first to marginalised groups. Once established, conditionality is then expanded to the broader benefit population. Finally, conditionality expands further by eroding the coverage of more secure and generous benefits by transferring people into residualised programs.

Conditionality is not cheap. Alongside restrictions in benefits, spending on privatised surveillance expands. As with the example of family benefits, while partisan differences remain, the broad trajectory of reform is consistent across both sides of politics. Comparing the two examples suggests very different experiences of 'residualisation' and opportunities for political contestation.

Social Payments in the Wage-Earner Welfare State

The model of flat-rate means-tested benefits was established early in Australia's history with the introduction of state-based aged pensions around the time of federation (Stebbing 2015, 118–119). Those payments were consolidated

into a national scheme in 1909 under the Deakin Liberal government relying on Labor support and at the time marked a substantial development in
Australia's 'social laboratory'. The development of pensions pre-dated today's
near-universal income tax system. Instead, the additional tax revenues used
to finance social policy expansion came from more steeply progressive forms
of taxation (*Ibid*, 121). This structure reflected a view in the labour movement that social protection should be financed by those with an ability to
pay, and the wages of ordinary workers protected (see Smith 2017, 178–179).
A conservative government almost replaced the model with an insurance
principle similar to European schemes before the Second World War, but
the legislation was never implemented, and the Wartime Labor government
instead entrenched the principle of funding social payments from consolidated revenue.

The expansion of social payments post-War built on the architecture of
early twentieth-century social policy. Following constitutional changes to
overcome constraints on Commonwealth powers, Labor established sickness and invalid, windows and unemployment benefits. All were flat-rate and
means-tested, although income taxation had been substantially broadened
during the Wars such that most workers now paid tax. The same constitutional change allowed maternity and family payments, facilitating a new
child endowment, which was also flat-rate, but universal. While most of the
benefits in the Australian system were means-tested, they were also understood to be unconditional. Labor's opposition to insurance-based schemes
reflected a commitment to universalism, because payments would not require
prior contribution (see Stebbing 2015). Flat-rate benefits reflected a more universal understanding of need, one tied to a common social position rather
than previous market income. Thus, payments constituted a higher 'replacement rate' for low-income blue-collar workers than for higher-paid professionals and managers (Castles 1985).

Regular payments were categorical, but not necessarily conditional.
There was no 'universal' payment. Instead, payments reflected the normative
commitments of the breadwinner model, with benefit categories reflecting
'acceptable', and highly gendered, social roles. Men gained access when they
were not expected to work, for example based on disability, illness or age.
Women gained access when they were not able to access support from a male
breadwinner. Payment rules were largely categorical, and reflected the dominance of full-time work. Either a person was in a benefit category (and not in
work) or they were not eligible at all. Benefits cut out quickly with additional
income, but there were few conditions and little enforcement within the categories. Together, benefits and arbitrated minimum wages created a relatively
solid floor for those fitting inside the system's socially determined categories.

For those who did not conform to the gendered and raced categories, life was far more precarious (Altman and Saunders 2018; Smith 2017).

Social payments also sat alongside occupational and fiscal welfare, which helped to contain overall social spending. Arbitration ensured minimum wages were relatively high and wages in general were relatively compressed (Castles 2001). Social protection was also built into the wage system itself. Sick leave, annual leave (and later leave loading) and workers compensation were all funded by employers and accessed by workers at the level of their ordinary wage. Alongside the wage-earner protections designed around the needs of blue-collar workers, a parallel system of fiscal welfare developed. Tax concessions for contributions to retirement income were introduced in the early twentieth century (Stebbing 2015), partly reflecting a political compromise with the high-income earners whose taxes funded means-tested public pensions. Similar deductions were later introduced for private health insurance (Smith 2001).

Tax rules also allowed deductions for a dependent spouse and family members. Income tax deductions for those with dependent children were introduced in 1915 and then for income earners with a dependent spouse in 1936. Child endowment, a social payment, was belatedly added in the early 1940s, in response to feminist calls for equity and to strategically reduce inflation and wage growth (Cass and Brennan 2003, 42).

The universal child endowment was not indexed and lost real value over time. Alternatively, tax deductions had an inbuilt growth mechanism, as they were implicitly linked to changes in wages and the tax system. Thus, by the 1970s, the value of tax concessions was considerably larger than for social payments (see Montanari 2000, 320). These tax expenditures were explicitly 'social', in the sense that they mimicked the role of social spending, and so are usefully understood as STEs.

Both fiscal and social welfare entrenched strong gender norms. A proliferation of payments was built around the normative role of women as mothers and men as breadwinners. Labour market rules either excluded women or mandated differential pay rates based on gender (Ryan 1984) ensuring a gendered division of occupational and fiscal welfare, received by male breadwinners to provide for female homemakers. In terms of income support, the wage-earner welfare state was both a 'dual' welfare state (Stebbing and Spies-Butcher 2010) and a 'breadwinner' welfare state (Mitchell 1998).

Reshaping Family Support

From the 1970s to the 2000s Australia's system of income support for families with children was significantly restructured. Dual welfare and breadwinner welfare was gradually, and still partially, reshaped to become more egalitarian and less gendered. Feminists were central to these changes, both through political and electoral mobilisation, and as 'femocrats' (Sawer 2016; Yeatman 2020) within state bureaucracies and policy machinery. It was the combination of political and technocratic mobilisation, I argue, that facilitated a hybrid model of reform. Political mobilisation created pressure to expand access and adequacy. Technocratic strategies helped navigate fiscal constraints, not by rejecting market principles but by extending them and applying them more consistently.

Feminists challenged the asymmetries of the dual welfare model to highlight the uneven support provided to (especially high income) breadwinner households. They instead asserted symmetry between taxation and social spending, advancing a common set of normative principles. Need was addressed through raising base payments in line with a monetary conception of the poverty line. Even as austerity eroded explicit universal access, arguments over competition and incentives helped prevent a slide towards severe forms of residualisation that aid retrenchment. Combined, these strategies proved relatively effective, and the new policy architecture relatively robust. However, the incorporation of feminists inside the policy machinery contributed to a longer-term demobilisation and weakening of the movement, while post-GFC austerity pressures have begun eroding coverage.

Liberalisation coincided with the transformation of family income support. The changes in Australia are not exceptional internationally. All welfare states have responded to some extent to the entry of women into paid work (Orloff 1996; Esping-Andersen 1999; Navarro 2020). Across the OECD women have become an important progressive electoral constituency in support of welfare state expansion in areas like family spending and childcare provision (Wren 2013; Navarro 2020). Indeed, Australia's work/care regime, as Barbara Pocock (2005) calls it, has been relatively slow to adapt to the new norm of women's equal labour market participation, with Australia lagging in introducing paid parental leave and increasing public spending on early education and care. Yet, amongst these changes, reforms to family payments have gone further, creating a stark contrast to changes in other benefit systems.

Expanding Family Spending

Family spending has increased significantly. Figure 3.1 outlines changes in social spending on families in Australia and as an average across the OECD from 1980 to 2017. Social spending on families with children became a central component of the social wage demands of the Accord, and was expanded

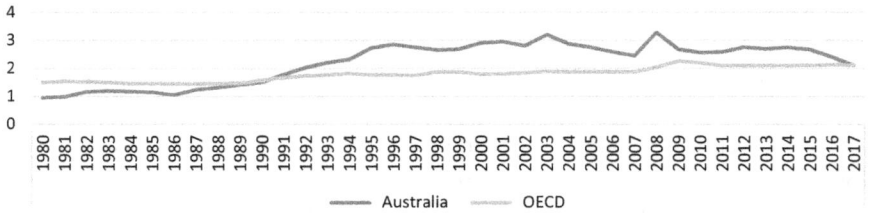

Figure 3.1 Australian social spending on families and OECD average spending as a proportion of GDP, 1980–2017. *Source*: OECD (2023), Family benefits public spending (indicator). doi: 10.1787/8e8b3273-en (Accessed on 19 January 2023).

further (although in ways that reflected different normative commitments) under the Howard Coalition government and then again under the Rudd/ Gillard Labor governments. Australia entered the 1980s spending less than two-thirds of the OECD average on families as a proportion of GDP. This rose substantially in the decade from 1986 to 1996, by which point the OECD average was less than two-thirds of Australian spending, and continued to rise until 2003. Changes in spending since have partly reflected broader economic conditions, falling against GDP during the mining boom and then recovering, except for a dramatic increase in 2008 associated with the Rudd government's economic stimulus package. The decline in recent years reflects freezes to indexation, discussed below, although spending did jump as EEC temporarily became free during Covid-19.

The women's movement played a key role in shaping this transformation. Despite the strong breadwinner foundations of the wage-earner welfare state, Australia has a long history of women's and feminist organising (see Smith 2017; Ryan 1984; Towns 2016). Australia followed close behind New Zealand as one of the first modern democracies to expand the franchise to women shortly after federation. Agitation for equal pay has a long history through the twentieth century (Ryan 1984; Smith and Whitehouse 2020); however, second-wave feminism brought a more visible and organised industrial and political voice. In 1972, the newly formed Women's Electoral Lobby (WEL) ran its first candidate survey for the federal election, creating a formal campaign platform and set of policy demands (see Sawer and Radford 2008).

The Australian women's movement, while diverse, was relatively more successful at pursuing state-orientated strategies through the bureaucracy, partly reflecting challenges in pursuing more aggressive strategies through civil society (Sawer 1993, 15). Those efforts centred on establishing a women's policy machinery within the state staffed by feminists connected to movement politics outside the state, dubbed 'femocrats'. A substantive literature has emerged around the importance of 'femocrats' to policy reform in Australia (Cass and Brennan 2003; O'Connor et al. 1999; Sawer 1996; Yeatman 2020). While operating within the state, individual femocrats maintained an uneasy solidarity with movement activists (Eisenstein 1992) and class politics (Yeatman 2020), and the new structures were themselves subject to political contestation and defence.

Marian Sawer (1996) argues feminists were more successful at advancing their interests within the bureaucracy than were women's movements in other countries, maintaining a more central position and more direct executive access than elsewhere (Sawer 1996). This coincided with the parallel rise of economic rationalism within the central economic agencies (Pusey 1991) and the rise of the 'guardian' role of these agencies in asserting fiscal limits within cabinet (Brenton 2016). The result, Sawer argues, was the unique interplay of 'femocrats' and 'econorats' that helps explain the somewhat technocratic trajectory of women's policy.

Importantly, the femocrat strategy was not only technocratic but relied on the political mobilisation of women as an electoral constituency. Sawer cites the public resignation of Sara Dowse as Head of the Office of the Status of Women, and Anne Summers' success in leveraging the 'women's vote' to gain funding commitments under the Hawke and Keating Labor governments as key examples of politicising women's policy from within the bureaucracy (1996, 5, 10). Finally, Prime Minister Bob Hawke's commitment to end child poverty reflected the success of political mobilisation inside and outside the state. While now seen as hyperbolic, over the next 15 years Australia's child poverty rate fell faster than in any other OECD country (Whiteford et al. 2011, 91).

It was the combination of politics and technocratic expertise, I argue, that fostered hybridity. Only by mobilising politics were governments obliged to act. The form of policy change reflected the relatively technocratic strategies of femocrats to highlight gender bias, and Australia's brand of fiscal politics, with its emphasis on quantitative economic measures. Family payments, in particular, reflected a two-step process of conversion that transformed gen-der-biased and inegalitarian tax concessions into a form of 'affluence testing'. Payments expanded and targeted poverty, but also remained inclusive and thus politically popular. However, the technocratic nature of policy reform potentially contributed to the deradicalisation and demobilisation of the women's movement, allowing more hostile governments to dismantle much of the initial policy machinery (Sawer 2007) and contributed to the delay in advancing other reforms such as paid parental leave.

Australian feminists were at the forefront of feminist economics and devel-oping accounting devices to help conceptualise and quantify gender bias, particularly using gender budgeting (see Sharp and Broomhill 2002) and tax expenditure data (Smith 2001; Austen et al. 2015). These tools assert symmetry between social and fiscal spending, and between paid and unpaid care, helping feminists highlight inequality. Gender budgeting highlights how benefits and costs from state action differentially accrue to men and women. Gender budgeting was an important tool for demonstrating the gendered impacts of market restructuring, for example, informing efforts by feminists, unions and the community sector to defeat a Treasury proposal to radically flatten the tax base in the mid-1980s through the introduction of a consumption tax (Sawer 1996, 7). Even more significant for the reform of family payments were efforts to calculate the fiscal impact of tax concessions in order to reform fiscal welfare (O'Connor, Orloff and Shaver 1999; Cass and Brennan 2003).

The dual structure of family support produced two types of inequality. First, vertical inequality benefited high-income earners more than low-income earners. Second, horizontal inequality benefited men as breadwinners (and income tax payers) relative to women. Bettina Cass and Deborah Brennan chronicle how this process evolved, emphasising the key roles of both the Australian Council of Trade Unions (ACTU) through the Accord and feminists, especially those within state policy-making machinery. By the end of Labor's rule, family payments had been broadly recast into the affluence-tested model. This reflected a number of interlocking pressures.

Cass and Brennan (2003) outline how vertical and horizontal inequalities were addressed together through reforms that converted STEs into direct social spending. Initially, concern over the impact of family STEs centred on the first of these inequalities, emerging out of the 'rediscovery of poverty' that coincided with the Henderson Inquiry into Poverty (Cass and Brennan 2003, 42). The Henderson Inquiry proposed a novel policy conversion, which later became important for overcoming fiscal resistance, recommending the abolition of STEs be used to fund an expansion of child endowment.

As discussed in Chapter 2, while fiscal welfare appears to reduce the scale of taxation, it expresses a form of state distribution. Yet it is typically hidden from conventional budgeting processes. As tax concessions were incorporated into more visible budgetary forms, so the spending became subject to egalitarian norms. Conceptually, this can be understood in two steps, outlined in Figure 3.2. First STEs were converted into a form of spending and accounted for within the budget. Second, that spending was reorganised according to two normative principles – need and pro-market incentives. In practice this produced 'affluence testing', where the base rate of payments increased alongside mild forms of means-testing (see Hodgson 2011; Spies-Butcher 2020b).

Dual Welfare	Conversion	Hybrid Welfare
Benefits delivered as tax concessions	Benefits delivered as social spending	Social spending reformed to target need
Finance is outside budget process	Finance is inside budget process	Finance is inside budget process
Proportional to private income/spending	Proportional to private income/spending	Proportional to need

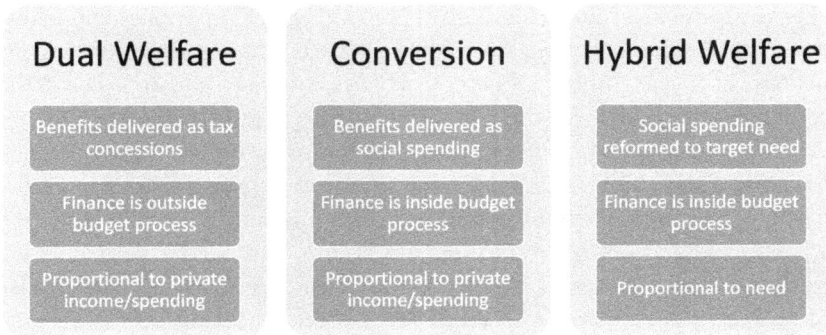

Figure 3.2 Conversion of dual welfare to hybrid welfare.

From Dual Welfare to Affluence Testing

The combination of expanding base payments to better reflect need alongside mild forms of means-testing can be understood as an expression of hybridity. Changes to means-testing reflected tensions over fiscal constraints, work incentives and value. Feminists fought to expand social spending for families with children and to direct those funds to primary carers. Their efforts increasingly focused on the Accord framework, where social spending could be framed as off-setting the impact of wage restraint on household incomes, and spending on early education and care could facilitate women's labour force participation (see Cass and Brennan 2003, 47; Cass 1994, 117–118; Brennan 2007, Chapter 9). The strategy challenged the binary categories of wage-earner welfare because household income was no longer equivalent to breadwinner wages, and benefits were not confined to those outside the workforce. Instead, part-time workers contributed to household incomes, while remaining eligible for 'needs' based payments.

The growing prevalence of part-time work made incentives at the margin – the net gain from taking on an additional shift – more important, and highlighted the poor incentives confronting part-time workers (see Saunders 1995). The focus on incentives reflects the principles of the tax system, and was often discussed in terms of effective marginal tax rates (EMTRs) (see Beer 2003). EMTRs combine the incentive effects of taxation and social benefits. For example, if a person on a government benefit also earns market income they likely face both means-testing and income tax. The net income they gain from an additional dollar of market income is thus reduced by both the means-test and the income tax rate. Both are also clearly the result of state law, which sets withdrawal rates and tax rules.

Framing welfare reform through the lens of EMTRs applies the principles of marginalist economics used to justify tax cuts more symmetrically. The logic of this argument is laid out by Patricia Apps and Ray Rees (2010), who show how means-tested flat-rate benefits are equivalent to the taxation of universal benefits. Marginalism is concerned with changes 'at the margin', for example the changes in net income that result from an additional dollar of gross income. Such an account assumes instrumental rational action, yet it also opens the way for an assertion of universal need. Conversion can be understood as reorganising payments around the principle of EMTRs. EMTRs integrate income tax rates and means-tests, breaking down the dualism between fiscal and social spending, making the 'taxation' of social payments visible. The equivalence treats all income, public and private, similarly, and all state claims on income, both means-testing and taxation, similarly. Thus, EMTRs reflect and facilitate a form of universalism.

In the case of family payments, the Whitlam government transformed family-based STEs into tax rebates, that is, flat-rate rebates to tax payers (Cass and Brennan 2003, 42). While more egalitarian then tax concessions, the rebates were only available to those paying income tax. The rebates were then converted into an expansion of endowments, which remained unindexed, under the Fraser government, and then finally into indexed payments under Hawke (*Ibid*, 44). This model of moving from STE to tax rebate to social provision has been repeated elsewhere, as we shall see in the next chapter.

Under the Hawke and Keating governments a number of different benefits were restructured into a form of affluence testing. Labor remained committed to strong fiscal restraint through its 'trilogy' promise, but also sought to increase female labour force participation as a mechanism to support household budgets during a period of wage restraint. Very tight forms of means-testing created strong disincentives for part-time work.

Femocrats used mainstream economic arguments to contest economically rationalist bureaucracies (Sawer 1996, 3). Feminists argued both to increase benefit rates to better reflect need and reduce poverty and to advance universalism, initially by resisting means-tests but then by highlighting the anti-work incentives of harsh means-tests (see Cass 1986; Cass and Brennan 2003, 43–45). Economic rationalists argued to means-test universal payments to reduce social spending. These pressures intersected around a model of provision usually described as 'affluence testing' (see Hodgson 2011, 259).

The two steps in restructuring family support outlined in Figure 3.2 can be seen through the overall impact of numerous smaller changes. The first set of changes converted STEs from the dual welfare model into social payments. Research by Ingalill Montanari (2000) estimates that the substantial increase in family spending achieved by 1990 only marginally exceeded the previous combination of spending and STEs provided in 1975. This appeared as an increase in family support because STEs remain invisible within public accounts, but is more properly understood as a restructuring in the form of assistance. States already used fiscal power to shape incentives and distribution, conversion made those powers more visible and subject to democratic oversight. The changes also achieved another movement goal of shifting the beneficiary of public support from (predominantly male) primary earners to (predominantly female) primary carers (Cass and Brennan 2003).

The second set of changes targeted and integrated different social payments. A multitude of payments were consolidated into a simpler family payments system. In effect, the previously universal child endowment became subject to means-testing, although initially 90 per cent of families continued to receive payments (Cass 1990). Simultaneously, higher payments, which were more tightly targeted, were made more generous and accessible by reducing means-tests. The restructuring and expansion of social spending shaped the subsequent politics of family spending. While means-testing advanced, it remained far more inclusive than for other payments. 'Affluence testing' reflected different normative commitments, where flat-rate benefits reflected something akin to a guaranteed minimum, while means-testing reflected enduring austerity. This entrenched a greater degree of universalism than reforms in similar countries that linked family payments to work (see St John 2006), and refocused political contestation around economic incentives.

Changes in Australian family payments accompanied similar proposals across liberal welfare states (Esping-Andersen 1999, 75–76). The best known, perhaps, is Milton Friedman's (1962) proposed negative income tax (NIT). Friedman's proposal sought to collapse the welfare system into the tax system by restructuring benefits as a tax refund, which was gradually withdrawn until no payment remained, at which point additional income was subject to income tax. Conceptually the refund represented the outcome of a 'negative tax rate', where individuals received an increasingly large refund for every dollar they fell below a given threshold. Friedman's proposal informed Nixon's family tax reforms and paralleled experiments in a universal basic income (see Woodbury 2017). While not fully dealing with the EMTR issue, the failure of Nixon's proposal was also the direct prelude to a shift within US politics to linking payments to work requirements (Moffitt 2003, 134–135).

Friedman's proposal also sought to limit social provision, funding his NIT through the retrenchment of public services, effectively 'cashing out' the welfare state. However, this is not a necessary element of NIT. Contemporaneous to Friedman, James Tobin proposed a similar scheme funded through an expansion of tax revenues (see Tobin et al. 1967), in practice very similar to Australia's conversion of STEs into social spending. What both schemes have in common is the integration of social payments and taxation according to a common set of principles. Both involve a base payment understood as a form of guaranteed minimum income. Both also involve organising contributions to fund the payment around a person's ability to pay.

Three elements of these changes are significant for understanding the political dynamics of welfare. First, contestation increasingly centred around universal categories of need and contribution, displacing the gendered social categories of wage-earner welfare. Base payments reflected a common definition of the social need associated with raising children. That common baseline built on the Henderson Inquiry into Poverty, which sought to translate the social claim of ending poverty into a monetary measure through the 'poverty line'. The poverty line was then mobilised electorally through feminists campaigns, and integrated into policy through Bob Hawke's commitment to end child poverty.

Second, renovation saw the integration of the social principle of income adequacy with the competitive principle of prices used to allocate resources via market exchange. While means-testing reflected fiscal austerity, the relatively inclusive model of affluence testing and continuation of a flat-rate benefit available to most families facilitated a shift in the locus of contestation. EMTRs created a conceptual basis for integrating the governance of social payments and income tax. The progressive income tax system, based on rising marginal tax rates, already reflected these dual imperatives. Increasing the tax burden proportionate to income reflects the principle of 'ability to pay', while marginal tax rates integrate with market prices (such as wages and profits) to minimise disincentives. EMTRs connect means-testing to similar principles, rather than limiting access to social categories or applying conditionality, reflecting the structure of affluence tested, rather than conditional, payments. Affluence testing constitutes payments as entitlements and makes means-tests functionally equivalent to changes in income tax rates.

Finally, renovation reflected attempts to mediate the political imperatives of fiscal constraint through innovative accounting techniques. Framed as a 'means-test', the reduction in the total resources (market income plus government payment) for higher income families was categorised as a reduction in public spending, rather than an increase in taxation. Of course, there is an important proviso. Unlike new tax rates, which apply to all income, means-tests apply to payments, which have a maximum level. EMTRs fall once the payment is exhausted and the withdrawal rate no longer applies. Thus, the highest EMTRs usually applying to middle-income earners (see Harding and Polette 1995). Likewise, conversion of STEs into spending facilitated an expansion of spending without deficit financing and an increase in tax revenues without an increase in tax rates. Importantly, the Hawke government introduced a new form of fiscal accounting – tax expenditure statements – to facilitate this process by tracking and quantifying the impact of tax expenditures (see Stebbing and Spies-Butcher 2010, 591). Both affluence testing and conversion of STEs 'framed policy change as *restructuring* rather than *increasing* government distribution' (Spies-Butcher 2020b, 596).

It is significant that changes to financing operate within a single social domain. STEs for dependent family members were converted into spending for a similar social group. Means-testing of family benefits financed increases to base rates of the same type of payment. This emphasises the connection between finances and specific social needs. As Esping-Andersen (1999) notes, the development of welfare states reflects a response to risk when individual misfortune is politically acknowledged as reflecting social risk. Equality is a by-product. While redistribution is a more explicit goal of Australia's welfare tradition, I argue hybrid strategies are most effective when they combine budgetary and economic equivalence (between means-testing and taxation, or STEs and social spending) with social equivalence between similar social risks. Converting STEs in one domain to fund general revenue is much more likely to be successfully resisted as a generic increase in taxation, as it seems occurred to Labor in 2019.

The politics of renovation combined mobilisation around a politics of need with an innovative technocratic politics of fiscal accounting. However, the results remained incomplete, while the political forces that aided renovation faded, in part due to the incorporation of feminist energies into the state (Sawer 2007). More recent changes have sought to reconnect family support to the tax system and to favour breadwinner families. A crucial test of hybrid policy is whether it proves resilient to retrenchment or is more easily reversed. The experience of family policy reveals important limitations, but also a shift in the underlying dynamics of contestation. Austerity has not disappeared, nor is it consistently dominant. Instead, affluence testing has facilitated a politics more favourable to equity and expansion than often assumed.

Retrenching and Defending Family Support

Labor lost office in the wake of a deep recession. The Coalition focused on rising debt and deficits, using a Commission of Audit to reinforce fiscal constraints and justify significant cuts (see Quiggin 2012, 126–127). Much of the policy machinery built by femocrats and other movements was dismantled through austerity. The Coalition also targeted social payments, seeking to reconnect the family payments system to the tax system and reinforce breadwinner incentives (Cass and Brennan 2003). Yet, as Helen Hodgson (2011) has argued, the structural shifts away from STEs remained largely resilient to retrenchment, while affluence testing continued. In new policy domains, such as parental leave, the demobilisation of movement politics hindered policy innovation. Insider strategies may be effective at advancing more egalitarian forms of liberalised policy, but by themselves lack the normative energy needed to politically contest liberalisation.

The Howard government restructured family assistance in two main steps, which are helpfully examined by Bettina Cass and Deborah Brennan (2003). Both sought to unwind the earlier changes, by reconnecting family support to the tax system and targeting support to traditional family models. Initially, the Family Tax Initiative effectively increased the tax-free threshold for families based on their number of children. However, the changes created two income tests: a household income test and a test that effectively applied to the *second* income earner. The second income test created a disincentive for second earners (largely women) to gain paid work. The changes reframed support as a tax policy and valorised breadwinner families; however, distributionally the changes did far less to reverse the impact of previous reforms.

The new support may have been framed in relation to the tax system, but effectively remained a payment. While the amount received was the equivalent of an increase in the tax-free threshold, parents could receive the income even if they were not in work. Jobless households would generally receive the benefit as a social security payment, while higher-income households accessed it via the tax system. As both components were means-tested, the additional support was strongly progressive and largely supported by the welfare sector. The new payment structure did create a disincentive for second earners in low-income households, and the shift in the structure of support to the tax system reinforced the economic dependence of carers on earners (Cass and Brennan 2003; Hill 2007). However, for the growing number of single-parent families, and those where neither partner had a significant market income, the structure remained highly redistributive.

Family support was then consolidated as part of the tax reform package associated with the introduction of the Goods and Services Tax (GST). A series of payments were restructured into two sets of benefits, broadly reflecting the structure of the Family Tax Initiative. Family Tax Benefit Part A was based on a household means-test that applied in two parts. Low-income households (up to approximately two-thirds the full-time wage) received the full benefit, which reflects the earlier targeted component of assistance. The means-test then paused to create a base payment, equivalent to the formally universal assistance, accessible to most households, up to a second threshold equal to about 1.75 times the average wage.

Alternatively, Family Tax Benefit Part B exaggerated the breadwinner bias previously introduced with the Family Tax Initiative. It was only means-tested against the *second* earner's income, with a threshold well below the full-time minimum wage. This allowed very high-income households with a single earner to access FTB B (while they no longer qualified for childcare rebates), strongly encouraging a breadwinner model (see Cass and Brennan 2003).

Because the family payments system mimics elements of the income tax system, it is well suited to managing policy trade-offs. When the Coalition sought broader integration of tax and benefit systems through the introduction of a Goods and Services Tax (GST), it facilitated a form of 'compensation politics' (Wilson et al. 2013). The regressive impacts of the GST could be offset by increases in benefits. It is hard to do this only through the income tax system, because those on low incomes pay very little income tax. If access to social payments is highly constrained, it makes it very difficult to target many on low incomes. Thus, the family payments system played a crucial role in the GST tax reform and again when Labor introduced carbon pricing in the 2010s (see Wilson et al. 2013, 633).

The structure of these payments has been broadly retained since. Policy change has eroded the shift away from the Australia's previously dominant breadwinner model, but has not reversed the key elements of the earlier renovation. Despite renaming family assistance as 'Tax Benefits', the payments remain highly redistributive between high- and low-income families. Because single-parent households typically only have one income earner, even FTB B is redistributive in this sense. There is no evidence of a successful shift back towards the structure of STEs. Instead, more recent changes reflect the ongoing salience of affluence testing. A subsequent Labor government introduced a twin means-testing rule for FTB B, initially at $150,000 for the primary earner, using the savings to finance an expansion of access to other families, and removed links to the tax system, returning all support to the payments system (Australian Government 2008, 370–371).

The Coalition reforms, which expanded access to family payments, were often decried as 'middle class' welfare. Changes did allow more middle-income households to access payments. However, these benefits were fundamentally different from other changes, also called 'middle class' welfare, that extended public support via the tax system or to private schools and hospitals. The confusion highlights difficulties in assessing political contests within liberalised welfare systems, where similar trends lead to different kinds of outcomes, and most differences appear technocratic. Indeed, it was the combination of Labor and Coalition governments that facilitated a more egalitarian form of affluence testing, as Labor prioritised increasing base rates (often funded by tighter targeting), and the Coalition loosened means-tests to expand access (often increasing total social spending, less impeded by the same fiscal constraint that apply to Labor).

Understanding this process strictly through the lens of distribution risks eroding the political mechanism that aids inclusion. Over the last decade access to family benefits has significantly declined. Without the revenues of the mining boom or the political pressure of the women's movement, both sides have sought to constrain costs (Stewart and Whiteford 2018, 224–225). Explicit retrenchment remains politically risky because of the broad constituency of recipients. Instead, both sides of politics have used a combination of pausing indexation, freezing payments and delaying access to gradually erode coverage (Klapdor 2022). Coverage remains significant, at over 50 per cent of families with children (*Ibid*), but it highlights the potential dangers of policy drift, where governments respond to fiscal pressure by using less visible and more technocratic means to gradually erode social entitlements, a dynamic that has seen the less popular unemployment benefit fall well below the poverty line.

The earlier, more progressive hybrid dynamic is also evident in the development of support for new parents. While the decline of women's economic policy-making machinery under the Howard government limited the influence of feminists, policy reform continued to be shaped by similar normative principles. Responding to demands for paid parental leave, the Coalition initially created a tax rebate for new parents who left the workforce. While not an STE, the model allowed higher income earners to claim a higher rebate. But this was short lived, with criticism leading the government to restructure the 'Baby Bonus' as a flat-rate, universal payment to parents – very similar to the earlier child endowment (Hodgson 2011, 280; Brennan 2009a, 24–25). The final distributional impact was highly progressive – offering low-income households a larger proportion of their income than high-income households. And as with family payments, a subsequent Labor government converted the spending to be both more targeted and more supportive of working women through a paid parental leave scheme.

Labor's changes reflected the model of affluence testing, reducing payments to higher income earners to part fund an expansion of a new paid parental leave scheme (see Baird and Whitehouse 2012). The new scheme combines elements of occupational and social welfare. The payment is set at the full-time minimum wage and paid through the employer, creating a normative link to work, but is flat-rate and (generously) means-tested, following the normative structure of social payments. It is also more generous than first appearance as many mothers (the main recipients) work part-time, while also retaining incentives for unions to win more generous terms through collective bargaining. It clearly builds on the hybrid principles of earlier reforms, incorporating the logics of different systems, although it remains limited in promoting gender equity between partners (see Baird et al. 2021).

Taken together the changes reveal an important political cleavage. The Coalition in office has done more to support breadwinner households, extend support up the income distribution and foster access via the tax system; Labor has favoured two-income households and targeting the greatest assistance to low- and middle-income households. These differences are important, reflecting the increasing feminisation of progressive politics alongside traditional class dynamics. Both parties also continue to use technocratic measures, such as indexation freezes, to impose austerity. Overall, however, the contestation of affluence testing appears conducive to welfare state expansion. Support for families with children has increased in scale and reinforced redistribution. The same cannot be said for changes to social payments more generally. 'Welfare reform' has instead seen the steady advance of a punitive variant of workfare.

Eroding Unemployment Support

Liberalisation has meant different kinds of changes for different types of benefits, despite technical commonalities. All benefits have seen forms of means-testing revised, benefit types consolidated and eligibility rules formally de-gendered. Yet in place of the logic of affluence testing that has emerged within family payments, benefits for the unemployment have become stingy, conditional and stigmatised. Australia's unemployment assistance has become amongst the most meagre and conditional in the OECD (Grundoff 2021). Changes to unemployment assistance also reflect changing patterns of political contestation, which as with family benefits appear durable despite changes in government. Unlike family payments centred on a universal conception of need and economic incentive, however, these new dynamics entrench the politics of dualism built around a form of 'wedge politics', where conditionality advances through incremental changes targeted to especially marginalised sub-populations.

Australia's system of social benefits had become remarkably complex by the 1980s. Covering all of the changes to benefits is thus beyond the scope of this analysis. Instead, I focus on the evolution of the primary unemployment benefit – formerly Newstart and now re-branded JobSeeker – charting changes across the benefit system in relation to it. A series of changes to all benefits removed explicit gender requirements and consolidated payments (Mitchell 1998), with several pension payments alongside the JobSeeker benefit.

Pensions are targeted to groups who were once presumed to sit outside the paid workforce, but who are now increasingly expected to engage in part-time work. This includes, single parents, those past retirement age and those with a disability. Pensions generally have few ongoing forms of conditionality, beyond establishing initial eligibility, have relatively higher payments and relatively more generous means-testing. The alternative model is exemplified by the unemployment benefit, which is subject to strong conditionality and ongoing surveillance, harsh penalties for non-compliance, a poverty level payment and steeper means-testing (Whiteford 2015a).

Pensions and benefits have developed distinct politics dynamics. Where campaigns to raise pensions have been modestly successful, a long-running campaign backed by business and a near-universal economic consensus (see Mendes 2021) has struggled to meaningfully raise the much lower JobSeeker rate.

Benefits for children and the elderly are typically more inclusive and generous than those expected to be in paid work. The differences between family payments and JobSeeker no doubt reflect this overarching politics of deservingness linked to expectations of work (see Mendes 2021). Yet, the differences between support for families with children, including single parents, and the unemployed is much starker than in other liberal welfare states.

Overseas benefits for families have often followed an explicitly dual model. For example, in both the United States and New Zealand reforms to social payments saw nominal cuts in benefit levels and strong new forms of conditionality, such as time limits or restrictions to those having subsequent children (see Kingfisher and Goldsmith 2001). More generous provision was organised through the tax system, as tax offsets, or bonus payments to those in paid work (Bitler et al. 2017; Neuwelt-Kearns and St John 2020). Australia's affluence-tested model stands out as more egalitarian and inclusive. Our treatment of the unemployed lies at the other extreme of the OECD. These differences suggest distinct political dynamics.

Wilson and Turnbull provide an analysis of some of the early changes under the Howard government that can be used to understand how deservingness has been mobilised and institutionalised in Australia's welfare politics, which they dub 'wedge politics'. While the term has wide currency in political debate, the authors use it in a more specific sense. For them, wedge politics is a 'calculated political tactic' that focuses on divisive social issues to gain advantage. In particular, it focuses attention on groups that 'attract resentment or antipathy in the wider electorate', and involves gaining advantage by dividing the 'support base of a political opponent' (2001, 386).

The distinctions between payment categories and the introduction of new forms of conditionality both emerged under the Hawke-Keating Labor governments, but have been sustained or increased subsequently. Labor established differential indexation, albeit by *increasing* the indexation of pensions to average wages (leaving benefits linked to inflation), a practice then codified by the Coalition (Klapdor 2014a). Labor also introduced the first forms of 'mutual obligation', the policy framework used to increase compliance and surveillance of the unemployed. Indeed, Labor initially claimed credit for the approach when first announced by the Howard Coalition (MacIntyre 1999, 107). Admittedly, Labor's extension of obligations (and penalties for non-compliance) came alongside substantial increases in resources for active labour market programs (ALMPs), formal commitments to industry policy and a rhetorical commitment to full employment through the *Working Nation* package (*Ibid*). This created a Job Compact that introduced case management and required recipients to complete a period of paid work experience after 18 months unemployment.

The subsequent expansion of 'mutual obligation' reflects a growing social conservativism with the Coalition and extension of a neo-paternalism similar to the welfare reforms advanced in the United States (Gatens et al. 2002) and to the advance of 'workfare' more generally (Peck 2001; Mcdonald and Marston 2005). Reforms to payments have advanced alongside a reorganisation of support for job seeking. Australia led the world in privatising employment assistance, creating a substantial industry of publicly funded private providers, who police many of the conditions imposed on payment recipients (Considine et al. 2011). Central to both changes was a process of 'welfare reform' led by two reports chaired led by former Franciscan Priest, Patrick McClure. McClure's reports not only emphasised 'mutual obligation' but also recommended a growing role for non-government organisations in providing welfare services (Cass and Brennan 2002). Changes to benefit rules paralleled a radical privatisation of employment services.

Wilson and Turnbull initially identified the logic of wedge politics in the first round of welfare changes shortly after the 1996 election. Alongside the more rigorous enforcement of existing conditionality, the Coalition restricted the eligibility of recent migrants (Wilson and Turnbull 2001, 396). Changes created waiting times to access payments, deny back pay and make it administratively difficult to apply; all features applied more broadly to JobSeeker recipients since. The same logic was repeated in subsequent changes. 'Work for the Dole', the scheme that mandates periods of work to remain in receipt of benefits, was initially applied only to the young unemployed (those under 25), a relatively popular target for paternalism (Eardly et al. 2000), although mandatory involvement has since been expanded for all long-term job seekers, and participation is no longer 'one-off' but recurrent (Casey 2020).

The most extreme examples have targeted Indigenous Australians. 'Income quarantining', where the government restricts how a portion of a payment can be spent, was initially introduced as part of the 'Intervention' (see Altman 2018; Staines et al. 2021). In the lead up to the 2007 election, the Coalition passed the Northern Territory National Emergency Response

Act, commonly known as the 'Intervention' into Indigenous communities in the Northern Territory (see Altman and Hinkson 2007). The militarised response involved the suspension of the Racial Discrimination Act and changes to reduce Indigenous control of land. Ostensibly it sought to keep children safe from abuse, although authors of the report used to justify the response opposed it (SMH 2011). Following the same pattern, quarantining of payment has since been extended more broadly (Maher 2020).

Conditionality has not only expanded through the introduction of new conditions to especially marginalised groups but also by changes in over-all eligibility that make it harder to access 'pension'-type payments. These changes accompanied major 'welfare reforms' and were justified as a mech-anism to encourage work. However, unlike family payments, this did not involve promoting work incentives for all, but rather re-emphasising differ-ent work expectations attached to different social roles and narrowing the scope of roles with reduced work expectations. Thus, access to pensions has been restricted to the 'most deserving' by changing the boundaries between pension and benefit-type payments. Parents with older children (Cortis and Meagher 2009), those with less severe, less predictable or harder to document disabilities (Mendes 2009, 105–106) and the young-old (Klapdor 2014b) have each been moved from pension entitlements onto JobSeeker.

Importantly, the advance of conditionality and the 'wedge politics' that underpins it has proven relatively resilient to changes in government. Not only have most of the conditions been maintained under both Labor and Coalition governments, elements of conditionality have been advanced under Labor. Welfare quarantining, for example, was first advanced through tri-als in remote Indigenous communities facilitated by the suspension of the Race Discrimination Act. When Labor won office it was committed to lifting the suspension of the Act. Yet, instead of unwinding conditionality, it opted to *extend* quarantining to non-Indigenous communities to ensure the scheme complied with the Act (Mendes 2019, 42).

Likewise, Labor has narrowed eligibility for more generous payments. The Coalition created an anomaly amongst single parents by grandfather-ing existing recipients onto more generous arrangements when it moved new recipients onto Newstart. Rather than reverse the decision, Labor responded by ending the grandfathering, forcing more parents onto the lower payment and increased conditionality (Bueskens 2019). Labor was also responsible for increasing the eligibility age for the age pension, effectively shifting 65- and 66-year-olds onto JobSeeker (Klapdor 2014b). Thus, while there are differ-ences in how parties have eroded income support, these twin processes – of extending the *scope* and the *conditionality* of the JobSeeker – have been at least partly bipartisan. Growing Indigenous representation in parliament and renewed civil society campaigns led by people on government payments offer some hope of a shift against extreme forms of conditionality. Labor has since partly reversed the eligibility restrictions for single parents and is reviewing and potentially unwinding some mutual obligations.

Comparing the evolution of unemployment and family benefits suggest very different models of liberalisation. Both involve elements of 'residualisation', in that payments are targeted via means-tests. Both also rationalise the number of payments, disconnecting entitlement from specific socially accepted roles. However, the distributional and policy consequences are divergent.

Family payments expanded significantly, as state distribution was restructured away from tax concession and towards the hybrid model of affluence testing. Policy changed by asserting symmetry, between STEs and payments, and between income tax and means-testing, reflecting normative claims for inclusion and adequacy, alongside market incentives.

JobSeeker has become an extreme example of the punitive politics of workfare. Conditionality has advanced through wedge politics, which reinforces distinctions between deserving and undeserving by targeting new conditionality to the most marginalised, and then extending the boundaries of paternalism. These different trajectories, each apparently self-sustaining, suggest a shift in the dynamics of political contestation under liberalisation. A shift that is echoed outside the benefit systems.

Chapter 4

MARKETISING WELFARE

Privatisation has been an important policy tool for liberalising the provision of goods and services. Around the world, utilities, transport systems and other industries nationalised during the twentieth century were restructured along corporate lines and sold to private owners. However, explicit forms of privatisation – that is the sale of a public provider – is far less common within the welfare state. Instead, welfare state services have been marketised – that is, reorganised to reflect elements of competition. Marketisation often advances commodification, yet it retains a visible role for the state. Where other neoliberal reforms explicitly advocate replacing states with markets, marketisation requires a more nuanced account of combining states and markets. Perhaps unsurprisingly, this ambiguity has seen a much greater political and academic acceptance of variety within the 'managed' or 'quasi' markets that dominate social provision.

The complexity of understanding marketisation is evident in popular political understandings of some of Australia's key social services. Medicare, Australia's system of universal public health insurance, is broadly understood as 'public', yet it operates alongside a 'private' system and actively facilitates private medical provision. This structure was not the result of liberalising a more public system; instead competition was a key strategy for achieving universalism. Alternatively, Australia's system of childcare gave rise to the largest for-profit private childcare company in the world, ABC Learning, during a period of rapid expansion of provision and public spending. In both cases, Australia's experiences of marketisation partly reflect its wage-earner history, which left a legacy of weak public provision within the welfare state. Liberalisation coincided with strong political pressures to expand provision.

This chapter uses these two examples – Medicare and Early Education and Care (EEC) – to understand the political economy of marketising social provision. Advocates of marketisation view its integration of states and markets as a source of dynamism, allowing efficiency alongside equitable access (see Barr 2001; Le Grand 1997). Marketisation often reflects the interplay of fiscal politics and accounting anomalies that favour private provision. Here, initial marketisation is orientated towards underwriting profitability in otherwise unprofitable sectors. These anomalies were clearly at play in the development of Australia's childcare sector. However, less recognised is how these same fiscal and accounting dynamics open space for the expansion of social provision, at least when combined with strong political pressure, as was the case for Medicare.

The chapter explores how Medicare advanced a form of *hybridity* by structuring state action in market terms, helping to overcome constitutional and fiscal barriers to the expansion of universal healthcare. Both healthcare and childcare expanded, in part, through the same strategy as in family benefits. Both made fiscal welfare visible and then converted it into social spending, alongside other novel fiscal strategies facilitated by the Accord. Medicare also mobilised monopsony power – the power of the state as a single buyer – to regulate private producers to facilitate universal access. Alternatively, from the 1990s childcare expanded through a form of financialisation that exploited accounting definitions and fiscal politics to entrench a dual welfare market.

These examples partly reflect the varied dynamics of social markets. Drawing on Jane Gingrich's (2011) work I explore how Medicare and childcare reflect aspects of 'state-managed' and 'two-tier' markets, which I argue respectively facilitate the politics of *hybridity* and *dual welfare*. While Gingrich emphasises how these various social markets express continuity with the post-War worlds of welfare, I use the Medicare and childcare examples to highlight contestation and the potential to change course, either towards universal healthcare or dualised childcare.

The chapter begins by situating marketisation within efforts at liberalisation. It identifies the central role economists played in shaping the politics of marketisation through innovations in welfare economics that informed Third Way governance. While grounded in mainstream concepts and methods, these approaches stand out from other efforts at liberalisation in focusing on specific industries, rather than broader competitive principles, and acknowledging significant market failure. Next, I examine how this kind of policy analysis intersected with strong movement pressure to advance universal healthcare, fostering a form of policy hybridity, which militated against retrenchment. I then examine the development of public support for EEC, dividing these developments into two. An initial campaign to expand more egalitarian provision was driven by a broad political coalition and mobilised new economic arguments about the value created through service provision. From the late 1980s, policy shifted to reflect more conventional modes of liberalisation, where concerns over 'middle-class welfare' created the conditions for a more dualised welfare market and facilitated financialisation. Finally, the chapter reflects on key lessons, which will be explored more fully in the final section.

Marketising Services

Marketisation more obviously provides a potential for hybridity. Marketisation infers the ongoing combination of state regulation and funding with market competition.While competition drives behaviour, the outcomes are not, in a Polanyian sense, those of a 'self-regulated' market. Instead, states shape incentives to guide competitive outcomes. It is unsurprising marketisation has found strong advocates within the Third Way. Efforts to redesign the state to 'steer' rather than 'row' (Osborne and Gaebler 1991; Keating 2004) suggest states govern through markets, rather than not governing at all. However, in most cases, these approaches situate marketisation between states and markets, imagined as an attempt to combine the virtues of each institution by somewhat reducing state control and shifting closer to market outcomes (Le Grand 1997). Such an approach is limited in two respects. As with fiscal welfare, it conceals the extent of state control within inegalitarian social markets. Second, framed only as liberalisation, it obscures how hybrid forms of marketisation mobilise competition to advance universalism.

Debates over marketisation are complicated by context. A key feature of liberalisation has been the influence of elite policy networks that allow new policy ideas to move quickly between countries – what Jamie Peck and Nick Theodore call 'fast policy' (Peck and Theodore 2015). The Australian Labor Party's success during the early phase of neoliberalism raised its profile overseas, particularly in the United Kingdom, leading to significant policy learning (Pierson 2003; Pierson and Castles 2002), which then fed back from the United Kingdom to Australia (Manwaring 2016). However, the context for marketisation differed significantly between the two countries. In the UK marketisation marked a shift away from largely nationalised forms of public provision. As Julian Le Grand, a key Third Way thinker and advisor to the Blair government, argued, the United Kingdom's welfare state was built on assumptions that professionals and policymakers acted like 'knights' to assist passive 'pawns' (1991, 1997). In Australia, health and social care were never nationalised and progressive movements were generally suspicious of professionals within service provision.

The complexity of marketised social policy has generated growing conceptual interest in the diverse ways states and markets interact. At the macro, social theoretic level this is reflected in literature on the 'regulatory state' (Braithwaite 1999; Moran 2002) and 'actually existing neoliberalism' (Cahill 2010; Peck et al. 2018). Within social policy it has produced nuanced accounts of how licencing rules, professionalisation and funding structures have the potential to create very different outcomes (see Meagher and Goodwin 2015; Fine and Davidson 2018; Meagher et al. 2022; Carey et al. 2018). In seeking to understand how politics shapes variation across marketised models, Jane Gingrich's (2011) work is particularly helpful. Through analysing different social markets in different welfare state contexts, Gingrich develops a typology of marketisation, arguing there is both continuity between existing welfare state structures and the trajectory of new market reforms and differences in partisan strategies within each context. While focused on continuity within worlds of welfare and broader in scope, Gingrich's work provides useful archetypes for this study.

Gingrich uses a case study approach like the one used here to understand marketisation within the welfare state. She focuses attention on where power is located within a market and on the degree to which access to services is understood in universal terms to construct a typology of marketisation. Two of the models within this typology map directly onto the broader conceptual framework of this study. Two-tier markets reflecting the dual welfare state emerge when producers have significant power, and there is some expectation of provision across the community, although no strong norm of universality. State-managed markets emerge where states retain strong control, and provide opportunities for hybridity via monopsony power.

Gingrich sees marketisation as a response to political constraints, similar to the fiscal and legitimacy constraints discussed earlier, which either require left-of-centre parties to engage with competition or right-of-centre parties to maintain forms of state financing. As Le Grand suggests, this means marketisation differs from outright privatisation in three important respects: providers are often not driven primarily by profit, demand is often supported by public finance specific to the individual market and choices are often made by, or heavily influenced by, actors other than the end consumer (1991, 1260). Rules governing who can enter the market, professional codes of conduct and licencing arrangements all complicate traditional profit motives. The structure of government spending influences market structures, while governments often act as purchasers on behalf of consumers (or create the entities that do).

The structure of quasi-markets creates policy levers that can be used to shape 'state managed' markets. Medicare mobilises monopsony power, the market power exercised by a single buyer, to increase government control. Monopsony facilitates an expansion of state power in a form associated with market regulation, reflecting a form of hybridity that mitigates both constitutional and fiscal constraints designed to limit the scope of state regulation. Unlike Gingrich's examples, where varieties of marketisation largely follow existing institutional patterns. Medicare shows the possibilities of expanding universalism through a combination of political campaigning and policy hybridity.

Public financing and regulation can also mimic market distribution and reward profit-orientation. This is typically the case where states subsidise consumers rather than exercising monopsony power by purchasing services directly. The inequalities of these 'two-tiered' markets are reinforced by many of the features of dual welfare, particularly linking public subsidies to the level of private spending and by providing public support via fiscal welfare, as was the case in the pre-Medicare health system. Because many social markets are subject to market failure, such arrangements not only reinforce market inequalities in distributional terms, but facilitate forms of producer power as consumers lack information or services act as positional goods.

The economic dynamics of these quasi-markets are structured by politics. Medicare's introduction followed a fierce union and public campaign firmly grounded in establishing access to medical care as a universal right. While the mechanisms for delivering that right were marketised, the strong norm of universal access helped weaken fiscal constraints and mitigated efforts at retrenchment. Alternatively, efforts to universalise a right to childcare were never fully successful. This both reinforced fiscal limits, in part driving forms of marketisation that would appeal to private capital, and complicated efforts to resist inegalitarian restructuring. Without a firm foundation in a universal politics of need, even policy reforms that aim to limit producer power and aid equity remain limited.

Medicare: Universalism Through Markets?

Despite a tumultuous history, Medicare is now entrenched as a pillar of the Australian welfare state. Medicare is a system of universal public insurance. It has two components. The hospital scheme provides free hospital care as a public patient in public hospitals. It is part-funded by the Commonwealth but provided by state governments, and operates in a similar way to forms of nationalisation. However, Medicare allows for private hospitals (and provision for private patients in public hospitals) to operate in parallel to the public system, alongside private health insurance. The medical scheme provides access to subsidised medical services, such as General Practitioner (GP) and specialist visits, most of which are provided by private medical providers. The medical scheme operates through a schedule of fees for different types of services. Patients are either reimbursed a set proportion of the scheduled fee (although they can be charged more than the scheduled fee) or the government pays the doctor directly on condition the patient does not pay a fee, a practice known as 'bulk billing'.

Medicare was originally introduced as Medibank by the Whitlam Labor government in the 1970s (Boxall and Gillespie 2013). The scheme was gradually eroded by the following Coalition government, a unique example of universal healthcare being retrenched in a democracy, before being reintroduced as Medicare by the Hawke Labor government in 1984. It replaced a system of subsidised private healthcare, known as the Page Scheme. The Page Scheme combined dual welfare, via generous tax subsidies, with regulation to promote risk sharing, ensuring cross subsidisation between the well and the sick. Medicare remained subject to explicit partisan opposition until the mid-1990s, when the Coalition committed to retain Medicare before winning office (Elliot 2006). It has enjoyed formal bipartisan support since. The Coalition even claimed to be Medicare's 'best friend' (*Ibid*), although proposals to increase co-payments and strengthen private health insurance signal ongoing partisan differences.

Medicare marks a contradictory shift in Australian health policy. For most of the twentieth century the Labor Party had campaigned to nationalise healthcare. Nationalisation remained a central part of Labor's platform until the late 1960s, when Labor's embrace of the Medicare model signalled its acceptance of a substantial and ongoing private health sector. Yet, unlike marketisation in the United Kingdom, or most marketisation in Australia, implementing Medicare involved a significant expansion of universal social provision. Not only is Medicare a 'less market' form of marketisation, its marketised structure successfully advanced universalism. That success parallels many of the features of 'affluence testing' discussed in the last chapter. Social Tax Expenditures were converted to expand social spending. Competition facilitated an expansion of access along egalitarian lines. Framed as a change to health pricing, Medicare's introduction contributed to fiscal constraint in other areas, reduced opposition to fiscal expansion within healthcare and overcame constitutional barriers to command and control forms of state regulation. It thus presents an important model for shifting Australia's dual welfare state towards universalism.

Failed nationalisation and dual welfare

Access to affordable healthcare was a central battleground of twentieth-century politics. Labor advanced a politics of nationalisation against producer and conservative resistance. Labor governments enjoyed some early success at state level; however, the most significant effort was advanced through Labor's post-War reconstruction plans. Labor sought to follow its British counterpart, which was simultaneously introducing the National Health Service (NHS), holding a referendum to gain new powers, which it used to directly control health provision (Gillespie 1991). When doctors refused to work in the new system, Labor instituted fines. Likewise, opposition to nationalisation centred on mass mobilisation and creating explicit limits to state power. Doctors mobilised against national healthcare as a form of socialism, building public campaigns, boycotting public services and creating constitutional limits. The British Medical Association (BMA), which represented Australian doctors, proved one of the most powerful unions in the country (see Gillespie 1988).

The BMA mobilised an extraordinary campaign against Labor's health plans (Gillespie 1991). Enormous funds were raised, materials distributed to local surgeries and clinics and a mass advertising campaign developed. Even after legislation passed the parliament, the BMA organised a mass boycott of the new public system, causing Labor to institute financial and even custodial sanctions. The success of the BMA's organising reflected not only ideological opposition but also the unifying effects of Labor's command-and-control politics. However, ultimately, nationalisation failed through the combination of political opposition and legal constraint. The limits imposed by federalism are set out constitutionally. Changes require referendums to gain overall majority support, and a majority in a majority of states, a task that has thus far proven near impossible without bipartisan support (Saunders 1994, 53). When Labor sought new powers over healthcare, the medical profession sought concessions, via their close alliance with the conservative parties, to create a new constitutional limit to prevent 'civil conscription' in return for bipartisan support for any referendum (Gillespie 1991, 223). A legal challenge successfully struck down Labor's penalties, while the campaign against nationalisation contributed to a change in government.

In place of nationalisation, the Menzies government instituted a system of subsidised, voluntary, private health insurance. The Page Scheme, named after the then Coalition health minister, entrenched a form of dual welfare, albeit one that limited market inequality through egalitarian regulation. Access to healthcare expanded via private health insurance, offered by non-profit funds. The model was integrated into both Australia's wage-earner and dual welfare models; health insurance premiums were tax deductible (Smith 2001) and considered in the basket of goods used in arbitration to determine socially acceptable wages (see Mahony 1978). Premiums were also subject to 'community rating', a regulatory framework that ensured all individuals/families would pay the same premium regardless of their risk profile (see Butler 2002) – either their age or medical history. Community rating was supported by an industry-wide funding pool to cross-subsidise insurers with riskier customers. These structures ensured a key role for the state as funder and regulator, while state financing was concealed by the exclusion of fiscal welfare from budgetary accounting.

In Gingrich's terms this was a two-tier market, where producers had significant power. Initially, however, like Australia's model of home ownership, most people had access to the subsidised private system, with only a small minority relegated to the 'honorary' system, where doctors voluntarily provided services for free to those deemed unable to pay. At its peak, more than 80 per cent of households had private insurance (see Figure 4.2). Over time, however, coverage began to decline. The non-profit insurance companies had high administrative costs and struggled to sustain adequate financial reserves. Most were run by doctors, making insurers reluctant to exercise strong discipline over prices. As a result, medical costs rose quickly, and this began to erode affordability. As insurance coverage began to fall, many were left risking serious financial difficulty or falling back on 'honorary' provision (see Scotton 1969).

Proposals for universal insurance emerged in response to weaknesses in private provision. The Medicare model was proposed by two health economists Richard Scotton and John Deeble (1968). They understood the problems of the existing system through the lens of market failure and used relatively standard neoclassical reasoning to promote a single insurer as the solution. However, as *health* economists, their approach differed from what later became the standard 'economic rationalism' of the central agencies in three important respects. First, they understood healthcare as a need. Thus, it was sensible to interpret a lack of needed medical care as a market failure, rather than simply the outcome of willingness to pay. Second, they paid close attention to the operation of the existing insurance market, rather than relying on simplified models of (near) perfect competition. Finally, they were not hostile to higher taxation in principle. Instead, their approach differed from advocates of socialisation in neglecting questions of status and class. The economists defined health 'needs' narrowly. They viewed many aspects of care that differentiate the quality of service, such as choice of doctor and accommodation, as legitimate consumer choices rather than mechanisms of class stratification.

Using markets to expand access

Labor's failure to universalise healthcare in the 1940s reflected the limits of statist strategies. Despite mass political support and an expansion of fiscal powers, the Commonwealth was hampered by constitutional constraints and federalism. In the less favourable context of liberalisation, marketisation proved a more effective mechanism for transferring power from producers to the state and expanding access. This success reflected a politics of hybridity. Medicare advanced state control alongside market competition, exploiting ambiguities in how 'state' action is defined to overcome constitutional, political and fiscal barriers to expanding provision and access.

Medicare reversed the usual logic of layering associated with liberalisation by constructing a new public system to erode private control (Spies-Butcher 2014). It left in place the existing systems of private provision; hospitals, medical care and insurance. Instead it created new mechanisms of state control through guaranteed free access to hospital care (echoing the earlier push for nationalisation) and by creating a public insurer (and single purchaser). Public provision expanded through successful competition, using monopsony power, rather than direct legal regulation, to discipline producers. Constructed as market power, these forms of state control bypassed constitutional constraints on overt regulation. The state is able to enforce outcomes through payment that it cannot through legal regulation. Secondly, fiscal constraints were overcome, in part, by equating taxation to market price and exploiting asymmetries in how arbitration accounted for the interaction of state regulation and market pricing.

Most obviously the insurance model of universal healthcare bypassed the constitutional impediment on civil conscription. Under Medicare public hospitals are run by state governments (who are not constrained by the constitutional prohibition), while medical services are based on a fee-for-service model rather than public employment. In both cases the Commonwealth used its power to pay rather than to regulate. While there are specific constitutional issues in healthcare, the model also reflects a broader feature of social services; vertical fiscal imbalance means that the Commonwealth collects most of the tax revenue, but has little experience running services, and is thus better placed to act as a funder than a provider. Federation entrenches a form of the purchaser/provider split within social policy making. Fiscal power can be exercised through tying block grants to policy commitments, as Labor did with Medibank to ensure free hospital access, but more recently fiscal power also operates via markets to fund consumers or providers directly.

Framing public healthcare in insurance terms not only overcame constitutional barriers, it helped to fragment political opposition and expand public provision. The medical profession once again mobilised an extensive campaign against public health. However, unlike the earlier campaign, medical opposition was less united. The AMA failed to reach fundraising targets and saw a fall in membership (Scotton 1993, 70). Eventually a breakaway group of progressive doctors formed an alternative pro-Medicare association, the Doctors Reform Society (Siedlecky 2005). Not only had attitudes changed within the profession, the market framing of Medicare made it more difficult to characterise as 'nationalisation'. Indeed, the new scheme enjoyed unexpected support from parts of the financial press for challenging the doctors' oligopoly, and this in turn contributed to gaining crossbench support from the anti-communist Democratic Labor Party in the Senate (Sax 1984, 79), an appeal with parallels to the current small-l liberal independents.

Using competition to expand universalism

Once established, Medicare was also much more effective than nationalisation at overcoming producer resistance within provision. In different ways, price competition drove a significant expansion of access and contraction in private provision. Bulk billing rates for all medical services rose from 45 per cent when Medicare began to reach 70 per cent by the mid-1990s, and are now just over 80 per cent (see Figure 4.1). Private health insurance coverage fell sharply with the introduction of Medibank and Medicare, and then continued to fall. Having been close to 80 per cent when Whitlam was elected, coverage fell to only 30 per cent by the late 1990s, before a series of counter-measures from Labor and Coalition governments sought to save the private sector (see Figure 4.2).

Medicare uses a combination of creating free alternatives to outcompete private provision and monopsony power to discipline private producers. It is unsurprising that free hospital admission undermines demand for private hospital insurance, although the pace of change makes industrial action like that undertaken in the 1940s much more difficult, and bypasses constitutional constraints. The private sector maintains some scope for competition,

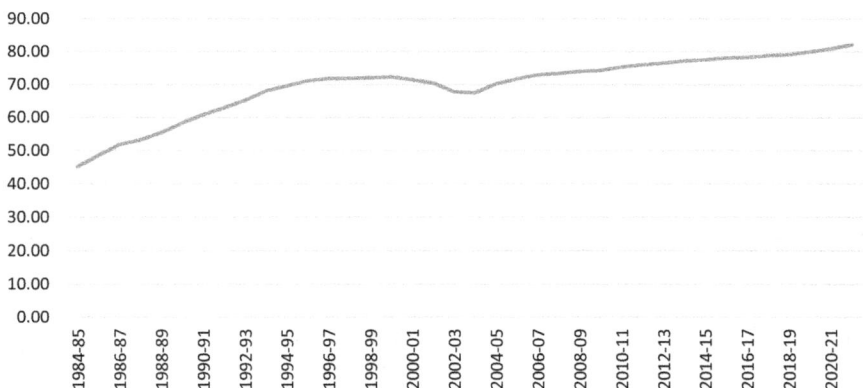

Figure 4.1 Bulk billing rates, 1984/85–2021/22. *Source*: Department of Health and Aged Care. 'MBS annual Medicare statistics 1984/85 to 2008/10' and Medicare annual statistics State and Territory 2009/10 to 2021/22'. Available at: https://www1.health.gov.au/internet/main/publishing.nsf/Content/Medicare%20Statistics-1.

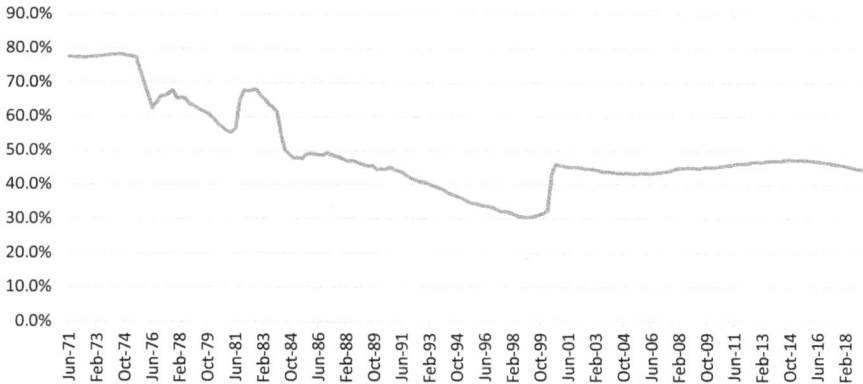

Figure 4.2 Private hospital insurance coverage, 1971–2019. *Source*: Australian Prudential and Regulatory Authority. 'Quarterly Private Health Insurance Membership Trends'. Available at: https://www.apra.gov.au/quarterly-private-health-insurance-statistics.

allowing choice of doctor, access to a private bed, more timely care and broader coverage, especially of dental and optical care. However, even these advantages are undermined by adverse selection, as the young and fit tend to drop out of private coverage first and risk sharing does not extend across the public and private sectors (see Deeble 1982). Restrictions on patient choice reduce marketing and administrative costs for the public sector while reducing the bargaining power of individual doctors (McAuley 2005). Monopsony power also provides much better cost containment compared to multiple private insurers, contributing to rising private insurance costs and falling coverage. These market dynamics point to new strategies for contesting public coverage, which I address below.

The medical side of Medicare facilitated a more subtle form of competition. Unlike hospital treatment, Medicare involves very little direct public provision of medical services. Instead, public control is fostered through bulk billing, which facilitates an expansion of free provision by private practice doctors. Bulk billed consultations involve an agreement between the doctor and Medicare not to charge the patient a fee. In return Medicare simplifies the reimbursement, allowing a bulk payment to the doctor, rather than a series of individual transactions. This substantially reduces administrative costs and allows payment for services that might otherwise be 'honorary', making it financially attractive to doctors (Gray 1991), especially those servicing low-income communities (Scotton 1980, 208–209). It also gives Medicare considerable influence over the fee levels that are charged, because Medicare sets the rate for bulk billed consultations. Doctors saw the potential of such a system to control medical incomes well in advance, explaining the low initial take-up rate.

Even with low initial take-up, however, competition has driven an expansion of bulk billing. Competitive pressures make it difficult to resist in areas where other doctors already bulk bill. Looking at the geographic pattern of bulk billing reveals that rates are higher not only where average incomes are lower but also where the number of doctors is higher and competition stronger, explaining low rates in some regional communities (see Spies-Butcher 2014, 29). Likewise, the rate of bulk billing amongst GPs is much higher (over 80 per cent) than that amongst specialists, where competition is reduced or absent. So strong is this competitive pressure, that general practice has started to become 'proleterianised', as GPs join larger medical centres organised along corporate lines (Collyer and White 2001).

Financing social insurance

The market construction of Medicare also helped to overcome fiscal constraints both initially as Medibank and then as Medicare. The introduction of Medibank followed a similar pattern to the expansion of family payments, identifying the cost of fiscal welfare as a source of public finance. As with family benefits, the expansion of public provision relied on making the state's role in providing fiscal welfare more visible. Labor prime minister Gough Whitlam famously remarked that he paid less for health insurance than his driver, because his higher salary and progressive income tax rates meant he received a larger tax deduction (Hocking 2012, Chapter 4). Labor drew out this equivalence, identifying how the Commonwealth already financed healthcare, to redirect funds into the new public insurance scheme. As with family payments, the politics of conversion involved making a rhetorical link between fiscal welfare and social welfare in the same policy domain, even though there was no formal hypothecation.

Following the dismissal of the Whitlam government and two crushing electoral defeats Labor became far more fiscally cautious, evidenced in its 'Trilogy' commitment. Medibank had proven more expensive than envisaged, driven by AMA efforts to push up prices via its 'recommended' schedule of fees (Scotton 1980). The Fraser Coalition government had used rising costs to help justify a roll back of public insurance, causing many in Labor to resist the scheme's reintroduction. Movement pressure was central to ensuring a commitment to 'universalism'. Unions organised a rare 'general strike' in response to Medibank's retrenchment and organised through the Accord to prioritise the scheme's reintroduction (Boxall and Gillespie 2013, 120–126). However, the market framing of Medicare as insurance was also pivotal.

Framing Medicare as a public alternative to existing insurance spending helped to address fiscal concerns in two ways. Labor now proposed additional funding framed as a form of insurance premium. The Medicare Levy suggested a direct tax payment for a service, even though the money raised went to consolidated revenue. Much like the additional funding raised by re-directing fiscal welfare, the changes only provided 'top-up' funding to supplement public spending already in place, making a formal social insurance fund difficult. The framing helped to demonstrate equivalence with the cost of private health insurance, which was much higher than the new tax for most households. Second, the construction assisted the Accord's macroeconomic goal to contain inflation (see Sax 1984, 241). Not only was Medicare used as social wage compensation to justify lower wage increases, its hybrid structure complicated accounting measures of public and private built into the arbitration system. As a (public) tax measure, the levy did not count towards inflation, the official measure of (market) prices, while the reduction in (private) health costs did. Thus, Medicare helped to reduce measured inflation twice, once by offsetting wage increases and then again by reducing health costs. Meanwhile, advocacy by the scheme's economic architects helped to persuade fiscal conservatives that monopsony power would constrain public costs.

Contesting Medicare

The initial increase in bulk billing rates and decline in private health insurance coverage have not been stable. While hybridity reduced resistance to expanding public provision and facilitated an ongoing expansion of universal healthcare, it is potentially less resilient to retrenchment than more overt forms of public provision. The largely uncontested continuation of a sizeable private healthcare sector provides opportunities to reinforce a dual welfare model. However, as with family payments, the introduction of hybridity changed the nature of contestation. Efforts to wind back public access have largely been unsuccessful. Instead, the layering of Medicare on top of private healthcare has facilitated an expansion of dual welfare, albeit along less inegalitarian lines than before. The most troubling features of contestation are the regulation of competition to favour producer interests and failure to expand Medicare to other areas of medical need.

Medicare has proven resilient to overt forms of retrenchment. Even as ideological support for public provision waned within parliament, public opposition to privatisation frustrated efforts to reintroduce user payments. By the early 1990s both sides of politics had agreed private health insurance had fallen too far, fearing the fiscal cost of entirely public provision (Colombo and Tapay 2003, 10). Initially Labor emphasised regulatory reforms aimed at increasing competition within the private sector to lower premiums; however, these proved largely ineffectual. Labor also considered unwinding bulk billing by introducing a co-payment (Leeder 1999, 35–36). The proposal faced fierce internal opposition and was withdrawn. Twenty years later the Coalition attempted a similar reform, which failed to pass the Senate after a fierce public campaign against it. Overt attempts to reintroduce fees within the public system or even hinting at 'privatisation' of aspects of health provision have since proved politically risky, with the Coalition crediting a union campaign against the privatisation of payments systems within Medicare – which it dubbed 'Mediscare' – as central to its loss of support in 2016 (Carson et al. 2020). Instead, contestation has involved more modest moves that gradually erode access and equity.

Having accepted Medicare would stay in place, the Coalition sought to strengthen the private health system. Initially this took the form of relatively conventional 'dual welfare', through subsidises for private welfare spending. The reforms were like those in family payments, seeking to rebuild a form of fiscal welfare without directly returning to a system of expensive tax concessions. First, the government introduced a rebate for low-income earners on their insurance premiums. Unlike a tax concession, where benefits are proportionate to tax liabilities, the rebate provided a flat-rate 30 per cent reduction in premiums. Despite the rebate doing little to increase coverage, the means-test was scrapped, extending subsidies to all private health insurance holders (see Colombo and Tapay 2003, 11). As premiums continued to rise above inflation the Coalition then increased the rebate for older people, who are both more likely to hold private insurance and the Coalition's core political constituency (Ratcliff et al. 2020). A complex tax offset was also briefly introduced for out-of-pocket costs beyond those refunded by private health insurance. These measures may have prevented decline, but did not significantly increase coverage (see Figure 4.2).

The public sector's competitive advantages have made private subsidies less effective, forcing new forms of dual welfare that impose tax-like penalties for opting-out of the private system. The most significant of these is LifeTime Cover (see Palangkaraya and Yong 2005). The reform reflected policy learning from Fraser Coalition government, which had been hamstrung in supporting private healthcare by the competitive dynamics of adverse selection. While ever the government retained free access to forms of catastrophic insurance, young, healthy people saw little benefit in private coverage. Instead, insurance was increasingly dominated by older people and those with chronic conditions, who were effectively cross-subsidised by healthier members. Undoing community rating, however, is politically challenging because the core beneficiaries – older people with private insurance – are the Coalition's electoral base. Instead, LifeTime Cover effectively created a tax on young people who did not have insurance, while a separate policy created an explicit tax, the Private Health Insurance Levy, on high-income earners without insurance.

Lifetime Cover modifies the principle of community rating so that premiums are set according to the age at which a person first insures. For every year a person delays insuring after 30, their premium is increased by 2 per cent, to a maximum of 70 per cent. The levy is effectively a tax rather than a price, enforced by legislation and levied at rates determined politically and unrelated to direct costs or risks. The pseudo-tax initially proved effective, leading to a surge in coverage. Alongside LifeTime Cover, the Coalition also introduced an explicit new tax, the Medicare Levy Surcharge, which progressively increases tax liabilities on higher-income earners who do not have private health insurance. The Surcharge's structure means that most for high-income earners, private insurance has a negative price, that is, they would be liable to pay more in tax than the cost of an insurance premium (McAuley 2005).

Both Lifetime Cover and the Surcharge suggest private health insurance is now only competitive when exit from the system is punitively taxed. However, only the initial introduction of LifeTime Cover has had a significant and lasting impact on coverage (Palangkaraya and Yong 2005, see Figure 4.2). Despite significant fiscal support from the Rebate and the Surcharge, coverage has again begun to decline.

The Coalition's expansion of dual welfare opens up the familiar path of conversion. The Rudd government begun down this path, means-testing the Rebate, albeit at very generous levels (see Biggs 2011). If the Rebate were abandoned, and the Surcharge incorporated into the normal tax code unconditional on insurance coverage, the changes could fund a substantial expansion of coverage in areas like dental or mental health.

The unrealised potential to expand Medicare speaks to the ongoing limits of the hybrid model. Medicare has entrenched health as a social right and legitimised 'free' healthcare as a principle. However, it also entrenches a private sector and bipartisan support for private health insurance. Dental, optical and mental health remain largely excluded. Specialist fees have proven substantially immune to the monopsony effects of bulk billing. And Australia continues to have high out-of-pocket costs by international standards (OECD 2021).

Growing out-of-pocket costs potentially threaten universality. Holding down the public schedule of fees reflects an attempt to exert monopsony power; however, it can also make it worthwhile for doctors to opt-out of bulk billing, as seemed to happen with declining rates of bulk billing in the 2000s, and again more recently. Labor has shown falling bulk billing rates can be an effective political tool to communicate the erosion of Medicare. However, higher bulk billing rates have now been achieved by providing selective incentives to bulk bill those on lower incomes and facilitating much higher out-of-pocket costs for those that do pay fees (Spies-Butcher 2024). While introduced under the Coalition, Labor announced in the 2023 Budget it will build on this 'targeted' model to expand bulk billing coverage. Medicare might reveal a strategy for combining markets with equity, but as it currently operates, it also reveals the limitations of that strategy without a more explicit politics to expand social provision.

Early Education and Care: Expanding Financialised Care

The expansion of EEC stands out as one of the most important additions to the 'social wage' negotiated through the Accord besides Medicare. Both required significant increases in public funding, generating fiscal concerns that informed efforts at marketisation. Yet, the two areas are also distinct. Health was well established as a public policy issue. Debate focused on universalising an already marketised system. EEC was far less developed. Public investment in healthcare drove a shift from private to public provision, while investment in EEC drove a shift from the informal to formal economy. As a result, EEC is much more tightly tied to the changing role of women in the economy and the reorganisation of social reproduction, despite both sectors being dominated by feminised care labour. The relationship between EEC and labour force participation also changes the economics of the sector, from one where spending is highest near the end of life and is often understood as a cost to one where spending is early in life and can be more easily understood as investment generating future economic benefits. Alongside this, childcare has increasingly been redefined as EEC, emphasising the potential to build human capital and connecting 'care' to a logic of productivity and investment.

From the 1970s feminists and childcare advocates fostered a powerful alliance of workers and parents to place childcare on the political agenda and drive public investment. The alliance politicised the need for childcare, linking it to an electoral strategy aimed at addressing Labor's underperformance amongst women voters, and mobilised novel economic arguments to frame public spending as 'investment' in EEC. These political efforts saw rising public funding, but funding did not expand rapidly enough to match demand. Instead of universalising provision, policy shifted to provide subsidies to supplement private spending. The rapidly increasing demand for EEC was not only for workers but for centres. Here, fiscal constraints intersected with budget rules favouring privatisation to fuel a speculative model of private centre construction. That model, developed most famously by ABC Learning, circumvented fiscal constraints by reimagining future public subsidies as collateral, accessing private finance by integrating social provision into circuits of global capital. As ABC Learning's collapse demonstrates, the model was neither sustainable nor capable of transferring long-term risk away from the public sector; however, it reflects an increasingly important dynamic, explored in the next chapter, connecting dualised social provision to global finance.

Establishing the right to childcare

The development of childcare policy in Australia has been skilfully told by a number of feminist scholars, most notably Deborah Brennan (1998, 2007). I draw on this work to help illustrate the similarities and differences between childcare and health policy, and thus help explicate the political and economic dynamics of marketised welfare. Like many social services, childcare was initially dominated by non-government provision. However, before the 1970s, most paid childcare was home-based child minding, rather than formal non-profit or for-profit centres (Women's Bureau 1970 cited in Brennen 2007, 214). Outside of wartime, formal childcare was targeted to those considered in particular need and highly residualised. The male breadwinner model built into Australia's arbitration system presumed most childcare would be provided in the home by a stay-at-home wife. However, the growing entry of women into the labour force, combined with second-wave feminism, challenged this, leading a Coalition government to establish the *Child Care Act* in 1972, along its traditional model of funding non-profit services (see Brennan 1998).

The 1970s saw a shift in movement politics. The previously dominant kindergarten movement was committed to preschool rather than childcare and sceptical of state control. A feminist-led childcare movement instead sought to establish access to care as a publicly funded right. Consistent with other new social movements, childcare activists sought funding for small, independent and community-controlled centres. This, feminists believed, would open space for parents to directly shape the provision of care, rather than care being the preserve of professionals, as happened in public health and education systems (Brennan 1998, 8–9). New feminist organisations successfully influenced Labor's platform in the lead up to Whitlam's 1972 election, marking the beginning of a substantial push to expand public funding along these lines. Ironically, the fiscal austerity of the Fraser government saw it relatively favour childcare over preschool, creating the conditions for greater collaboration between parents and workers to defend and expand funding (Brennan 1998, Chapter 5).

Brennan (1998, 9) notes that while feminists did win 'political' victories through public campaigns, the failure to translate these victories into practice saw a growing focus on bureaucracy. This 'femocrat' strategy was twofold – operating both through the bureaucracies of the state and through the bureaucracies of the Labor Party and trade union movement. It was in the later that the gender bias of the breadwinner model was perhaps most fundamentally challenged. A cross-factional alliance of feminists successfully shifted union and Labor support from the family wage model towards support for equal pay. The Nurses union campaigned strongly for work-based childcare centres, and feminists continued to use campaign tools, like WEL's scorecard, to mobilise women voters. The efforts to turn around the labour movement, and to establish a strong base for child care's expansion in Labor's platform, became central to femocrat success in the long period of Labor government under the Accord (Cass and Brennan 2003, 47; Brennan 1998, Chapter 7).

Through both the ACTU and the ALP, feminists successfully framed childcare as a key component of the Accord's social wage. Feminists won greater funding and a restructure of provision. Additional childcare places were the single largest budget initiative promised by Labor during the 1984 election (Brennan 1998, 176), a commitment echoed in Labor's less ambitious 2022 platform. The continued expansion of child care funding, especially in the face of the strong fiscal constraints of the 1980s, owed much to conventional economic arguments used to counter Treasury pressure to constrain spending. However, because childcare involved a move from the informal to formal economy, it mobilised different kinds of arguments than the shift within health from private to public. Childcare was framed as a *new* economic investment, with macroeconomic returns through the development and maintenance of human capital (ALP 1988; Brennan 1998 Chapter 9) and, later, the creation of new jobs in the industry itself, rather than the reorganisation of (hidden) public spending.

Particularly important was the ability to highlight direct *fiscal* gains. Arguments over public finances have tended to be more powerful than those over the economy as a whole. Brennan claims one of the most significant parts of the campaign within Labor to expand childcare was a report from ANU's Centre for Economic Policy Research, and the most influential part of the report was its fiscal analysis. The report highlighted how women's entry into paid labour improved public finances, both by increasing income tax receipts and by reducing public support for the older breadwinner model, primarily provided through STEs to the primary earner. It found childcare spending of $190m created $290m of fiscal benefits (Anstie et al. 1988, quoted in Brennan 1998, 197–199). Similar arguments, now echoing a well-developed international literature on social investment (Esping-Andersen 2002; Hemerijck 2015; Garritzmann et al. 2022), were mobilised by the Gillard government to expand funding, and are increasingly central to mainstream policy analysis in the area (Deeming and Smyth 2015).

Labor's Child Care Act also changed the structure of provision. Public funding only flowed to non-profit organisations, with community control a condition of the block funding centres received. The Act linked funding levels to the number and qualifications of staff, facilitating an important alliance between childcare workers, parents and feminists to argue for better training, pay and conditions for workers as a mechanism to improve the quality of care for children (Brennan 1998, Chapter 6; Brennan and Mahon 2011). That alliance was resurrected to win higher pay for feminised work in the 2010s, and lies at the centre of changes to industrial relations legislation to more easily recognise the undervaluation of care labour, which Labor took to the 2022 election (Ravlic 2022). While access to centres was not means-tested, those on low incomes qualified for fee subsidies. The model used base funding of centres to reduce all fee levels and additional funding to target financial need.

Publicly funded expansion was never strictly based on a socialised model; however, it was premised on supply-side funding of centres rather than demand-side funding of parent-consumers. Community-controlled centres received base funding to provide services. The structure of independent centres reflected not only movement aspirations for participatory democracy but also the structure of federalism and the Commonwealth's role as funder rather than provider. Fees were a normal part of the model from the start.

Expansion followed a planning principle, based on geographic and demographic data. However, expansion did not match demand, leading to the expansion in an unsubsidised private sector. Access to the different systems was largely a function of capacity, not need. Many low- and middle-income families were forced into the more expensive private system, allowing fiscal conservatives to raise equity concerns (Brennan 1998, 190–191). The structure of public funding, the existence of fees and the failure to universalise provision facilitated a shift from supply-side to demand-side finance.

From community control to dual welfare

The shift to a demand-side funding model, across both Labor and Coalition governments, gradually transformed childcare into a quasi-market. Initially, the trend reflected the pro-market thinking of the central agencies, Finance minister Peter Walsh in particular, and the influence of an established private industry lobby (Brennan 1998, Chapter 9). The shift also reflected the interplay of austerity politics and the women's movement success in making access to childcare a mainstream political concern. Rapidly growing demand for public funding confronted budgetary and accounting rules that limited public investment. Thus, each step towards marketisation accompanied an increase in public *spending* (i.e. purchasing services) and private *investment* (i.e. expanding provision).

The first significant move towards a demand-side model came in 1985 when increased funding was restructured away from grants to centres and towards fee subsidies for lower-income parents. The change reflected the dominance of targeting in Australian social policy. Publicly funded community centres were framed as 'middle class welfare' because access was neither universal nor formally based on need (*Ibid*, 190).

Concerns for equity interacted with gender bias. While community centres disproportionately serviced less advantaged families, critics of the sector, especially the economic dries in Labor and the media, argued its universalist entry policy favoured professional working women. The interplay of attitudes to work, gender and professionalisation represented in these criticisms remain a key barrier to progressive reform. Ironically, the shift to funding parents facilitated more overt dual welfare as the Coalition restructured funding to provide uniform rebates. In any case these changes reorganise the structure of provision, given public funds remained within the non-profit sector, and largely influenced the distribution of costs. That changed in 1991 when another increase in funding extended access to parents in for-profit centres (see Brennan et al. 2012, 386).

Opening funding to for-profits triggered a substantial shift in industry structure. The shift reflects the impact of technocratic forms of neoliberalism, which reshaped public accounting rules to impose austerity and favour private interests. The rapid growth in demand for childcare required considerable capital investment. Accounting rules constrained public debt finance, while obscuring public support for private debt finance. This has encouraged governments to restructure public finance as streams of income rather than direct investment. Broader policy changes reinforced these constraints. National Competition Policy (NCP) restricted access to low-cost public debt finance, while compulsory superannuation created a growing pool of private funds looking for investment opportunities (Newberry and Brennan 2013).

Changes to public sector accounting practices have been an important element of neoliberal austerity. A series of accounting changes made it difficult to increase public investment, either through explicit restrictions on public borrowing or by reinforcing political constraints on the size of public debt. (Net) private borrowing could be offset against the new assets the funds created, a privilege denied ordinary public agencies and only extended to corporatised and 'off-budget' entities. Access to future streams of income can secure private finance, but do not appear in public accounts. Thus, public investment in new childcare centres appeared as a current cost, while the new 'public assets' represented by the centres remained invisible in budget documents. Alternatively, private businesses could borrow money to invest through their capital account based on their expectations of future returns. Private finance was not cheaper or more efficient. Instead, accounting practices and fiscal politics combined to drive privatisation.

Financialising childcare

The new funding model fundamentally changed the way public funding operated, facilitating a process of financialisation. Effectively, the government was encouraging private centres to invest capital on the expectation of future returns largely comprised of government rebates. Where childcare funding in the 1970s and early 1980s provided capital to build centres, now funding established streams of public subsidies that could be used by the private sector to secure access to private capital. This is not an unusual model, and it is essentially how private toll roads are constructed.

The shift to demand side funding is designed to allow innovation on the supply side. Market advocates argue that by specifying the outcomes government wants, and paying for those directly, the market can develop more efficient ways of delivering those outcomes. However, as public funding continued to increase, Newberry and Brennan (2013) chart how firms began to innovate, not in the delivery of quality EEC but in how they could leverage dual welfare.

Shortly after the Howard government announced an expansion of childcare funding, a small childcare firm in Brisbane, ABC Learning, indicated it would list on the stock exchange. Its prospectus outlined a novel company structure, comprising two separate companies that were effectively dependent on each other. One company, the propco, would own childcare centres, while ABC Learning, the opco, would run the centres. This model facilitated an extraordinarily aggressive expansion strategy. Over the next seven years ABC Learning grew from its initial holding of 31 centres when listed to over 1,000 centres in Australia and similar numbers internationally (Newberry and Brennan 2013, 235). However, the model meant that while ABC Learning's share value was increasing, it had few tangible assets to match. In the place of the tangible assets a company might ordinarily own, ABC Learning listed a very valuable set of intangible assets, which were consistently over 70 per cent of the company's total asset holdings. The largest of these intangible assets were publicly issued childcare licences (*Ibid*, 237).

Childcare licences are issued by state and territory governments to certify a centre complies with relevant regulations. Licences are not expensive, but the conditions they set out involve significant initial costs. The licences are non-tradable. The apparent value of the licence does not come from compliance with state regulation, but from access to the stream of federal government subsidies that require licencing. ABC were upfront that the company's value was directly tied to these rebates. Their accounting practice effectively capitalised a future stream of government spending, converting those future payments into capital today. As became obvious, this practice was extremely risky, and implied a form of government guarantee, but it overcame a constraint on accessing the large-scale investment needed to expand the sector. In this sense, accounting practices, both public and private, constructed the politics of childcare and facilitated corporatisation. It is an important example of financialisation, and the technocratic politics of neoliberal reform, which reconstructs a real social choice – the structure of childcare provision – as a pseudo-technical choice, gaming an accounting system.

From 2005 new financial rules made it hard for ABC Learning to maintain its model (*Ibid.*, 237–238). The rules prevented a company from revaluing its self-created intangible assets, and so prevented the company from continually increasing the book value of its licences as childcare rebates rose. However, this is not what stopped the company's expansion. Instead, it simply 'innovated' again, establishing yet another related company, a developmentco. This allowed a new set of arrangements that made it appear ABC Learning was purchasing its licences from the related entity at inflated prices, and thus constructing the licences as an asset based on expected future returns (*Ibid* 238–239).

ABC's model was not only about financial engineering, it was also about monopoly power. The company's rapid expansion reflected a strategy to use its 'first mover advantage' to dominate the market. Similar strategies underpin the rise of many 'innovative' tech companies (see Fernandez et al. 2020), such as Uber. Implicit in the strategy is that a dominant private provider will come to exercise market power. However, unlike the monopsony power exercised by Medicare, which holds prices down, monopoly power is used to increase future prices and profits. Newberry and Brennan argue the related company structure, and contract arrangements were designed to ratchet up childcare fees, by building in higher future rents for premises, that would create political pressure to increase government subsidies (2013, 240). Alongside this market power, large private players clearly also exercise some degree of direct political power, especially in a system that places few limits on political donations (see Evans 2010). That influence has implications not only for funding but also for standards.

In a highly marketised environment, where there is little direct control from government, standard setting becomes an important site for politics. Efforts to strengthen state regulation and to implement a federal system of accreditation have consistently been opposed by private childcare providers and their industry body (Brennan 1998). Promoting these processes has brought together a very similar coalition of forces to those behind the initial expansion of childcare provision – childcare workers and their unions, feminists and parents. Ensuring quality provision by attaching conditions to accessing federal funding has been an important element of union campaigns to improve pay, qualifications and recognition of childcare workers (see Cook et al. 2017).

Funding childcare

The rise of ABC Learning not only reflects the importance of fiscal politics in facilitating privatisation, it also reflects the success of politicising the need for care. EEC provision has expanded rapidly, underpinned by public spending. As with many areas of social need, left purely to market forces, supply grows slowly. It is only with the commitment of public funds that a functional and substantial market develops at all. The expansion of funding has been bipartisan, reflecting an emerging consensus that childcare is a social and economic need and government has a responsibility to ensure access. That consensus, only emerging from the 1990s, was strongly contested by both market dries and conservatives and represents a significant movement victory. However, while the need for EEC is now widely acknowledged, universal access is not, reinforcing a 'soft' form of dual welfare.

The dynamics of funding also reflect ongoing partisan dynamics, similar to those observed by Gingrich, and in changes to payment systems discussed in Chapter 3, as rebates have been organised according to the principles of 'affluence testing'. Labor governments have tended to provide more support for lower-income households, whereas the Coalition has tended to extend support to higher-income households. Labor has tended to construct support as payments to primary carers through payment systems, while the Coalition has tended to construct support as concessions to primary earners through the tax system. Yet, in both cases, there are exceptions to these rules, suggesting policy is as much the product of responding to short-run political contingencies as longer-term and more deeply held commitments. Again, this is consistent with the technocratic politics of neoliberalism, which is now less clearly tied to strong movement actors.

The growth of public support for childcare has often been described as 'middle class welfare', and there are certainly aspects of the various funding models that match Adam Stebbing and my (2010) description of dual welfare. However, this assessment is complicated by the relationship between demand side subsidies and the organisation of provision. Unlike healthcare and school education, there are not distinct public and private sectors, each with their own funding mechanisms. Had block grants remained in the community sector while flat rate rebates were extended to private providers, this would have more closely resembled a dual system. Instead, choice of provider is genuinely limited for virtually all parents by capacity and geography. There is little status hierarchy between private and community providers (see Press and Woodrow 2018); indeed, community providers typically offer higher-quality care (Rush 2006), but they are difficult to access. In this sense, childcare has come to operate more like the medical side of Medicare, where government funding attempts to provide some equity of access to expensive services provided in a market. Of course, unlike medicine, quality is less regulated and more contested in childcare, and the direct providers of care – childcare workers – are less collectively powerful.

Analysis of childcare is also complicated by its relationship to the labour market. Many services in the welfare state are targeted at addressing the costs of misfortune. Our health system, as many critics point out, is really a sickness system (Gardner 2008). The vast bulk of spending goes on treating illness, not promoting health. The social determinants of health – and of poverty, crime and family breakdown – mean that spending in these areas tends to target those on lower incomes. Medicare is universal, but the distributional effects of health spending are highly progressive. That is less clearly the case with childcare and other forms of education. In the short run, EEC is disproportionately accessed by those with more hours of paid work. In the long run, EEC, like education generally, increases earning potential. It is precisely these features of EEC that led many fiscal conservatives to oppose public provision, because EEC was perceived to cater to the 'middle class'.

Critiques of middle-class welfare resonate with Australia's welfare model, but are often misleading. As with Medicare and family payments, once tax concessions have been converted into social spending it has proven extremely difficult to change them back. Even the less egalitarian structure of uniform rebates, which make public subsidies proportional to private spending, is rarely *regressive*. Understanding this can help to make sense of why most measures of inequality show it falling in the early 2000s (Whiteford 2015b, 85) as the Coalition expanded less means-tested family spending.

The Coalition's universal 'baby bonus', increased family payments and childcare rebates were less targeted than other spending. However, the amounts received by low-income earners were a higher *proportion* of their income than those received by high-income earners. As the measures increased aggregate social spending, they acted to reduce inequality in much the same way predicted by the paradox of redistribution (Korpi and Palme 1998). More visible 'middle-class' welfare has proven more equitable than the main alternative – less visible fiscal welfare.

Targeting public spending can also undermine state control. Historically, rebates targeted at low-income earners for both childcare and health insurance have been converted into universal rebates and do little to aid state power over private providers. Recent changes, informed by the Productivity Commission (2015), attempt to address these challenges by creating a progressive scale of rebates linked to a family's income and a schedule of fees. As Corr and Carey (2016) show, the Productivity Commission's preference for targeting in childcare appears to be the outcome of an inbuilt bias against universalism, which privileges an abstract commitment to markets over a detailed understanding of the dynamics of a specific sector.

The new model does little to address the economics of childcare. Without the competitive pressure of free services generated by bulk billing it is doubtful the schedule of fees will aid public control. The more generous 'affluence testing' form of targeting now applied to childcare also has very different implications than when the principle is applied to income. As discussed in Chapter 4, EMTRs reveal the 'tax-like' qualities of means-tests. Likewise, the means-tested structure of childcare support resembles a tax, but one applied selectively based on a household's need for the specific service. In effect, the current system serves as a form of gendered taxation, a system which is both discriminatory in principle and that creates obvious disincentives for women participating in paid work (see Stewart and Whiteford 2018). Predictably, reframing childcare support as a form of targeted welfare assistance also reinforces the wedge politics discussed in the previous chapter. Access to funding is explicitly tied to labour force participation. In practice, the new system potentially creates two types of undeserving parents – those on low incomes without work and those on high incomes who should pay for themselves. Both reinforce austerity.

Markets and Financialisation

Marketising services is complex, especially in a country where state-subsidised, non-government provision has long been the norm. Australia's dual welfare history has meant marketisation is not uniformly privatising. Competition can be harnessed by the state to advance access and equity. Framing Medicare as an insurance scheme, rather than nationalisation, almost certainly assisted universalism through a politics of hybridity. It allowed a new tax to be framed as a price and the conversion of fiscal welfare into social welfare. Establishing forms of free public provision allowed the state to use competition, rather than regulation, to erode private control. However, high out-of-pocket costs suggest limits to hybrid policies.

Marketisation has also advanced in a more conventional manner, through the politics of austerity. As with Medicare, access to EEC also advanced through movement action to politicise need. Initially, those normative demands connected technocratic politics inside the state and labour movement to political campaigns by feminists. Femocrats used the Commonwealth's fiscal powers to tie funding to community control and workers' rights and mobilised an economics of 'social investment' to weaken fiscal constraints. That framework fostered a successful political coalition in favour of universalism. However, the capital demands of shifting provision into the paid economy proved too great in a context where austerity biased accounting structures against public investment. Instead, funding shifted to parents, and the same accounting rules facilitating a financialised model that allowed private companies to convert future public subsidies into investment today and market power tomorrow.

Restructuring public support as private subsidy reinforces the broader trend to financialisation. Subsidising user payments appeared cheaper to governments than guaranteeing universal provision, at least in the short run. But it also established a stream of payments that could be financially reengineered into higher capital values. ABC Learning provides a dramatic example of this speculative logic. The real money behind the asset economy lies elsewhere; in the reorganisation of how we support citizens to manage life course risks through pensions and housing. It is in debates over population ageing that an asset economy has been born, and a deep generational divide has emerged in the organisation of welfare, gradually ratcheting up inequalities within each new generation. But here too there is complexity making it difficult to judge public from private and social from individual. The financialisation of the life course, from student fees to house prices and superannuation, is increasingly the main frontier between hybridity and dualism.

Chapter 5

FINANCIALISING THE LIFE COURSE

Financialisation is potentially the most significant, yet challenging, aspect of liberalisation to assess. Where residualisation and marketisation can be understood through discrete changes within areas of social policy – payments and social services – financialisation involves a more complex interplay between policies we think of as 'social' and changes that are ordinarily understood as 'economic management'. That interplay reflects how finance reworks and reimagines 'risk', the social relationship at the heart of the welfare state. Financialisation also describes a shift in the organisation of the economy, towards a model of profitability increasingly centred on capital gains and asset ownership. This asset economy is, ironically, increasingly underpinned by the streams of money households spend on social needs in the absence of a strong welfare state (Adkins et al. 2020; Bryan and Rafferty 2018).

Australia's retirement income system has proven particularly susceptible to the processes of financialisation. Our wage-earner model created modest pensions and a reliance on home ownership, leading households to rely on private savings in asset-based welfare (ABW). Deregulation of housing finance has made borrowing cheaper, but housing much more expensive. Efforts to expand the narrowly means-tested pension have focused on building a new market-based pension system – superannuation. Unlike other areas of social policy, where fiscal welfare was converted into social spending, retirement incomes have grown by encouraging private savings, which has expanded fiscal welfare. As money has flooded into super and housing, dual welfare has steadily increased. Retirement incomes have increased for many as a result, reflecting the success of union demands. But that increase has come through a much more technocratic and individualised system, tied as much to macroeconomic goals as tangible social needs.

The rise of 'asset-based welfare' within social policy mirrors a shift in how risk is imagined and economies managed. Rather than managing *social* risks by redistributing *income* in the *present*, states increasingly see their role as helping citizens manage their *individual* finances *over time*, by saving and investing in *assets*. This is most obvious in retirement incomes policy, where pensions and superannuation are explicitly framed around the life course, but it is also true of changes to higher education, framed as an investment in 'human capital'.

State and corporate accounts have been remade. They are now less useful for understanding and managing the contingencies of today and instead orientated to creating and profiting from an imagined future. Where Keynes scoffed that in the long run 'we are all dead', fortunes are now made by unlocking the magic of capital gains. Corporate books are dominated by *intangible* assets, which reflect expectations about the future. Chicago school economists advanced complementary accounting models within social policy to highlight the dangers 'population ageing' presented to the interests of future taxpayers. It is ironic indeed that the very problems most young people decry today – expensive housing, student debt, insecure work – are born of a political project ostensibly aimed at 'generational equity'.

Financialisation, however, opens opportunities as well as risks. There have been successful attempts to make fiscal welfare visible, and to reconnect public spending to its ultimate purpose of meeting social needs, rather than balancing the books. Nor are the policies of financialised welfare – super, student loans and support for home ownership – purely the product of markets. All remain connected to tangible social needs, and of necessity, each involves a degree of hybridity, combining markets with elements of social protection. While facilitating 'privatisation' and dual welfare, each involves new forms of provision whose function is far less 'privatised' than they appear. Home ownership provides security to pensioners. Super is built on 'employer contributions' that look very similar to European social insurance payments. Student fees are funded through a 'loan' system that is entirely public and repaid to the tax office using an income tax scale.

The chapter explores the politics of social policy and financialisation through retirement incomes and higher education. It begins by situating Australia's post-War retirement income system internationally and within the wage-earner model and then explores how this settlement was reworked by the advance of financialisation. It then explores how efforts to contest social policy have been linked to changes in public sector accounting – both to retrench social protection by constructing social rights as future fiscal liabilities and to expand protection by making visible fiscal welfare. Finally, it examines the reintroduction of university fees and student loans. Where super was driven by macroeconomic concerns, student fees reflected concerns over 'middle class' welfare. Both resulted in marketised policy models, but also hybrid policy forms, raising possibilities for 'social' investment. Financialisation may have left social policy in a much more precarious position, yet even here, contestation remains.

Remaking Retirement

Older people have always been key to the welfare state (see Castles 2004). Ageing is a universal experience. Unsurprisingly, in most countries older people are the primary beneficiaries of the largest spending programs, pensions and healthcare. Australia's aged pension emerged at the turn of the twentieth century and became entrenched nationally soon after federation, well before other cash payments. As discussed in Chapter 3, the flat-rate and means-tested pension, funded from general revenue rather than social insurance contributions, became the model for most of Australia's payments systems. From the 1970s researchers and policy makers increasingly acknowledged an interplay between pension policy and housing policy, not only in Australia but across the OECD (Kemeny 1977, Castles 1998). In economic terms, housing and pensions can be seen as complementary because they both involve income smoothing, as households save during their working lives to support post-work living standards.

Exactly how the structure of housing influenced the development of welfare has been subject to significant debate, with Australia's wage-earner model playing a prominent role. Jim Kemeny (1977) argued home ownership mitigated against the solidaristic politics needed to expand social protection. Home purchase can only be accessed via mortgages. Large debts discipline wage demands because workers cannot afford to strike. Mortgage repayments also increase tax resistance from workers, reinforcing market dependence. Kemeny's thesis was reinforced by an empirical relationship. By the 1970s, countries with high home ownership rates did tend to have lower overall taxation and social spending, while those built around rental housing, either via social housing or strong tenant protections, developed more extensive welfare states.

Australia appeared to fit Kemeny's model relatively well, much as it fit the liberal version of Esping-Andersen's welfare regime typology. Francis Castles, however, developed an alternative account, building on his analysis of arbitration, that viewed home ownership as a more inclusive and egalitarian institution. Castles argued access to home ownership did not emerge spontaneously as a market response to uneven life course earnings. Instead it was part of the broader wage-earner model, which focused on market regulation as much as taxation and spending. Extensive capital controls ensured first-home buyers had preferential access to loans at predictable interest rates, wages were set to allow modest savings and development was managed to provide affordable housing stock. Home ownership operated alongside a public housing system, which while relatively small, managed to cater for a significant proportion of long-term non-home owners and provided a stepping stone into ownership for others. Both systems were built around the normative family model. Home ownership came via the wages of the white male breadwinner, and public housing was only available to married couples. For those outside this model, extreme poverty remained (see Gilmour 2018). Nonetheless, security of tenure was ensured for both owners and public tenants, and private rental was dominated by short-term leases for the young and the transient.

The politics of housing differ somewhat from arbitration. From early on, the Labor Party and union movement prioritised wage regulation over social spending. The institutions of arbitration were the direct result of union campaigns and Labor action in parliament, even if the system was subsequently maintained and adapted by Coalition governments. In relation to housing, Labor and the unions followed their British counterparts more closely. Initially Labor focused on regulatory measures, like rent caps and tenancy protections. The Wartime Labor government then committed to a mass expansion of public housing (MacIntyre 2018), opening an explicit partisan cleavage. The Menzies' Coalition instead advocated home ownership, which Labor initially decried as a strategy to turn workers into 'little capitalists' (*Ibid*, 273). Over time rental protections were also unwound as the expansion of home ownership eroded the constituency of long-term renters.

Still, housing remained part of a social model of liberalism (Forrest and Hiryama 2015; Yates and Bradbury 2010). Policy design, macroeconomic management and social norms reinforced home ownership as a normative aspiration rather than housing as an investment vehicle. Ownership paralleled an ideal life course, where workers would save a deposit, before buying a home to start a family, and would ideally acquit their mortgage before retirement, when they could then live in the home rent-free (Castles 1997b). This social model emphasised the 'use value' of housing as tenure rather than the exchange value of housing as an asset. While it overlapped an economic understanding of saving across the life course (Ando and Modigliani 1963), it did not position housing as a form of liquidity, to be drawn down in retirement to fund consumption. Instead, the family home was excluded from the pension means-test to reflect its status as a form of direct provision, rather than a source of income. The ideal was to own a home outside financial relations, a norm that persists amongst the 'old old' (those over 80), frustrating economists who see potential welfare gains from accessing housing equity (Whait et al. 2019).

Liberalisation of finance and the decline of wage-earner welfare have slowly transformed this social model, interacting with an existing system of fiscal welfare to produce increasingly unequal outcomes. Financial reforms have made it easier to access cheap finance, especially for those with existing assets and good credit histories (Yates and Yanotti 2016). Insecure work and changing family formations have stratified household risk and savings profiles. More households rely on irregular or low market incomes while managing significant care responsibilities. Many others now have two market incomes. Thus, home ownership rates are falling for younger age cohorts, with the falls greatest for those on low incomes and with greater caring responsibilities (Stebbing and Spies-Butcher 2016).

Superannuation balances reflect similar changes, which are directly influenced by lifetime earnings and thus reduced by either periods of under-employment or primary caring responsibilities. It is unsurprising the wealthiest 10 per cent of Australians hold over 40 per cent of total super savings (Davidson and Bradbury 2022, 30), and that women typically retire with less than 60 per cent of the super savings of men (Australian Super 2022). Both trends are made significantly worse by the interaction between financial markets and the tax system, a product of both greater marketisation of retirement incomes and a failure to wind back or convert fiscal welfare.

Building a New Retirement Incomes Model

Reforming the retirement income system is difficult. Pensions are understood in relation to working life and reflect an implicit social contract between generations. Restructuring retirement policy involves reworking the relationship between current and retired workers and how we imagine those relationships into the future. ABW creates an additional set of challenges by linking our future incomes to our past behaviour. It is hard to reform the system without creating seemingly 'undeserving losers'. The ubiquity of retirement ensures the sums involved are enormous.

From the 1930s through to the 1970s several efforts were made to expand provision beyond the means-tested public pension. A social insurance model was legislated in the 1930s, but was overtaken by the Second World War before it could be implemented. The Whitlam government also looked to extend the pension system along these lines, by creating a publicly controlled insurance-based pension scheme (Stebbing 2015). In the absence of earnings-related social insurance, the 1970s saw moves to universalise the pension. However, none of these efforts was complete when policy momentum in the 1980s swung back towards targeting.

Where efforts to replace wage-earner welfare had failed, reform instead turned to adding a new 'layer' of social policy on top. However, instead of strengthening the public pillar (public pensions) by removing tax concessions on the private pillar (private pensions), superannuation strengthened the private alternative. Expanding private superannuation promised workers a better retirement without expanding taxation or social spending. Indeed, public spending would fall as workers' retirement incomes rose and the means-test reduced their public entitlement (see Kingston and Thrope 2019; Stebbing 2015, 123). There is some truth to this story, but not much. Despite the enormous resources super now controls it cannot guarantee adequate incomes, housing or care in retirement. Nor is there a widespread expectation that it should.

Privatisation and hybridity: Layering super onto the pension

The absence of an existing earnings-related public pension scheme was central to the development of super in Australia. More so than almost any other policy domain, the principles of pension policy invoke long time horizons. Market schemes take considerable time to establish because current workers are understood to be making contributions to their own individual entitlement in the future (see Bryan and Rafferty 2018, Chapter 4). Shifting from a public scheme (where current pensions are effectively paid by current worker-tax payers) to a market scheme (where workers also fund their own future pension) generates resistance. In contrast, superannuation was an *addition* to existing public pension entitlements in Australia. As with the private health insurance rebate, new private benefits were layered on top of the existing system. There was no need to unscramble an existing scheme.

As a new layer in the retirement income system super both reduced resistance and generated new support. Superannuation universalised an existing system of private pensions that had been largely confined to white collar and public sector workers. Pension policy not only set the model for social payments, it also established the model of fiscal welfare. Alongside the targeted public pension Australia had implemented tax deductions for contributions to private pension schemes (Stebbing 2015). The model expanded under Menzies, with many white-collar firms offering tax-subsidised employer-based schemes, and was integrated into Australia's brand of Keynesian macro-management through a link to public investment; tax concessions were only available to funds that held sufficient public bonds (*Ibid*).

The shift towards super was distinctly 'Australian', developing through arbitration and the Accord to mediate fiscal and macroeconomic constraints. Superannuation integrated an existing system of private employer pension funds into the broader welfare state, through a mandated and more universal model covering almost all workers. Following the election of the Coalition in 1996, the system then evolved into a more traditional form of dual welfare.

Initially, the claim to universalise access to private pension funds came through wage arbitration. Frustrated by the lack of success in advancing an earnings-based public pension, the union movement looked to arbitration as a vehicle to incorporate pension schemes into awards. The model they developed reflects elements of the Scandinavian Ghent model. Employers were required to make contributions to specific funds co-managed by workers, via unions, and employers, now known as 'industry funds' (see Stebbing 2015, 122–123).

The model proved useful to the macroeconomic goals of the Accord and the constraints of fiscal austerity. After 1985 the pressures for wage restraint grew. Labor and the unions saw expanding the new employer pension contributions as a solution. Employer contributions would count as a deferred wage rise, allowing total worker compensation to keep pace with inflation even as money wages declined in real terms. This was similar to the trade-off between money wages and the social wage used in other aspects of the Accord, but here the trade-off was temporal, between current and future wages. The temporal shift avoided fiscal constraints by defining super in financial terms – as private savings – rather than as taxation. However, the shift to market definitions also changed the structure of the schemes, from defined benefit schemes, based on the social principle of income maintenance, to defined contributions, based on the market principles of investment.

Establishing the funds as separate entities was important for how the funds were understood, accounted for and operated. Super is understood as a private industry, regulated by the state, rather than a public system. In practice, it involves a degree of hybridity, which allowed state control to expand despite fiscal politics constraining the introduction of new taxes. Contributions are mandated and deduced from wages much like income tax. Likewise, access to payments is restricted by social principles reflecting the idea of 'retirement' from paid work. However, because super is managed by separate, non-government entities, contributions and payments are considered 'private'. The OECD does provide alternative figures, which include superannuation in social spending, where it adds 4 per cent to GDP, raising Australia's tax take from well below to around the middle of developed countries (OECD 2020, 5–6).

Hybridity, however, is limited by the political dynamics that led super to be layered onto the pension. Rather than primarily reflecting political campaigns to address social needs, super was driven as much by efforts at macroeconomic liberalisation, where super would aid national savings (Gallagher et al. 1993) and address a persistent current account deficit (Coates and Vidler 2004). Unions may have advanced super, but there were no mass protests in support, as with Medicare, limited grassroots movement activism, as with feminism. Indeed, unions were initially divided on the proposals (*Ibid*, 10). Thus, superannuation reflected much more strongly the pro-market sentiments of both Treasurer Paul Keating and Sawer's econrats. Dual welfare remained. The scheme's hybrid structure turned the very technical regulation of super into a key battleground of the welfare state.

Super funds operate according to market rules, enforced by trust law and prudential regulation (see Markey et al. 2014). This effectively prevents democratic control, even of industry funds. Fund managers are obliged to maximise individual returns, rather than to use their investments to advance other social principles, even if their members wish them to. Savings are radically individualised. There are no restrictions on where funds can be invested, no requirements for minimum levels of return and no requirements that the money be accessed as a regular pension (annuity) rather than a lump sum.

Union representation appears to have successfully mitigated the worst excesses of private finance (*Ibid*), but have done little to prevent 'financialisation' of pensions (Bryan and Rafferty 2018; Broomhill et al. 2021). Super is now much closer to a market investment vehicle than a social policy. Super has a much 'riskier' asset profile than many comparable pension systems, reflected in the much larger drop in superannuation accounts during the global financial crisis (Whitehouse 2009, 536–537). The growing pool of super funds also created pressure to expand long-term investment options. Rather than spurring new private investment, super funds were increasingly invested in what had previously been public works, especially in transport infrastructure and more recently housing. It is no coincidence that private-public partnerships developed alongside superannuation (Jefferis and Stilwell 2006, 53–58, also see Newberry and Brennan 2013; Kindston and Thorp 2019). Where post-War taxes supported nation building and public payments, superannuation has helped remake a privatised economy.

Reworking fiscal welfare: Super and housing

In healthcare and family benefits policy, the shift from the wage-earner and dual welfare model to hybrid policies was financed by converting fiscal welfare into social spending. No similar conversion occurred with retirement incomes. Superannuation advanced by expanding occupational welfare, which in turn facilitated an expansion of fiscal welfare. Policy reform within retirement incomes was not primarily driven by guaranteeing social rights. It was instead shaped by economic arguments that understood retirement incomes in market terms, as a problem of income smoothing across the life course. That framing has tied retirement incomes into larger capital markets, where fiscal welfare plays a broader role in tax minimisation.

Retirement incomes are not only integrated into capital markets; housing and pension funds are two of the largest asset categories in the market.

Changing the taxation of either involves reworking taxation of capital in general. That is a challenging task, and one made more difficult by new financial models that emphasise capital gains as a source of profit (see Adkins et al. 2020). Homeownership and super have partly spread the windfall gains of the asset economy, even amongst many older working-class households, but have also disguised just how much has flowed to the very wealthy. Even with Australia's relatively equitable distribution of housing assets and compulsory superannuation, the 'asset economy' has significantly widened wealth inequalities (Davidson and Bradbury 2022, 28–29).

The 1980s saw Labor restructure the broader tax system. Progressive unions had successfully pushed to include efforts to close tax loopholes as part of the Accord. However, changes to the tax system were largely decoupled from discussions of social protection. Unlike the dynamics in other policy domains, which allowed the conversion of fiscal welfare into social welfare, the tax reform process set out a formal and explicit commitment to offset any additional tax revenues through tax cuts (see Tilley 2021, 8–9). Potentially this advanced equity and efficiency by removing concessions and loopholes disproportionately used by the rich, but it decoupled the politics of tax from the politics of social protection, and thus severed one of the primary political mechanisms that has proven successful in advancing social protection. The structure of retirement incomes policy confounded the process further. Instead of tax loopholes being used to fund welfare, the financialisation of retirement incomes saw social needs used to justify tax loopholes.

The rise of superannuation was somewhat incidental to the broader tax packages, but also clearly intersected with them. Taxing super is not straightforward. Conventionally, economists argue governments should either tax money on the way in (via contributions and fund earnings) or on the way out (via withdrawals) (see Yoo and de Serres 2004, 6–7). Australia began by only taxing withdrawals, albeit on concessional terms. Contributions and earnings were tax free. Directing more money into super (instead of current wages) thus threatened to reduce overall taxation by turning taxable wages into tax-free super contributions, and thus threaten the budget balance. Labor's solution was to create new taxes on contributions and earnings to 'bring forward' tax revenues (see Marriott 2009, 486). However, a simple switch, by eliminating taxes on withdrawals, would create windfall gains for those who made tax-free contributions in the past. Instead, the tax changes meant concessional tax rates were applied at all three stages. The changes were progressive, but they did not retrench fiscal welfare per se, instead leaving a complex model that at once appeared to tax super too many times while retaining concessional tax treatment overall (see Sharp 1992).

A more direct and challenging situation confronted Labor when it came to housing. Labor's efforts to broaden the tax base and reduce opportunities for tax avoidance involved introducing two new taxes. The Fringe Benefits Tax targeted the emerging corporate practice of offering executives and clients a host of 'non-salary' benefits, like school fees, cars and boozy lunches. The Capital Gains Tax (CGT) aimed to target precisely the kind of speculative tax avoidance that has increasingly driven the asset economy, by taxing the income earned when you buy low and sell high. Both taxes targeted the top end of town, those that think seriously about how to 'organise their affairs' to minimise tax liabilities. However, home ownership potentially extended the logic of capital gains to the vast majority of Australian households who owned a home (and benefited from capital gains as house prices rose). In 1980 the Coalition ran a successful scare campaign suggesting Labor would tax the family home (see Carling 2016). While business could be compensated through the broader Tax Reform process, it is much harder to make complicated changes involving millions of people with little financial training, especially when you are targeting their life savings.

The political solution for Labor was to exempt the family home from capital gains tax and grandfather all existing investments. It was potentially a political necessity. In the old world of wage-earner welfare, where most workers expected to own a home, it potentially simplified things. But as the world changed and house prices rose, it entrenched an increasingly unequal set of advantages for those that could make it into home ownership. The CGT exemption also reinforced the existing exemption for the family home from the pension means-test, creating strong incentives to invest more in the family home (see Neilson 2010 for chronology of policy changes). In retirement there are also few restrictions on how to access super, creating incentives for those with substantial savings to invest more in their home (where for tax and means-test purposes the money disappears).

Investment in social housing moved in the opposite direction. Rather than expanding the social housing stock, Labor shifted the budget to support rent subsidies in the private market by expanding eligibility for, and increasing the level of, Commonwealth Rent Assistance (Prosser and Leeper 1994). Just as with childcare, governments met growing demand, not with increased supply, but with a shift in funding towards streams of public subsidies that could support private investment (i.e. private landlords buying investment properties to rent out) (see Lawson et al. 2022). Where public housing placed downward pressure on rents, rent assistance is associated with rising rents, especially in poor neighbourhoods (Ong et al. 2020).

The impacts of these changes are gradual. People acquire housing equity slowly, as they pay down their mortgage. Many of the beneficiaries of asset inflation remain average workers who entered the labour market 30 or 40 years ago. In wealth terms, Australia remains one of the more egalitarian countries in the OECD (Bryant et al. 2022, 7–8), reflecting the windfall gains experienced by many older working-class households. Over time, however, it promises to produce rising inequality as less affluent younger households (at least those without family wealth) are locked out (Stebbing and Spies-Butcher 2016; OECD 2022c). Perhaps more importantly, these tax and pension changes set up a partisan political dynamic that exaggerates the inequalities of dual welfare. ABW connects social needs to markets, tying the interests of millions of households to rising house and stock market prices through complex tax rules that even many of the beneficiaries do not fully understand. Efforts to wind back asset inflation potentially create millions of losers.

Unlike the successful models in health and family payments that have withstood sustained efforts at retrenchment, the dynamics within retirement incomes policy appear to drive greater dualism and weaken the forms of hybridity that initially existed. The complex tax models created by Labor's reforms opened the door to much less equitable tax changes. Those changes were often defended as protecting younger generations by helping households save.

First, in 1999 the Coalition introduced the Capital Gains Tax discount. This changed the way capital gains were calculated and tax applied. Instead of discounting an asset for inflation, an owner could halve the rate of tax on the nominal gain on the condition the asset was held for at least 12 months (see Kenny 2005). It purportedly created an incentive for long-term investment. In housing, the largest market for such funds, it simply created a tax dodge and set off a surge in house prices (see Shi et al. 2016).

The new rule also interacted with another anomaly of the tax code, colloquially known as 'negative gearing'. Negative gearing allows losses on an investment to be deducted from labour income for tax purposes. The combination of negative gearing, CGT concessions, low inflation and rising house prices drove a new highly geared investment model. Fiscal welfare not only delivered the largest gains to those wealthy enough to invest large sums, it drove up house prices too, undermining a key social right and complicating monetary policy.

Second, in 2006, the Coalition cut taxes on withdrawals from superannuation accounts for those over 60 (Nielson 2010, 10). The changes significantly simplified super's complex tax treatment. However, because the previous tax system applied concessional taxation on contributions and earnings, and only applied tax to withdrawals from larger accounts, the distributional impact of the changes was starkly regressive. Most workers now face a flat-tax system, where everyone pays the same 15 per cent tax rate on super. Other changes deregulated the operation of super funds, allowing entry to for-profit providers and self-managed funds. Neither fund type performs well compared to the older industry fund model (Markey et al. 2014; Phillips 2011). Instead, these models grew through the promise of tax lurks and aggressive marketing.

As the new dual welfare model has matured it has reinforced an apparent generational cleavage. Rising house prices may have benefited many working-class people and many on low incomes, but only for the overwhelmingly older Australians who were already in the market. Changes to the taxation of super and new tax offsets to encourage older people to work longer mean older households routinely pay less tax than younger households on the same incomes (see Pattugalan and Ellis 2010 for overview of offsets). Increasing fees for education and rising house prices, alongside climate change, reinforce generational grievances.

Ironically, many of the tax changes made to support Australia's asset-based model were justified on the grounds of generational equity. Generational Accounting (GA) was central to the fiscal reform agenda of the Coalition government, influenced similar changes under Labor and reinforced other pro-privatisation accounting changes. Billed as defending generational interests, GA also justified an increase to the eligibility age for the pension, reinforcing a class divide between the poor old who are force to work longer through a threat of poverty and the rich old who are able to access superannuation much earlier. Understanding how accounting shaped the politics of welfare can help explain contradictory generational politics, why inequality is likely to rise in the future and more optimistically the potential for hybrid alternatives.

Generational Accounting: Financialising the Social Project

Changes in retirement income policy reflect the financialisation of social policy, which is increasingly tied to capital markets. Financialisation is connected to changes in accounting that normalise the speculative characteristics of financial markets, such as a shift to financial and less tangible assets and fair value measures (Zhang and Andrew 2014). In the public sector an accountability agenda emerged around new public sector management that sought to import norms and processes from the private sector into government (see Dunleavy and Hood 1994, 10).

Where the Keynesian consensus was built on separating 'public' and 'private' money (see Chapter 2), financialisation blurs these boundaries by attempting to remake public finance in the image of private finance. Importing private sector accounting and governance models often involves a degree of asymmetry because states retain unique powers associated with sovereignty that disappear in private accounting models. Instead, accounting changes obscure these powers and reinforce fiscal constraints.

The Keynesian model of state finance focused attention on macroeconomic management. State budgets emphasised flows of income, or 'cash accounting', which made it easier to identify whether and how much state money was stimulating or contracting the economy. Public expenditure was understood as spending, assessed according to public benefit rather than only financial benefit. Public debt continued to be important, but it made less sense to think of 'net' and 'gross' debt, given the state did not often make market investments.

State management of finance was often integrated into central banking, with access to credit managed administratively within the state. Liberalisation saw this change, with the separation of 'independent' central banking focused on reducing inflation. New rules policed how states could manage their finances, changing real accountabilities. Actions that could once be organised internally within the state were increasingly accountable to non-state actors concerned with evaluating the 'fiscal sustainability [...] creditworthiness [...] (and) solvency [...]' of states (Lemoine 2017, 313).

Social policy was a key target of these neoliberal governance strategies. Social spending is a large proportion of total public spending and has tended to increase over time. A new set of strategies sought to constrain social spending by applying the financial logic of solvency to the state. Both private financial actors and pro-market economists began to use projection techniques to anticipate future public spending, constructing this spending as a form of liability on the future state (see Lemoine 2017). Just as corporate restructuring sought to reduce the liabilities of the firm, especially tax and employment liabilities, by avoiding obligations to states and workers, now the state itself would be restructured to reduce its 'liabilities' to its own citizens (Baker et al. 2020). Within social policy, a notable expression of these changes came through 'truth in budgeting' legislation, which entrenched a method of reporting only recently invented – GA (Spies-Butcher and Stebbing 2019).

Population ageing and welfare

Concern over the fiscal implications of population ageing emerged alongside pressures towards liberalisation. In the United States, debates that had focused on aged poverty during the 1960s and early 1970s gave way to concerns over the budgetary impact of new spending programs targeted at older people by the late 1970s (Hudson 2014, 7). A similar shift took place in Australia between the priority afforded poverty in the Henderson Inquiry and the assertion of strong fiscal constraint in Labor's 'trilogy' commitment.

By the 1980s a broader debate was emerging amongst international institutions, informed by awareness of declining fertility rates and rising life expectancies (Gee 2002; Gutman 2010). The most notable contribution came from the World Bank (1994), which urged pension privatisation to limit exposure to future public deficits.

Within the welfare state GA formed a core technique for changing how state finances were imagined and managed. GA was developed by Auerbach, Kotlikoff and colleagues in the United States, and became the most popular of a range of forecasting models (Kotlikoff 1992; Spies-Butcher and Stebbing 2019). The technique was proposed as politically neutral and less open to manipulation than deficit budgeting models, because it recorded 'unfunded liabilities' (Auerbach, Gokhale and Kotlikoff 1994). Unfunded liabilities were typically government commitments to future social spending. While appearing technocratic, the accounting changes were not neutral, but explicitly normative. A key tenant of GA is that 'generations born in the future should not pay a higher share of their lifetime incomes to the government than today's newborns' (*Ibid*, 84); public finance must never be allowed to grow.

GA is a method for projecting future budgetary costs. It combines analysis of current policy settings and demographic projections to create estimates of future social spending. GA provides estimates of the expenditure likely to be generated if current policy settings remained in place and demographic projections prove accurate. It is not surprising that GA techniques began to emerge through the 1980s and were often promoted by market advocates. Earlier in the twentieth century the same techniques would have produced very different results. Demographic ageing is a product of rising life expectancies and declining (or not rising) fertility. The initial impact of population ageing is not to expand the cohort of retirees, but rather to expand the workforce as more infants and children live into adulthood. These effects were magnified by the impact of war, which both reduced the number of adults and then led to a dramatic rise in fertility. A GA assessment in 1950 would have shown the proportion of workers on the rise 20 years hence (see Esping-Andersen 1999).

By the 1980s demography was increasingly framed as a fiscal challenge (Pierson 2001). Assisting older people had proven a powerful political strategy for welfare state advocates. Aged pensions were often the first mass welfare state policies enacted. Pensions and healthcare, which is also disproportionately targeted to older people, remain the largest areas of social expenditure across the OECD (Spies-Butcher and Stebbing 2019). GA refocused debate from addressing need to managing finances. Together with the service transition, population ageing created structural pressures to expand social provision. The normative commitment underpinning GA, to ensure each generation paid no more tax than the last, created a countervailing pressure to reassert fiscal constraint.

The structure of Australian social policy, however, already reflected many of the fiscal principles of GA. Initial claims that population ageing would lead to fiscal crisis were firmly rejected by the Cass Social Security Review in the 1980s (Foster 1988, 51). Similar analysis by the Economic Planning Advisory Council (1994), now using GA techniques, confirmed the result (see Spies-Butcher and Stebbing 2019, 1416). By the 1990s Australia's retirement income system combining the 'three pillars' of a flat-rate and means-tested public pension, compulsory market-based superannuation and voluntary savings was being heralded as world's best practice (see World Bank 1994; Borowski 2013). The hybrid structure of superannuation – compulsory but private – had pre-emptively solved the problem GA aimed to pose. Compulsion ensured more resources would be available to older people, but constructed as occupational welfare it did not increase measures of public finance and so avoided GA's prohibition on higher average tax rates. Unlike in Europe, it proved exceedingly difficult to demonstrate any real fiscal problem.

Generational equity as austerity

Assessments of generational equity, however, changed significantly with a change of government. The Howard-led Coalition had focused on the budget deficit during the 1996 election. After coming to office, it established a Commission of Audit, which laid the groundwork for significant austerity (Spies-Butcher and Stebbing 2019, 1418). The Audit was charged with exploring generational equity, eventually arguing the government should explicitly seek to 'moderate community expectations of government assistance', in anticipation of 'radical and lasting' demographic change (National Commission of Audit 1996 chap. 6, cited in Spies-Butcher and Stebbing 2019, 1418). It also proposed changes to budgetary standards and rules to ensure the future cost of spending programs were calculated and made visible.

The changes proposed by the Commission formed the basis for the Coalition's 'truth in budgeting' reforms (*Ibid*), which applied financial accounting techniques (initially asymmetrically) and instituted a regular Intergenerational Report (IGR). The IGRs reinforced existing asymmetries in public budgeting. The Reports focus on social spending while ignoring fiscal welfare, and reframe future social spending as a liability, without any equivalent accounting for rising revenues or public ownership as assets. Importantly GA did not seek to increase efficiency (i.e. better social outcomes per dollar spent), only to minimise spending. Unsurprisingly, GA created incentives for privatisation and retrenchment, promoting the expansion of dual welfare.

The first IGR, released in 2002, echoed the key themes of the original Commission. By focusing on demography, it narrowed attention to social spending, largely ignoring other large components of the budget like defence. Instead, both documents argued demography made key components of social policy – healthcare, pensions and aged care – fiscally unsustainable (*Ibid*). It encouraged policy responses that would support citizens to make their own provisions in these areas or to require user charges to cover costs. The first IGR helped frame proposals to reduce tax on superannuation and to advance user charges for aged care, as well as praising subsidies for private health insurance (Howe and Healy 2005).

The structure of the IGRs encourages proposals to privatise welfare. Assuming tax receipts will remain stable as a proportion of GDP implicitly assumes a series of tax cuts, to reverse the impact of rising incomes and a progressive tax structure. As the recent Coalition governments of the 2010s demonstrated, simply leaving existing tax rates in place leads to rising revenues from bracket creep (Weisser 2015, 19). Rather than projecting how a given tax structure will interact with demography, the IGRs assume stable revenues, removing any consideration of fiscal welfare.

The reports only focus on fiscal costs, rather than broader economic or social costs. Changes that reduce public spending may increase private spending by an even larger amount for the same set of outcomes. The goal is not efficiency, productivity or well-being; it is simply reducing social spending. This fiscal goal is then framed as generational equity. Fiscal austerity was achieved by promoting private savings to address life course risks. Thus, generational equity increasingly came to mean reducing tax on savings, exacerbating the global shift towards asset price inflation.

Changes to retirement incomes now have an enormous fiscal cost. Tax concessions for superannuation reduce revenues by $45b a year, while capital gains deductions cost $70b, the bulk of which is caused by the exemption for the family home (Treasury 2023, 5). In comparison, the aged pension and other income support for older people now costs $54b (Treasury 2022, 155). Yet, these arrangements have failed to ensure positive outcomes for older people. The number of older women facing homelessness is on the rise (Reynolds et al. 2018). Serious issues remain in aged care. While the total quantum of public support for older Australians has increased, its distribution increasingly favours the well off. Over 70 per cent of non-owner occupied dwelling capital gains tax benefits flow to the top 10 per cent of income earners, as do over 30 per cent of super tax benefits (Grudnoff and Littleton 2021).

As Adam Stebbing and I found (2016), changes in home ownership are better explained by income and care responsibilities than by simple generational effects. Over time, many, if not most, of today's young people will come to own a home. Those that miss out will overwhelmingly be poorer or single parents. Likewise, the size of inheritances is growing, but the largest benefits flow to the already wealthy (Wood and Griffiths 2019).

GA has helped restructure retirement policy away from egalitarian forms of social provision to a dual model of welfare that favours the very rich. Rather than a broad concern for the welfare of future generations, its narrow focus on social spending advances only the interests of those seeking to reduce their tax liabilities. The result is a slow erosion of social protections alongside greater freedoms and privileges for those with means. The changes may affect across generations, but the result is a return to older divisions based on class, care and colonial expropriation.

Contesting generational austerity

The rise of financialised accounting models reflects efforts to impose fiscal austerity, yet these technical moves can be contested. Often, austerity and privatisation were advanced through the asymmetric application of financial accounting techniques. Perhaps unsurprisingly then, efforts to contest these implications have partly focused on developing alternative accounting technologies. This progressive challenge to liberalised models of accounting is not simply technocratic. It reflects a broader philosophical and political challenge to mainstream economic understandings of value, summed up in Marian Waring's influential book *Counting for Nothing* (Waring 1999). Waring's research reflected her experience with the political implications of asymmetric economic and fiscal rules, which obscured the valuable unpaid work performed primarily by women, and the ecological and social costs of economic production (see Saunders and Dalziel 2017). Similar efforts inform alternative economic and well-being measures, as well as gender budgeting and fiscal welfare tools.

Perhaps the most significant challenge to rising inequalities within the retirement incomes system has come from the development of regular tax expenditure data. Focusing on tax expenditures, or fiscal welfare, is not specific to retirement incomes. As we have seen, social tax expenditures are central to many elements of the dual welfare state that developed as part of Australia's wage-earner model. Converting STEs has also been a key strategy to expand social spending on health and family support. Identifying tax concessions is therefore central to promoting social protection and to the politics of hybridity. However, fiscal welfare is now dominated by policies linked to the retirement incomes system, particularly housing and superannuation, and so has become central to the politics of financialisation.

Reporting STEs is not straightforward. Tax concessions are designed to be invisible, as they involve *not* collecting taxes. Traditional public sector budgeting does not record the taxes that would have been collected without the concession, only the total that was collected. Prior to the development of a Tax Expenditure Statement (TES) there was no list of concessions within budget documents. Mapping the scale of tax expenditures first required trawling through the operation of the tax system to identify the myriad ways that tax rules allow exemptions and deductions. Even once a list is compiled there is some disagreement on how each item should be quantified, given that the exemption itself might change how finances are organised. This makes it difficult to chart how tax expenditures have impacted fiscal aggregates over time (see Stebbing and Spies-Butcher 2010).

Efforts to map and measure tax expenditures have developed steadily since the 1980s. Initial estimates by the Economic Planning and Advisory Council suggest tax expenditures fell as a proportion of the economy during the 1970s (EPAC 1986, 9). From the mid-1980s Treasury began to produce more systematic and regular reports of tax expenditures, which consolidated into the Annual TES. Over time the TES has expanded in scope, including more tax expenditures that were previously overlooked. The number of exemptions included in the Statements increased by 75 per cent in the first 20 years of its existence (Stebbing and Spies-Butcher 2010, 591). The growing fiscal scale of tax expenditures partly reflects these changes in reporting. However, changes in legislation, which expanded tax concessions for superannuation and created the new capital gains tax concessions in the 2000s, saw a substantial rise in the cost of STEs (*Ibid*, 591–592).

Recording the scale of tax expenditures has facilitated a broader policy debate. Treasury released estimates of the distributional impact of superannuation concessions (2010, 2012), which showed high-income earners were overwhelmingly the main beneficiaries. The government effectively provided more financial support to someone in the top 5 per cent of the income distribution than to a full pensioner. Since then, tax expenditures have received growing and critical attention (Grudnoff and Littleton 2021; Daley et al. 2015).

Analysis of tax expenditures played an important role in the Rudd/Gillard governments and again now under the Albanese government. However, rather than converting fiscal welfare into social spending, Labor has closed off tax concessions to reduce the deficit. Following the global financial crisis, reducing fiscal welfare became a generic measure to allow Labor to reduce the deficit without cutting social spending, rather than a specific means of funding new rights. In opposition, Labor went to the 2019 election promising to reduce fiscal welfare to fund an array of general spending commitments. Reducing fiscal welfare both aids the budget bottom line and improves economic incentives. Thus, many of the changes came with Treasury approval, and indeed the strategy of reducing fiscal welfare to inch back to surplus continued under the Coalition once their more radical plans for spending cuts proved politically unachievable.

The political salience of what appear technical accounting changes was reflected in the Coalition's decision to change the name of the TES to the Tax Benchmark and Variation Statement. Similar struggles emerged over GA itself (Spies-Butcher and Stebbing 2019). The 2010 IGR (Treasury 2010), the only one produced under a Labor government, involved a significantly different structure. The report included a substantial section on the generational costs of climate change, echoing the Garnaut Report (2008) commissioned to explore the introduction of carbon pricing. This shifted the focus from a narrow construction of fiscal costs to macroeconomic costs caused by ecological damage.

The Report also focused on the cost of supporting private health insurance through rebates, identifying this as the fastest growing component of the federal health budget (Treasury 2010, 53–54). As with STEs, this comparison also reflected growing policy critique (McAuley 2005) of the relative costs of public vs subsidised-private provision. The comparison challenged an implicit assumption of the IGRs; that pubic provision was a cost to be managed while private provision acted to lower public spending by shifting costs onto households. The IGR was used to justify means-testing the private health insurance rebate. Interestingly, however, even the 2010 IGR excluded fiscal welfare and retained the normative assumption that tax receipts should remain constant.

The 2010 IGA introduced an alternative form of budgeting associated with a broader international shift in accounting for value (2010, Chapter 6). The final section of the report explored how to account for changes in well-being, rather than narrow fiscal impacts, an approach Labor has returned to recently (Chalmers 2022). Well-being accounting attempts to reconnect public finance to lived experience. The use of well-being accounting is one component of a broader challenge to understandings of economic value, which collectively connect to what is potentially a new 'paradigm' for understanding the welfare state centred on 'social investment' (Hemerijck 2015).

Social investment uses the same imaginary of financial accounting to reconstruct social spending as an investment rather than a cost. On this view, the welfare state creates capacity through investments in human capital and avoids costs by managing life course transitions. As Michel Foucalt (2008) famously observed, 'human capital' was a central component of early neoliberal thinking, where individuals are reimagined as entrepreneurs of the self, making investments in their future earnings potential.

The social investment approach is not always linked to such a radically individualist ontology. In Northern Europe social investment is more commonly used as a macroeconomic concept, referring to investments in collective capacities. In the Anglosphere, where social investment is understood in more narrowly fiscal terms, it is often used to explore avenues to provide returns on private investment (Baker et al. 2020).

In Australia, the 'social investment' metaphor appears to have opened another avenue for hybridity. Constructing public spending as an asset potentially removes it from headline budget calculations. The shift reflects an accounting logic generally used in business, which differentiates between recurrent costs and revenue (to calculate a profit) and investment in assets (which contributes to net worth). Connecting social spending to future fiscal benefits creates a budgetary link that transforms its status in new public accounting models. While more contradictory than changes in family spending and healthcare, the construction of income-contingent loans as a financial asset, facilitated by the very budget reforms used to advance fiscal constraint, potentially highlights new strategies to support social provision.

Financialisation by Other Means: Student Loans and Higher Education

The reintroduction of student fees for higher education is usually understood as an explicit component of generational inequality. The baby boomers accessed university for free, their children and grandchildren face ever higher levels of debt (see Martin and Roberts 2021). Marketisation has transformed higher education. Putting a price on individual units and degrees no doubt encourages students to prioritise economic returns from study and encourages administrators, teachers and students to see themselves as part of a market, where services are provided to consumers. Changes in the funding model create other pressures. As block funding decreased, funding from international students soared, creating strong competitive pressures for high rankings and an emerging culture of the 'enterprise universities' (Marginson and Considine 2000; Bryant 2022). Alongside marketisation has come a form of financialisation as student debt has increased. However, student debt has developed and is governed quite differently to the expanding financial markets connected to housing and pensions.

The reintroduction of university fees shares several parallels with childcare. On the one hand, unease within Labor ranks at committing public funds to 'middle class' recipients grew, especially in the context of tight fiscal constraints. Structural change increased demand for both sectors, creating pressures for rapid expansion. At first glance, the outcomes were also very similar. Both saw the expansion of the system along broadly 'public' lines during the 1970s and early 1980s. Then as the costs of expansion increasingly confronted the limits of fiscal austerity, Labor moved to marketise provision, enforcing user payments to fund private investment. However, the model of marketisation was different, particularly in its relationship to finance.

Universities have also made large debt-financed investments in facilities. However, at least for most domestic students, the income universities receive comes directly from the government, not from students. It is governments that transfer funds to universities, but in a new role as *creditor* rather than *purchaser*. And unlike the experience of ABC Learning, investment was undertaken by 'public' universities.

At the centre of this transformation was a policy innovation that has since spread across the world and increasingly across policy domains (Chapman et al. 2014), income contingent loans (ICLs). The adoption of ICLs shares much in common with the examples of Medicare and affluence testing from earlier chapters, and is also identified as a hybrid policy model in mainstream policy literature (Fabian and Breuig 2018). The main proponent of the scheme, Bruce Chapman, is an academic economist. The model emerged out of two trends within economics: first, to reimagine education in economic terms and secondly, to take seriously the extent of market failure within the 'education market'. The result was a kind of policy hybrid that involved elements of a market loan and elements of traditional tax-financed social spending. Changes in public sector accounting then changed how Higher Education Contribution Scheme (HECS) was recorded. Rather than reinforcing fiscal constraints and providing imperatives for privatisation, these changes facilitated greater state discretion to access capital. The reintroduction of fees was clearly marketising. Student loans, however, hinted at an alternative model of public finance.

Education as 'human' capital

From the 1960s economists began to focus attention on education. A group of Chicago school economists argued that rising educational attainment was crucial to explaining economic growth. They reconceived higher education as an investment in 'human' capital, which generated a future return through higher wages (Becker 1964). This facilitated a shift in policy thinking, so that education spending was understood as an investment. By the 1990s OECD governments had reconceived education as an 'arm of economic policy' (Marginson 1993, 20). It also drove the subjective re-imagination of the individual at the heart of neoliberalism, as people became '(their) own capital' (Foucault 2008, 226).

The logic of human capital fed into Labor's thinking. Economists argued public spending on universities was potentially regressive, because its recipients went on to earn higher incomes (Psacharopoulos 1994). If education provides the individual student with private financial benefits, then it seems more reasonable to charge students for their 'investment'. However, most students are young people with low incomes and little wealth. Charging students for education creates barriers for students coming from poorer backgrounds, which concerned Labor and its constituents (Chapman and Pope 1992). Ordinarily, economists might argue investment can be financed by borrowing; however, private capital markets had proven problematic in making student finance available.

Market failures reflect the limits of the 'capital' metaphor. Unlike other forms of capital, human capital is embedded in people. It cannot be repossessed and so cannot act as collateral. That makes lending money to students risky. Interest rates are often exorbitant, or loans are not offered at all. Building on the 'human capital' metaphor developed by his colleagues, Milton Friedman argued for a form of private investment in students, which would entitle investors to a share of a graduate's future earnings (see Barr 2016). Later, others suggested a role for government as a source of student loans. Grout (1983) proposed measures very similar to the ICL model as a mechanism to improve allocative efficiency in higher education. John Quiggin showed the same measures also aid equity (2003).

By the late 1980s Labor was searching for funds to rapidly expand the number of university places, as part of what was later called the Dworkins reforms. Chapman proposed the ICL model through an inquiry charged with finding new sources of funds, including from student beneficiaries (Chapman and Pope 1992, 275). However, student fees created serious access and equity issues. First introduced as the HECS, ICLs allowed students to defer upfront payment. Repayments were then made through the tax system, based on annual income. Those on low incomes paid nothing, and the level of repayment then increased with income, much like income tax. Chapman later noted that ICLs were distinctly state instruments because they required the surveillance and enforcement powers of the state to link repayments to income (Libich 2015, 112, see Bryant and Spies-Butcher 2020, 118).

While HECS facilitated the reintroduction of student fees, it also mitigated the consequences of marketisation. There is little evidence the system discourages working-class students from study or reduced the proportion of students from disadvantaged backgrounds (Chapman 2014, 18–19), while the repayment mechanism mitigates the risks of default. Still, ICLs narrow the tax base, applying continuously rising debts apply to each new generation rather than financing from broader taxation, reflecting the generational unravelling of social protection typical of financialisation.

Accounting for income contingent loans

ICLs played an important role in managing the fiscal politics of expanding university funding. By describing the new system as a 'loan' scheme, it explicitly tied *current* spending to *future* repayments. Current spending on universities was now understood to be financed by repayments students would make in future years, not, as most public finance is understood, by revenues raised today. Thus, the level of new funds made available to universities could reflect the level of fees charged, but the new income received by government was much lower, reflecting only upfront payments and initial loan repayments.

Initially, the temporal link between public spending and student repayments was illustrative. The budget recorded the funds transferred from government to universities as spending and only recorded current payments made by students as income. Even so, the promise of future revenue helped satisfy fiscal hawks. This changed through the 1990s as elements of accrual accounting were applied to the federal budget, transforming ICLs into financial assets. ICLs began to be recorded as an advance, not spending, and eventually disappeared from the annual budget (see Spies-Butcher and Bryant 2018, 775).

The accounting changes mimicked the financial 'innovation' of the ABC Learning model in childcare; however unlike in childcare, the risks, benefits and costs all stay within the public sector. Accrual accounting allowed HECS to be treated as a loan, outside headline budget balances. In a world of fiscal constraint, this provided two important elements of discretion. First, the spending was now deemed 'private' not 'public', so it did not increase the size of government and could meet Labor's trilogy commitments. Second, it allowed the future stream of repayments to be brought forward by counting HECS as a financial asset and thus removing it from the yearly budget balance. In practice, the increased funding received by universities continued to come from government. And because the state retained the asset, as part of a student loan book, the conditions of HECS continued to be controlled by government on non-market terms.

The change in accounting practice has had real impacts on the politics of HECS and higher education. Prior to the changes, policy sought to increase repayments. After the changes policy increasingly sought to increase the size of the loan book (*Ibid*, 775–777), that is, increase student debt, but not necessarily increase repayments. Labor typically expanded funding (and total student debt) by increasing the number of places. The Coalition typically increased funding (and student debt) by raising fees. Accrual accounting effectively allowed the state to overcome fiscal constraints by becoming its own creditor, nationalising the financial model developed for private gain by ABC Learning.

Technical accounting changes did not remove more overt politics, but changed the nature of political contest. The asset appears on a new accounting document, the balance sheet. Here the performance of ICLs is monitored and assessed. Critics argue the concessionary features of ICLs undermine its performance, suggesting the face value of the ICL assets should be discounted to 'fair value' (see Parliamentary Budget Office 2016).

The public balance sheet has been used in student loan debates in much the same way as the IGRs, to make a political argument for austerity (Norton 2014; Norton and Cherastidtham 2016). This was summed up in the Grattan Institute's report on 'doubtful debt', which argued for measures that would make ICLs look like traditional financial products. Loans would be charged market interest, repayment thresholds lowered and debts recovered from estates (Norton 2014). Many of these proposals were then proposed by the Coalition. The United Kingdom has even begun to privatise ICL debt, a move that signals the risks of the policy model (Bryant and Spies-Butcher 2020, 121–122) but also affirms the *public* nature of loan finance.

Still, the nature of this politics differed fundamentally from the discipline being exerted by financial actors over governments in southern Europe after the GFC or US students with market loans. There is no private financial actor demanding ICLs perform financially or that government compensate them for a lack of performance. The government has no difficulty raising funds or borrowing from private markets in general. Despite clearly incorporating the logic of financial calculation, HECS did not expand the finance sector or any private financial market.

Like the money raised from the Medicare Levy, HECS effectively contributes to general revenue. As a result, the state retains control over loan conditions. This does not prevent thresholds being lowered or interest rates increased. Instead it places those decisions within the realm of politics, subject to ministerial and parliamentary discretion. Efforts to make regressive changes to HECS have generated a political response very similar to responses to welfare state retrenchment generally. Students and unions have mobilised to defend equity, successfully lobbying the Senate to reject deregulation and narrowly conceding changes to fee structures, which may yet be reversed.

Very little of this politics is captured by traditional social policy concepts. Over time, governments have changed the composition of funding to expand the proportion of funds coming from ICLs. This shows up as a substantial

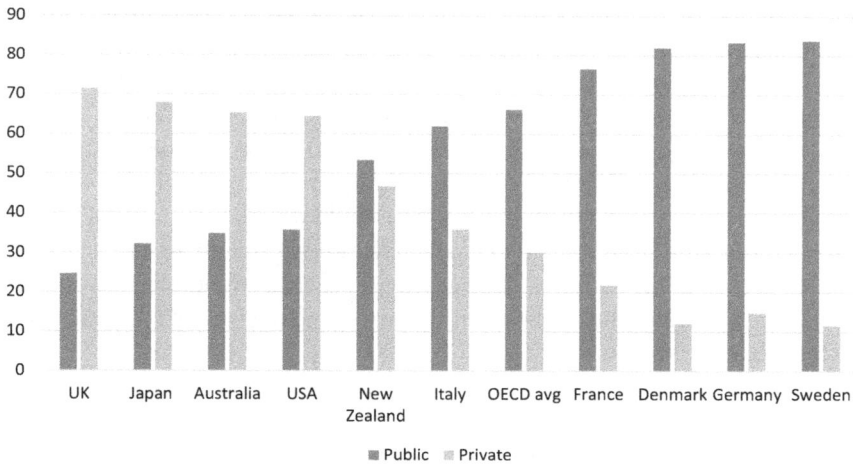

Figure 5.1 Public and private spending on tertiary education, selected OECD countries, 2020 or most recent. *Source*: Compiled by author from OECD Data. 'Public spending on education' and 'Private spending on education'. Available at: https://data.oecd.org/edusource/public-spending-on-education.htm#indicator-chart and https://data.oecd.org/edusource/private-spending-on-education.htm#indicator-chart.

privatisation of spending. Figure 5.1 reports public and private financing of higher education. It reveals Australia now rivals the United States as having one of the most privatised university funding models. Yet, the social consequences of privatisation are muted. Access to Australian universities is far less stratified than the United States and income contingency effectively mitigates loan default.

Distinguishing between policy logics helps to untangle changes within university finance.

The introduction of student fees, especially the effective deregulation of fees for international students and postgraduate study, has seen a real privatisation of university finance. ICLs, however, reflect a hybrid logic. ICLs mitigate aspects of privatisation while creating new political risks. Market advocates draw on the market framing of ICLs to apply market norms. Governments use budget tricks that expand provision, but avoid entrenching the right to higher education. However, the fiscal implications of treating social spending as an asset also open opportunities.

Beyond finalicialisation

The financialisation on welfare across the life course is perhaps the most troubling aspect of liberalisation. Managing the financial risks of age and retirement has always been central to the welfare state. Those same risks are key to financialisation. Reforming Australia's pension and housing systems while finance was liberalised has proven especially challenging. Efforts led by unions for better retirement incomes were always more closely tied to technocratic concerns with economic management and less embedded in political mobilisation than similar campaigns for family spending, healthcare or EEC. Trillions of dollars and an explosion of household wealth have failed to secure any social *rights* in retirement. For many older people adequate incomes, care and housing remain insecure. More depressing, these dynamics continue to worsen. The social rights of the older welfare state are eroding a little more in each successive generation.

Financialisation has also brought with it nascent forms of hybridity that offer opportunities for egalitarian reform. Super funds are not simple market actors. Tying superannuation more closely to social purposes and democratising its governance could radically change the Australian economy without adding a single dollar in social spending. More likely, reforming the immense and inequitable fiscal welfare tied to retirement incomes could fund tangible new social rights. Likewise, the new imaginary of social investment offers opportunities to highlight the economic benefits of equity and inclusion. For any of these possibilities to advance, however, requires a strong normative politics. Tying policy and politics together is the challenge of the final section.

Chapter 6

HYBRID POLICY MAKING

How can the lessons of our case studies be applied? In this section, I identify a set of common features from the successful case studies to develop a broader account of how to contest liberalisation. In each case, welfare state expansion appeared to involve a combination of strong political pressure to address social needs and technocratic expertise to incorporate these goals through novel policy design. This chapter focuses on policy design, emphasising strategies that respond to the growing power of neoclassical economic knowledge and fiscal discipline. The next chapter will focus on political mobilisation, emphasising strategies that connect citizens to democratic governance, although both chapters touch on both themes.

The case studies were selected to reflect three strategies of neoliberal welfare reform; residualisation, marketisation and financialisation. These strategies are commonly identified as driving rising inequality and insecurity. Each chapter presented evidence for that conclusion. Income payments were transformed into workfare and used to discipline rather than protect vulnerable workers. Marketisation in childcare entrenched producer power, unequal access and led to the collapse of ABC Learning. The integration of retirement policy into financial markets has produced growing inequality and eroded security of tenure in housing.

As welfare state scholars have noted, liberalisation rarely involved overt *retrenchment* of social programs. Instead, restructuring transformed provision to transfer risks from states and corporations onto citizens, managed through private markets and finance. These transformations reflect the declining power of traditional social democratic politics in the public sphere and the growing role of central economic agencies and of market economic ideas inside government. The result is neoliberal technocratic governance.

Yet, understanding each of these transformations is made more complex by other changes that appeared to extend social protection, both quantitatively and qualitatively. Family spending increased significantly, was highly redistributive and expanded under both Labor and Coalition governments. Medicare marked a breakthrough in equal access to healthcare.

Income-contingent loans (ICLs) play a contradictory role, facilitating the reintroduction of student fees, while increasing access and mitigating the social risks students face from market loans.

Each of these hybrid cases points to possibilities for expanding social provision along egalitarian lines, using policy instruments – means-testing, market power and asset/debt relations – that look remarkably like those correctly identified as widening inequalities and intensifying insecurities in other domains. Each example remains limited. More traditional social democratic policy options would likely prove more egalitarian. But in a context of broader liberalisation, these options not only mitigated insecurity, they actively expanded social protection.

Successful policy strategies involved forms of hybridity, engaging with the logic of market competition, while advancing socially defined goals connected to universal needs. Each case employed traditional neoclassical economic reasoning, but did so in specific policy contexts, which made it easier to identify market failure. Market failure was itself defined in social terms, including recognition that a lack of access or provision is a form of market failure.

Each of the examples blurred the boundaries between 'state' and 'market', incorporating market logics, but socialising risk. Means-testing and student debts were restructured to mimic the normative principles of progressive taxation. Payments to private providers were used to expand access and restrain profits. In each area, policy design intersected with the politics of budgeting to allow public finance to take advantage of privileges otherwise confined to private finance to remove political barriers to exercising sovereign power or to make state power more visible and subject to democratic pressure.

The chapter begins by comparing these strategies to those of the older wage-earner model. While both engage with the tension between capitalism and democracy, they do so in different ways. Rather than regulating markets directly to achieve social goals, hybrid policies extend market logics alongside democratic claims to social protection. In each case hybridity problematises the boundary between state and market by extending and remaking market rationalities. Such strategies take advantage of the claim to technical neutrality within both economics and accounting to unwind the dual welfare state. In each case policy adapts to competitive principles to mitigate fiscal constraints, while advancing universal conceptions of need.

The chapter applies this analysis to the three cases. First, it explores how reformers mobilised the logic of economic incentives to compare payment and taxation systems, making visible fiscal welfare and high-effective marginal tax rates and thereby opening opportunities to expand payments by converting Social Tax Expenditures (STEs). Second, reformers applied the logic of efficiency to compare private and public provision of care, identifying advantages of monopsony to solve market failures and financing public insurance through tax-based levies. Finally, a neutral application of capital accounting reframed social spending as productive investment, unlocking finance from 'future' returns.

Each hybrid strategy incorporates market logics while taking advantage of the state's unique sovereign capacities to set incentives, compel insurance and issue credit. Each strategy appeals to universal needs, which can mobilise broad coalitions. And each can be integrated with the principles of technical neutrality underpinning neoclassical economics. Where liberalisation often advances market logics asymmetrically to constrain state finances, hybrid policies appeal to neutrality to expand fiscal power alongside competition. The chapter concludes by applying these principles to practical policy reforms.

A New Politics of Welfare

Liberalisation, which reasserts fiscal constraints on social policy, emerged in response to the success of a previous politics of fiscal expansion. Exemplified by Scandinavian social democracy, fiscal powers expanded to limit the inequalities and insecurities of market competition. Public spending created a distinct public sector, governed by democratic norms. Spending took the place of ownership. As political resistance to nationalisation grew, public spending offered a complementary means of democratising the economy.

Many social democrats saw public finance as 'functional socialism'. Increases in taxation and social spending made the 'rights of private property [...] divisible and capable of being stripped away one by one' (Tilton 1990, 6). This model fits Polanyi's (and later Esping-Andersen's) understanding of the double movement, where 'the extension of the market organisation in respect to genuine commodities was accompanied by its restriction in respect to fictitious ones' (2001, 79). Competition continued to rule the market, but public finance established normative limits on commodification via democracy.

Australia's wage-earner model took a different path. It was not simply that Australia was less advanced down this social democratic welfare state road. Instead, Australian social policy achieved its ends through 'other means' (Castles 1989). Rather than relying on fiscal policy to create public space 'outside' private market competition, it instead emphasised the regulation of factor markets according to social norms.

Australia's regulation of factor markets is most obvious with arbitration, industry protection and migration restrictions. But it is also true of the community rating principle in health insurance (Chapter 4) and financial regulation to promote home ownership (Chapter 5). Regulating market processes ensured the initial distribution of income (pre-distribution) was more equal. But it less clearly separated 'public' and 'private' spheres. Instead public power shaped market outcomes.

Market regulation reflected social norms, but not necessarily egalitarian values. The norms that lay at the heart of this wage earner compromise applied a patriarchal model of the family and a 'white' conception of the nation. As feminists identify, it was both wage-earner and breadwinner welfare (Mitchell 1998; Pocock 2005), and both were strongly racialised (Altman and Saunders 2018).

The strategies developed elsewhere to address these intersecting inequalities were less obviously applicable to Australia's form of market regulation. Where Scandinavia set about increasing taxation and social spending to expand public provision of, and support for, care (see Curtin and Higgins 1998), the entire architecture of the wage-earner model required refashioning. Initially, the Whitlam government sought to shift towards a more traditional tax and spend model of fiscal politics.

The timing and execution of Whitlam's attempted shift informed how neoliberalism advanced in Australia and particularly the strong version of the 'politics of budgetary surplus' (Brenton 2016) evident in neoliberalism here. The savage electoral backlash against Labor saw a shift in strategy to self-imposed fiscal restraint, despite the need for significant welfare state renovation. The politics of hybridity, I argue, responds to the constraints of wage-earner welfare by shifting Australia towards a different fiscal politics. Rather than advancing social protection by limiting competition in labour and capital markets, hybrid strategies advance alongside competition, playing to the claimed neutrality of economics and accounting.

Liberalisation reflects a familiar pattern, where resistance to more radical reform leads to models of incrementalism. The 'risk shift' of recent decades (Hacker 2019; Quiggin 2007) mirrors the earlier effort to make the rights of private property 'divisible and capable of being stripped away' one risk at a time. However, where social democracy targeted the privileges of private ownership by socalising risks in the welfare state while minimising overt nationalisation, liberalisation targets the welfare state, individualising risks while avoiding overt privatisation. When managed through the methods of financial calculation, the result is a state increasingly governed by a 'derivative logic' (Bryan and Rafferty 2014).

Hybridity helps to contest liberalisation. It allows the resources of the dual welfare state to be refashioned into more efficient and equitable social protection. Like earlier social democratic models, hybrid policies combine political claims for universal provision with statecraft designed to mitigate the constraints on expanding the democratic state.

The techniques of statecraft, however, have shifted. As economies moved from industrial to service production and as the welfare state and public budgeting have been restructured by liberalisation the boundaries of public and private have blurred. Hybridity re-socialises risk by more symmetrically applying orthodox budget and economic conventions within the public sector. Australian experience here is not unique, but is likely to be an exemplar because it sought to move from a pre-distributive to a redistributive politics, and confronted liberalisation with a particularly 'economic rationalist' approach.

The femocrat experience is especially useful because its proponents were engaged in an explicit and self-reflective political project directly connected to unwinding the breadwinner features of the older Australian model (Sawer 2016; Yeatman 2020). Femocrats later explained how they employed the language and logic of mainstream economics to advance their case and how they aligned the interests of women and economic efficiency to win policy outcomes (Sawer 1996). Their strategy engaged with economic rationalist priorities, but it was not a simple process of co-option.

Femocrats extended economic logics in new ways to shine light in new places and draw different conclusions. Gender budgeting, for example, helped to rework the categories economists used to evaluate gains and losses. The new accounting device allowed bureaucrats (and citizens) to 'see' inequalities that were otherwise obscured within the 'household'. Feminists challenged the economists' 'language of valuation' (Martinez-Alier 2008).

Likewise, the concept of STEs made visible government support usually hidden in the complexities of the tax code. The tax expenditure concept extends principles of neutrality and horizontal equity, the principle that similar actions or people should be treated similarly, which underpin most free trade rhetoric. But identifying STEs envoked neutrality to new ends – to advance equal access to social rights, rather than equality of property owners to trade in the market.

An alignment of social rights and economic logic proved effective even where movements were less explicitly connected to state bureaucracies. In healthcare and higher education the new marketised policies succeeded in part because they reflected political imperatives shaped by democratic claims outside the state. The passage of these schemes – Medicare and ICLs – was, admittedly, different, but also reflected some similar dynamics.

Medicare may have used market mechanisms, but it did so to address obvious market failures. It credibly and practically advanced a social claim for healthcare to be delivered according to need. Thus, it could both mobilise the public and navigate an economic rationalist bureaucracy. The policy's hybrid features mitigated growing fiscal constraints and constitutional barriers, but its passage is more clearly the result of democratic pressure.

ICLs, in contrast, mitigated the impacts of user payments. The protection ICLs offer, and the greater responsiveness of ICLs to political contestation, is clearer in the United States, where conversion from market loans to ICLs has both been the outcome of political mobilisation and has since allowed the terms of student loans to be moderated (see Bryant and Spies-Butcher 2020). In Australia, resistance to user payments and privatisation played an important role in shaping ICL policy, reflected in the formal equity requirements placed on any financing reform through the inquiry process (see Chapman and Pope 1992).

Building a New Statecraft of Welfare

Connecting strategies inside the state to movements in civil society requires concepts and language that make policy practices visible to citizens. During the twentieth century, Keynesian 'economist technicians' built a new language and practice of statecraft, focused on revealing alternative political choices, which informed the fiscal strategies of social democrats (Mudge 2018).

The interplay of democratic politics and statecraft created a language of *full employment* and a system of national accounting capable of operationalising that claim within market economies by tracing and quantifying aggregate demand. An earlier iteration of the same logic in Australia had produced the language of a *living wage* and the technology of arbitration and indexation capable of operationalising the connection between money wages and social needs.

Neither development was specifically anti-capitalist, and both were rationalising. As Schumpeter complained, post-War reconstruction reflected the 'mechanistic attitude of economists' (Schumpeter 2003, 388). Both examples solved broader systemic problems confronting business as well as aiding citizens. But many solutions were possible, and these solutions were far more egalitarian than most alternatives.

The case studies suggest a similar combination of politics and statecraft is emerging. Within the welfare state, sovereignty complicates the advance of competition. The ubiquitous role of the state in social policy, both in supporting dualism and hybridity, ensures social markets are not 'self-regulating'. The outcomes are not strictly the result of market integration, but nor does hybridity only reflect state distribution. Instead, sovereignty constructs market exchange, setting incentives, compelling insurance and issuing credit.

State action mimics market forms of organisation and is designed to work alongside ongoing forms of market competition, while retaining the unique characteristics of sovereignty to shape markets according to social principles.

Hybridity mirrors the dual welfare state by applying the liberalised rationales used to justify private provision more symmetrically. The negative incentive effects created by taxation are compared to the withdrawal of benefits. The fiscal constraint imposed on funding for social insurance is applied to subsidies for private insurance. The financialisation of fiscal power, imagining social spending in the future as a state liability, is applied symmetrically to envisage current social spending as investment.

Applying economic principles symmetrically infers strategies for policy reform. Payments should be reformed to be universal in principle, adequate and minimise disincentives. Social services should follow a single-insurer model, again universal in principle, financed by tax levies. And social spending in general should be understood as investment, orientated to sustaining revenues, increasing output and, potentially, maximising well-being.

Remaking Social Payments (and Taxation)

The Australian Settlement reflected an important alignment of interests. Protections and benefits for wage earners were co-designed with a gendered order of paid and unpaid labour. Payments were built in explicitly gendered ways (Gordon 1988). Men were expected to work unless they could demonstrate a socially acceptable reason not to, such as illness, unemployment or age; women were expected to be dependent, and so qualified for payments by virtue of losing access to their male breadwinner. Family support was built into the tax code, to be received by men for dependent women and children. The structure of payments reflected the norm of full-time work, which effectively made means-tests redundant. Payments were effectively categorical – the employed received full-time wages, those receiving benefits were presumed to be outside paid work, with little in between.

The 'rigidities' of the labour market largely overlapped with the 'rigidities' of the gender order. This did not mean labour market deregulation aided gender equity. Individual bargaining, for example, exaggerates gender inequalities (Van Gellecum et al. 2008). Reconstructed as individuals, but without broader institutional reform, women continue to face other inequalities. But in the context of fiscal austerity, liberalisation facilitated strategies that advanced gender neutrality alongside economic neutrality.

The gendered and raced categories used to protect (largely white, male) workers from competition, thus came under a double attack from liberalisation and new social movements (see Fraser and Jaeggi 2018, 77). These attacks interacted with the politics of enduring austerity, which was generally expressed through two distinct, though related, budgetary measures. The first focused on the net budget position and emphasised the need for budgetary surplus as a proxy for the state's impact on national savings and credit. This reflects Scott Brenton's term the 'politics of budgetary surplus'. The second focused on gross measures of public spending as a proxy for the size of government, and was mobilised politically as tax resistance in favour of 'small' government.

The strategies of social policy advocates can partly be understood as attempts to increase the capacity for the state to respond to social demands within these constraints. This tension fostered an alignment between social goals advanced by movements and the focus on competition and productivity emphasised by the central economic agencies. The resulting strategies responded to fiscal constraint by revealing and democratising the state power hidden within dual welfare.

First, advocates equated tax concessions to social spending, legitimating the conversion of tax concessions into social spending. Second, they equated means-testing to taxation, a strategy that advanced affluence testing in the place of taxation, and made visible 'poverty traps'. A third strategy from the older wage-earner tradition also continued. Superannuation subverted budget rules entirely by expanding occupational welfare. This increased retirement incomes but without addressing the class and gender inequalities caused by the liberalisation of labour and financial markets.

Fiscal conversion

Equating tax concessions to social spending potentially expands the pool of resources available for social provision through a process of policy *conversion*. In response, to pressures for budget surpluses social policy advocates sought to make visible the fiscal impacts of tax concessions. This strategy was employed to fund Medicare, family benefits and more recently pension increases. The Hawke government introduced a Tax Expenditure Statement (TES), and the tool has become an important element of budgetary politics. Most recently, the 2023 Statement (Treasury 2023) immediately preceded the Albanese government's proposal to create a higher tax rate on earnings within super funds for those with very large accounts.

The tax expenditure concept applies rational choice theory, emphasising the role of incentives and net losses or gains. From this perspective, it is irrelevant whether the net gain is the result of a tax power or a spending power, both reflect a state claim over resources and both produce economic incentives. The logic resembles the equivalence between tariffs and subsidies in trade theory. By quantifying and documenting concessional arrangements, the TES makes fiscal welfare visible to policy makers and citizens.

Visibility is a powerful political strategy. Australia's wage-earner model produces particularly strong support for targeted welfare (Wilson et al. 2009). Tax expenditures invariably violate this normative framework, providing more to high-income earners than low-income earners. Once these distributional impacts are made visible, political pressure builds to limit access for top earners.

The tax expenditure concept also highlights budgetary impacts. Reducing tax expenditures raises new revenues, facilitating new social spending with no net impact on the budget balance. The strategy of conversion, however, relies on connecting the market logic of equivalence to the politics of need that drives social provision. It is most effective when the tax concessions and social spending are directed to the same social purpose, as with concessions for a dependent spouse and family spending, or private health insurance deductions and Medicare. Where the equivalence is more abstract, as with Labor's 2019 proposals to limit franking credits, it is much easier to caricature as a tax grab.

Progressive incentives

Liberalisation emphasises the negative implications of increasing taxation on economic incentives. Welfare advocates extended this logic to state action generally, analysing how states shape incentives across both tax and spending powers. The result is the concept of effective marginal tax rates (EMTRs), which effectively challenges an implicit dualism in the treatment of taxation versus social spending. Applying the same rational choice logic, EMTRs treat the loss of income from either taxation or benefit withdrawal as equivalent. Whatever the policy instrument, both imply similar changes to the distribution of income and the incentives actors face.

Initially, critics of dual welfare analysed incentives to challenge tax concessions. Concessions for a dependent spouse created disincentives for second earners because the primary earner lost the concession as their partner gained income. The analysis of incentives then informed interactions with the central economic agencies, who used means-testing to fund higher base payments for families (see Whiteford et al. 2011, 86–88). Using means-tests to limit access to payments play an equivalent role to tax-finance and required some attention to the incentive effects of the means-test.

A focus on incentives fosters a distinct politics around 'affluence testing'. Different policy frames reflect commitments to either dual or hybrid policy models. Framed as an incentive, means-tests facilitate a politics of universalism. Policy focuses on changes at the margin. All income, whether from government or market, is treated similarly. Judged by similar standards, incentives tend towards the social principle of 'ability to pay'.

Framed as a means to ration scarce public resources, means-testing facilitates greater targeting to limit social spending. Targeting accepts the size of the state is constrained and then seeks to limit the use of public dollars, reinforcing a distinction between 'public' and 'private' finance that does not neatly align with the extent of state power. Ironically, policy is no longer judged by economic criteria – such as impacts on incentives or distribution – but on a normative criteria that privileges private over public.

Targeting reflects a similar asymmetry to STEs. Both rely on accounting definitions of public finance, rather than an assessment of state power, to constrain the use of some policy tools in favour of others. Just as STEs create a dual welfare state accessible to those with means, targeting creates a dual tax state applied to those on low incomes. In both cases the asymmetry allows different norms to apply to different policy tools, reinforcing a distinction between market incomes, treated as deserved and managed through visible income tax rates, and social incomes, offered conditionally and managed by less transparent benefit withdrawal rates.

Emphasising incentives appeals to an economic logic of efficiency while aiding access. If means-tests and tax rates are equivalent, then both create the same incentive problems. However, the structure of EMTRs is very different to marginal tax rates. The highest EMTRs apply to low- and moderate-income earners, particularly those receiving payments that are withdrawn at very high rates, and to second earners.

Economists also recognise that low- and middle-income earners tend to be more sensitive to these incentive effects. Those in casual and part-time work, often primary carers, are especially sensitive as they have more potential to adjust their work time and earnings at the margin (Stewart 2018, 6). Thus, a focus on EMTRs can be used to expand access to benefits, while aiding economic flexibility.

If EMTRs are understood as a revenue raising mechanism, however, their relative lack of transparency ensures governments have incentives to extract revenues from the middle, rather than the top. Because most benefits are already targeted, attempts to fund higher payments through tighter targeting effectively redistribute income from the middle to the bottom. Tighter targeting also reinforces gendered inequalities because it often impacts primary carers. Far from managing the politics of austerity, targeting explicitly divides the constituency in favour of social protection along class and gendered lines.

EMTRs offer a potentially useful strategy for navigating fiscal politics, but it is yet to be incorporated into politics or policy making in an equivalent way to income tax rates.

EMTRs lack the visibility or universality of tax rates. Unlike the tax system, with a single set of rates, there are multiple means-tests applying across a range of different payments. The lack of visibility makes means-testing an easier vehicle for retrenchment when fiscal pressures dominate. Means-testing also reinforces austerity by limiting state claims. Once a benefit is withdrawn the means-test no longer applies. In contrast, marginal tax rates apply to infinity.

As with the conversion of STEs, it is difficult to separate the technocratic politics of policy instruments from contentious welfare politics. A key example was Labor's decision to suspend indexation of family payments, a move that explicitly decoupled the techniques for setting payments from need, and has facilitated a slow erosion of adequacy and access (Klapdor 2022).

Expanding (Social) Insurance

Providing citizens with access to needed services is more closely aligned to the principles of social insurance. Unlike Australia's flat-rate benefit system, which remains distinct compared to most European schemes, Medicare's model of universal insurance appears to replicate traditional social democratic politics.

Universal health insurance was partly funded by the conversion of tax concessions in the 1970s. More recently, Medicare has become the exemplar of another successful model, named tax levies. Such levies can also be understood as hybrid, in that they mimic both an insurance premium and a hypothecated tax, both of which apply mechanisms of market exchange, but do so within public finance. The Medicare Levy allowed a direct comparison of fiscal cost and social benefit of increased public provision, without separating health insurance from the wider public budget.

Medicare differs from efforts at nationalisation by confining the public role to finance rather than direct provision. Unlike nationalisation, insurance creates opportunities to layer a public option onto an existing privatised system, reducing initial political resistance and avoiding constitutional limits. Framing public provision as insurance also fits neatly with welfare economics scholarship, which distinguishes between redistribution and risk pooling (Barr 2001).

Liberalisation often seeks to limit state action to the redistribution of income, supporting markets to provide insurance functions. In practice, markets are often poorly equipped to offer efficient insurance. Welfare economists point to problems of adverse selection, complex contracts and incomplete or asymmetric information (*Ibid*; Quiggin 2007). As in other areas of social provision, these market failures have been important in advancing social provision. However, Medicare-style levies work precisely because they blur and recombine the insurance and redistributive functions of social insurance.

Social insurance levies mimic features of insurance premiums but organise financing according to social rather than individual risk. The levies create a link between paying an ongoing contribution and coverage in times of need. However, the levy is structured according to social rather than market principles, inverting the distributional impacts of market insurance.

Market insurance assesses contributions based on actuarial estimates of individual future costs. Most forms of social risk follow a social gradient. Future payments are not random; they reflect different life chances. The same social structures that stratify market incomes also stratify exposure to social risks. The poor are more likely to be sick and to die young than are the rich (Marmot 2005). Market insurance, therefore, tends to charge higher premiums to those least able to afford them. If we understand the purpose of health markets in terms of needed treatment, it is precisely this incompatibility of need and access that creates a market failure.

The Medicare Levy reflects actuarial assessments but undertaken at a collective rather than individual level. The initial proposal for the Levy in the 1980s reflected the estimated additional cost to the state of universal insurance. This collective assessment is well designed to inform political choices, by comparing the fiscal costs and social benefits of moving from the status quo to a new universal system.

The fiscal costs are collective, allowing distribution according to ability to pay. However, because the Levy is only designed to cover the *additional* cost of the policy change, it resists a strict financial relationship. Unlike hypothecation, where the funds raised by a tax are separated from general revenue and create an exclusive pool of resources available for provision, the Medicare Levy simply adds to general revenue. The structure may infuriate some economists, who implicitly understand its purpose to be applying fiscal discipline, but it aids its democratic purpose, helping citizens understand policy trade-offs.

The Medicare Levy was successfully expanded to facilitate the introduction of the National Disability Insurance Scheme (NDIS). The logic of this connection also reflected a hybrid model of insurance, although one taken from the Rawlsian perspective of not yet knowing one's position in society (Rawls 2001). The NDIS also reflected a hybrid logic in a second sense. Appealing to the model of social investment, its architects argued a single insurer could better act to manage risk, intervening earlier to prevent higher costs in the future or to enable future productivity (Productivity Commission 2011, 2).

Unlike Medicare, however, where public insurance mobilised economic arguments to increase public monopsony power against powerful producer interests, the NDIS reinforced and extended market relationships. The logic of social insurance helped bring together well-coordinated civil society support and existing producer interests, while mitigating fiscal constraints. It did less to militate the potential for growing producer power (see Miller and Hayward 2017).

Medicare and the NDIS both face rising costs, which create new fiscal tensions. While population ageing is responsible for some of this pressure, it is primarily a result of changing norms. As new medicines, aids and interventions are developed, Medicare and the NDIS act to continually universalise access. Rising costs are often a sign of the success of these schemes in ensuring broad access to the benefits of collective research.

The lack of strict hypothecation facilitates an ongoing political negotiation over the management of these costs, through debates over waiting lists, drug listings, diagnoses and so on, rather than imposing market discipline. Rising costs can foster austerity and pressure to stratify consumption, but can also exert pressure to extend hybridity by asserting monopsony power and challenging producer interests. 'Soft' hypothecation not only facilitates an initial political choice, it moves ongoing contestation into a more democratic sphere.

From insurance to investment

Payment systems and service provision connect social needs to social spending relatively directly. Claims are contested – dual welfare advances by depicting the unemployed as 'undeserving' of payments and by advocating consumers exercise 'choice' in social markets – but the alternative positions are reasonably transparent. The hybrid strategies used to advance social spending in these areas facilitate further transparency, by directly linking funding sources, whether tax concessions or income tax levies, to social provision to facilitate democratic choice.

Financialisation, however, reconstructs concrete social needs, like shelter, into complex financial products. It is unsurprising that those areas of social provision impacted most by financialisation are driving the most significant inequalities. Yet, even here, hybridity potentially mitigates these challenges by reducing the influence of private creditors on social provision. Instead, the 'investor' state retains a degree of democratic discretion.

As we saw in the last chapter, accounting changes have been central to how financialisation has impacted the state. Accounting reforms have shifted the imaginary of the state from one grounded in a Keynesian logic of the present, focused on managing aggregate demand as it occurs, to one focused on a speculative future (Adkins et al. 2020).

Two sets of accounting changes have significantly reinforced privatisation and retrenchment. First, the uneven application of accrual accounting techniques creates incentives to organise public investment through corporatisation, facilitating an expansion of funding for private contractors and the privatisation of public tax powers (like tolls). Organised along market lines, borrowing to finance high upfront costs is shifted off the headline budget balance. Second, forecasting techniques like Generational Accounting (GA) construct rising social spending as a liability, while explicitly rejecting complementary tax increases and obscuring the fiscal impacts of tax concessions.

These accounting changes facilitate privatisation and retrenchment by applying principles asymmetrically and by refocusing attention on fiscal limits in the distant future and away from social needs today. GA, for example, predicts higher social spending precisely because social need (for care and retirement incomes) rises, but devotes almost no time to outlining what those needs are or how they can be met. Instead, its focus is on the social spending devoted to addressing them. Likewise, accrual accounting has meant that borrowing undertaken by entities that look like private firms (even if they are publicly owned) does not contribute to headline deficit calculations, while borrowing undertaken in traditional public structures does.

It is less surprising, then, that forms of hybridity that facilitate greater fiscal discretion have tended to apply accounting principles more symmetrically and frame social spending as investment in future benefits. The shift is sometimes understood as paradigmatic, in the same sense that neoliberalism created a broad shift in state thinking and organisation compared to the era of the Keynesian welfare state.

The social investment state (Deeming and Smyth 2015) follows a logic of hybridity. It complements changes in payment systems and service provision linked to broader accounting changes that impact how the state 'thinks' and 'sees' (Spies-Butcher and Bryant 2024). These changes are embedded in new public sector accounting techniques that potentially open fiscal space, but also create pressures towards further liberalisation.

The contested politics of social investment

Social investment has been heralded as a new policy paradigm, replacing neoliberalism, and capable of revalorising the welfare state (Hemerijck 2015). The 'investment' frame engages with the terrain of financialisation, imaging the social in terms of the economic and orienting the present towards a speculative future. This creates the space for hybridity by imagining the state as a financial actor, while continuing to embed it within the powers and constraints of sovereignty.

Social investment challenges the conception of social spending as a 'cost' to be minimised and the constraints on public investment caused by 'competitive neutrality'. Within liberalised accounting practices, reframing social spending as investment facilitates taking social spending outside the fiscal constraints of the headline budget. Yet, both the conceptual and accounting strategies are limited, creating pressures for future fiscal returns or efforts to construct 'investments' in market terms.

Education, and its reimaging as 'human capital', has unsurprisingly been at the heart of social investment. As early as the 1970s Foucault outlined the importance of human capital to neoliberal subjectivity (2008). It was part of a broader shift, he argued, to reimagine the individual as an entrepreneur of the self, investing in one's own productive capacities (understood as capital) to maximise future income potential.

Human capital exemplifies the logic of social investment, extending the imaginary of the 'economic' to take in virtually all human endeavour so that any choice might be understood in terms of its economic potential. Foucault identifies these dynamics from the viewpoint of the individual neoliberal subject. Framed in fiscal terms, however, a focus on collective future benefits and costs has the potential to expand social protection.

Education also exemplifies one of the fiscal pressures facing the state as the economy transitions from industrial production to knowledge and care employment. Rising demand for skilled service workers creates pressures to expand provision, both directly through higher completion rates at high school and the massification of university, and indirectly through the incorporation of women into paid work and the reorganisation of care. Increased spending for both early education and care (EEC) and universities was justified through the 1970s and 1980s in economic terms, as enabling higher productivity and expanding the fiscal base (see Chapter 4).

Advocates advanced fiscal arguments grounded in potential future benefits. Initially, they drew on research that linked higher earnings and productivity to people's past education and care experiences. This evidence was then used to challenge fiscal constraints on the basis that future state finances and economic performance would benefit from expanding current spending. For EEC, this initially focused on enabling women to enter paid work, but has increasingly come to focus on the future benefits for infants and children. As I discuss in the next chapter, advocates have framed benefits in collective, macroeconomic terms. Alternatively, the expansion of dual welfare for school education reflects the potential to convert education into a positional good and private asset.

Higher education provides a more (neoclassical) textbook understanding of human capital, and has subsequently been more explicitly incorporated into fiscal accounting. University education has a longer history of being associated with economic and social stratification and higher lifetime earnings.

Even so, it has been subjected to a process of economism, as the broader democratic, intellectual and status dimensions of universities have been increasingly reduced to price.

Higher education is undertaken by adults, and thus more easily framed as an individual choice. The class dynamics of higher education played into internal Labor politics, creating greater resistance to expanding public spending on what was perceived to be 'middle class' welfare. Thus, an economic understanding of education as individual human capital formation legitimated the introduction of student fees as one component of increased funding to reflect the 'private benefit' that education entailed (see Chapter 5).

The pressure to reintroduce university fees, to facilitate user payments and the 'privatisation' of knowledge as human capital might be understood generically in neoliberal terms. The organisation of fees as ICLs, I've argued, reflects hybridity. Like Medicare, ICLs were proposed by economists as a solution to a market failure, which was understood in social terms, as a lack of equitable access. And like Medicare, the solution was not to socialise the market, but to use state power to correct the market.

The state's role might have been confined to underwriting private loans, as was initially the case in the United States (Bryant and Spies-Butcher 2020, 115). Such an approach explicitly facilitates the inclusion of private financial actors, providing state support to ensure risky markets are profitable. Instead, ICLs involve the state as creditor, a role that explicitly displaces private finance. Thus, ICLs may advance financialisation as a 'calculative device or mode of thinking' (Bryan and Rafferty 2014, 891), but they do not involve expanding finance as an industry.

As Gareth Bryant and I have argued, ICLs reflect hybridity precisely because the state plays a market role, in which it is understood to be contracting with student debtors (Spies-Butcher and Bryant 2018; Bryant and Spies-Butcher 2020). Hybridity is facilitated by the structure of higher education, where universities are organised as separate accounting units with autonomous governance, usually under state rather than federal law. Because the state is creditor, the loan terms become subject to democratic pressures, rather than being strictly governed by market contract. Repayments are organised through the tax system according to the normative logic of taxation (ability to pay). ICLs are at once a loan and a tax (Spies-Butcher and Bryant 2018).

The interaction of ICLs and accounting reforms shift hybridity from a discursive tool into an accounting practice. The initial effort to expand university finances associated with the introduction of student fees used the promise of future repayments to justify larger increases in public finance than would be initially raised by student contributions; however, there was no formal budget link between current spending and future contributions.

Changes in public budgeting transformed the conceptual link between government funding and student debts into an accounting practice. The loan funds were taken off the headline budget, offset by a matching 'asset' in the state's newly created balance sheet, a shift facilitated by the separate accounting status of 'public' universities. In cash terms, student loans operate in much the same way as block grants – governments transfer an amount to universities based on the number and type of students they teach. Students do not pay universities, either up front or through repayments, but pay government via the tax office. But in accrual terms, the funding is privatised, understood entirely as user charges (eventually) coming from the student. This accounting process also explains resistance to a more orthodox graduate tax, which would count as an expansion of state finance.

The case for funding both EEC and higher education as 'investment' reflects not only an economism of education but also a mobilisation of the future. Claims for resources are no longer grounded in immediate social needs, but rather in the productive capacities that spending enables. As Adkins et al. explain, this logic of financialisation is inherently *speculative*, not in a pejorative sense, but rather in the sense that the future in inherently unknowable and thus orientating action to the future can only ever prove speculative (Adkins et al. 2020).

Hybrid financial strategies mirror the logic of GA. By applying the future orientation of finance symmetrically, through investment in assets alongside 'liability budgeting', social investment loosens fiscal constraints on an increasingly entrepreneurial state.

There is a parallel to earlier Keynesian budgeting, which reorganised state finances to facilitate macroeconomic management. The investor state, too, is focused on macroeconomic dynamics, moving beyond the individual calculus of traditional rational choice theory, but this orientation is now to future macroeconomic outcomes to maximise public net worth or well-being, rather than managing immediate 'animal spirits'.

The investment metaphor has been extended beyond education. In Northern Europe, the model broadly covers spending that expands the fiscal base, by building the capacity of workers and mitigating the risks of labour market transitions (including to provide care). Finland's widely praised 'Housing First' strategy used exactly this logic to justify increased public spending on housing and homelessness (Baker and Evans 2016, 32). Social investment is increasingly tied to proposals for a 'wellbeing' economy, where the macroeconomic outcomes achieved by the investment state are understood in more explicitly social terms, rather than reduced to Gross Domestic Product or net worth.

In the Anglo world social investment is applied more narrowly. Public budgeting practices that open space for ICLs also create pressures to apply market discipline. Critics use 'fair value' estimates of the student loan book to argue loans are not performing. Underperformance justifies efforts to strip away the concessionary features of ICLs by applying market interest rates, collecting debts from student estates and potentially privatising the student loan book. However, it has proven more difficult to retrench the egalitarian features of ICLs, reflecting the 'public' nature of the spending.

A potentially more radical strategy has emerged from movements for racial equality. Critics of neoliberalism identify a link between fiscal constraint on the welfare state and fiscal expansion of the 'carceral state' (Gilmore 2007; Wacquant 2009). Where workfare forecloses entry into social protection, its punitive aspect parallels growing entry points into prison. Rising incarceration intersects with spatial and racialised hierarchies. In the United States, incarceration is concentrated in inner-urban communities with significant Black populations, whereas in Australia, prisons are dominated by First Nations people.

From the 2000s a model of 'justice reinvestment' began to apply the logic of social investment to these debilitating dynamics by explicitly tying prison expansion to social *dis*investment (Tucker and Cadora 2003). By linking social and carceral spending, justice reinvestment implicitly extends the fiscal constraints on the welfare state to prison spending. Prisons and police are recast as fiscal liabilities to be managed down. Increasing the resources available to and controlled by Communities reduces the 'need' for police and prisons. Emphasising the fiscal cost of police and prisons has implications for law reform, framing punitive bail and sentencing legislation as fiscally expensive and identifying how reforms that prevent incarceration free resources to be used elsewhere.

Trials have enjoyed some success, most notably the Marranuka program in Burke, NSW, led by the Burke Tribal Council and supported by Just Reinvest NSW, an organisation initially auspiced by the Aboriginal Legal Service NSW/ACT (Riboldi and Hopkins 2019). A KPMG (2018) study estimated $3.1m in fiscal and economic benefits from Marranuka, supporting successful appeals for public and philanthropic finance. A formal and ongoing funding mechanism is yet to be agreed; however, strong campaigns have seen commitments from both the Coalition NSW (NSW government 2022) and Labor (ALP 2022b) Federal Governments.

Social investment is potentially also a site to advance financialisation. The most prominent example of a novel financing mechanism introduced in social policy is the Social Impact Bond (SIB). SIBs effectively identify marginalised populations as 'risky citizens', likely to generate high future spending (Baker et al. 2020). The state uses these anticipated costs as the financial basis for funding private provision.

Entrepreneurial social service providers are encouraged to propose novel interventions that might reduce future spending through forms of early intervention. The state then offers contracts (called bonds) to private investors. Investors purchase 'bonds' to provide upfront funding for services, and are then paid returns out of the notional fiscal savings created if contract targets are met (Lilley et al. 2020).

In practice, SIBs have enjoyed limited success. Assessing fiscal savings is based on complex actuarial and scientific 'control group' models. These have proven idiosyncratic, making it difficult to create default contracts and thus increasing the administrative costs of bonds. The outcomes are also very uncertain and difficult to assess. The complex contracts deter most investors, creating thin markets, and typically see the government underwrite the risk by agreeing to pay out even when the fiscal benefits are dubious (Harvie et al. 2021). Finally, the desire for very strong causal links between intervention, social outcome and fiscal savings not only increases complexity and cost, it also narrows the potential scope of bonds to highly individualised interventions, where a program can be said to cause an individual to become less fiscally risky, rather than addressing broader social dynamics (Lilley et al. 2020).

Justice Reinvestment may offer a hybrid alternative to SIBs. Indigenous efforts at reinvestment are more clearly tied to a collective claim for self-determination. By framing the investment relationship as between states and Indigenous communities, rather than private investors, both the desired outcomes and the way these outcomes are monitored and assessed can potentially be subject to norms of self-determination.

Led by Indigenous communities, justice reinvestment is better able to tie financing to social principles, including more fundamental challenges to bureaucratic practice and authority. Justice reinvestment has advanced alongside the assertion of Indigenous Data Sovereignty (Walter et al. 2021), which rejects the authority of Settler institutions (states and markets) to unilaterally assess outcomes and thus set rewards. Instead, oversight and control should be returned to Communities. Framing spending not only as 'investment' but *re*investment also lays claim to future financing, essentially claiming the fiscal resources of the carceral state to support Community governance (Bryant and Spies-Butcher 2024).

Reshaping Liberalised Welfare

Liberalisation has remade the Australian welfare state. The protections of wage-earner welfare, which placed explicit boundaries around the commodification of labour by limiting price competition, have gradually been unwound. Inequalities in market earnings have followed. The ubiquity of home ownership has also eroded, undermining security of tenure and intensifying the consequences of low labour market income. Australia's welfare state has come under attack from overt efforts at retrenchment and from enduring fiscal constraints now deeply embedded in Australia's political norms. Residualisation, marketisation and financialisation have all contributed to a more punitive and privatised 'dual welfare state'.

Against the trends to residualise incomes, marketise services and financialise the life course, hybrid policies offer counter-strategies. In each of these three cases, rather than rejecting market logics, hybrid policies partly mobilised competition to advance more egalitarian alternatives by applying economic principles more consistently and symmetrically.

Residualisation is challenged by moving social payments towards the structures of income tax, eroding the dualism between tax and welfare that supports workfare and entrenching norms of income adequacy. Marketisation is challenged by applying the principles of efficiency to private provision, reinforcing the efficiencies of public finance. And the emerging inter-generational inequalities of the asset economy are challenged by asserting the future possibilities of social investment against the constraints of liability budgeting.

These strategies do not simply extend market logics within the state, but instead embed competition within public control. Hybrid policies challenge fiscal constraints by highlighting 'hidden' forms of state power and applying supposedly neutral economic tools, such as incentives or efficiency, to the dual welfare state.

Spending on social payments is not constrained by a small state, but by a sizeable and aggressively punitive one. Consumer choice in social markets is largely a product of public subsidy. And liability budgeting seeks to constrain state spending by selectively applying its gaze to erode social entitlements, while concealing how fiscal welfare and the punitive carceral state are both expanding. It is precisely because Australia's experience of neoliberalism reflects the 'roll out' (Peck 2010; Cahill 2010) of a dual welfare state, rather than the shrinking of the state, that hybrid strategies are effective; restructuring existing state commitments in egalitarian and democratic directions.

Technocratic strategies play a key role in advancing hybridity. Just as tools of macroeconomic management and structures of national accounting supported the development of Keynesian welfare states, so too a new set of economic tools inform hybrid policy making. Economists have been key to all the reforms examined here, from femocrats reshaping payment systems, health economists informing Medicare and welfare economists crafting ICLs.

What distinguishes hybrid policy from other forms of equally technocratic liberalisation is a connection to social definitions of need. Hybridity reflects a different 'language of valuation' (Martinez-Alier 2008). In each case, value and adequacy are defined socially. Typically, social principles are also framed in universal terms. Universalism facilitates broader political coalitions while remaining compatible with market logics, which emphasise neutrality between actors. Rather than asserting distinctions, such as between gender roles or domestic and foreign labour, universalism asserts common principles. Hybridity facilitates equity by enforcing symmetry in the application of universal principles between public and private finance.

Analysing hybridity should not be read as championing technocratic skill over contentious politics, but rather building politics on the foundation of universal principles. Hybrid policies only advance where social needs have been established politically. Medicare's insurance model may have mitigated fiscal and constitutional resistance, but it was a political campaign to treat healthcare as a right that ensured it was adopted. The structures of hybrid policies, however, have implications for politics.

The focus on symmetry and neutrality favour universal claims. The history of reforms suggests implicit universal principles. Hybridity implies universal access to adequate or basic incomes, against conditionality premised on distinctions between deserving and undeserving. It implies universal access to care and education, rather than stratified choices that allow some to lack access altogether. And it implies a degree of future security, especially of tenure, against the discipline of debt relations. These political claims are far from new, but their political power is reinforced in the wake of liberalisation, and their advance is often tied to hybridity.

Campaigns over income support follow universal principles based on the right to an adequate income. By asserting equivalence between means-tests and marginal tax rates, hybrid strategies treat market and state income as equivalent. Individual income is not yet subject to a norm of universal adequacy, but there is evidence of a similar norm for families with children and for older people. The partial integration of means-tests with the income tax system reflects successful resistance to residualisation.

In principle, 'family income' itself is incompatible with the individual model of income taxation. The ideal form of such a policy is a universal child payment. For individuals, however, means-testing is potentially compatible with income tax. Establishing a norm in favour of individual adequate incomes is not a technical, but a political question, exemplified in the recent $80 a day campaign. Incorporating such a claim into existing policy structures would likely involve a degree of 'affluence testing', reducing the fiscal cost of a basic income and adapting the claim to Australia's long tradition of targeting (see Spies-Butcher, Phillips and Henderson 2020).

Not only does affluence testing reflect the principles of hybridity – treating means-testing and income tax as equivalent – it also implies a policy trajectory. Such a model implies four types of changes to current payments: to raise base payments to the poverty line, remove conditionality, individualise payments (removing partner and parent tests) and moderate means-tests. Change in favour of any of these dimensions likely strengthens pressure for changes to the others. Changes to JobSeeker during Covid reflect exactly these changes. Even as these changes were wound back, numbers on JobSeeker remained much higher (Whiteford and Bradbury 2022), suggesting conditionality and stigma reduce access far more than the rules themselves might suggest.

Campaigns for universal access to adequate services have a clear model from Medicare and to a lesser extent the NDIS. However, there is reasonable concern that further levy increases target current workers, who have been subject to stagnating wages and rising housing costs. Particularly for social provision targeted to older people, there are good reasons to adapt the levy principle to the realities of the asset economy. Superannuation, for example, holds over a trillion dollars of assets and enjoys tens of billions annually in concessional tax support, yet it cannot guarantee access to adequate incomes, care or tenure in retirement.

A future levy might apply to the income earned within super funds rather than wage income (see Howe and Spies-Butcher 2022). Such a levy could be directly tied to the social purpose of superannuation – to ensure adequate living standards in retirement – by providing a universal right, via social insurance, to aged care or retirement housing. Targeting investment income, as the Albanese government has begun to do through super, is radically more egalitarian than a levy on wages. An insurance levy would mimic similar market insurance (for death and disability cover) already required within the super system.

The welfare state must also recon with growing wealth inequalities generated by the asset economy. While Australia's older model of home ownership complicates a simple reading of inequality, the evidence of growing inequalities across generations is clear. The financialisation of housing – promoting its ability to generate income from rents, mortgage payments and capital gains over its social function as secure tenure – creates significant challenges for reform. Insecure tenure in the private rental market underpins rising rents and house prices.

Increasing renters' rights redistributes rights from property owners to tenants directly, rather than via state budgets. However, given the political and economic significance of house prices and the broad constituency of landlords such a redistribution is more likely if complemented by budget action. Here, the state's hybrid roles – as creditor, investor and underwriter – are already emerging as central. Commitments for the state to 'co-buy' houses with low- and middle-income earners, or to structure social housing via investment funds and non-profit providers, reflect the fiscal logic of hybridity. Expanding the state's role as owner of housing can potentially socialise capital gains while supporting housing and stock market prices.

The expansion of housing debt already places pressure on the state to act as an implicit underwriter of house prices. Converting tax concessions could fund a transition in the housing market as tenant rights are restored. If private investors cannot manage their housing investments without the right to radically increase rents, reduce maintenance or evict tenants, then the state can acquire their properties, managed as market investments but with these rights guaranteed.

State intervention during both the GFC and Covid-19 revealed the enormous potential fiscal powers states possess. The political backlash against the bail out of Wall St in 2008 already appears to have influenced policy responses in the next crisis, where states acted in very similar ways to secure liquidity, but did so by underwriting households as well as finance (Spies-Butcher 2020a). It is likely policy makers will reach for similar policies in future crises.

Incorporating the social protections implied by crisis interventions into explicit and ongoing guarantees will likely involve hybrid models. This may see social protection guaranteed by the central state, but delivered through devolved governance. Investing in housing, underwriting cooperatives and providing citizens with income contingent credit all mitigate fiscal constraint by devolving governance. It is because universities, superannuation funds and social housing providers are separate entities that state support can be imagined in financial forms.

Devolution has many advantages, especially if the distribution of resources and rights continues to be organised centrally, but it also highlights how liberalisation displaces political contestation to the governance of devolved entities. Devolution of justice reinvestment to Indigenous communities can aid claims for self-determination, but the corporatisation of university governance reveals an equally important counter-example.

Ensuring the governance of the entities that receive fiscal support reflect social, rather than purely market, values must be central to any egalitarian politics. Efforts to democratise super investments, university executives and housing providers complement the extension of the state's social investment powers, just as it once insisted on non-profit, parent run childcare. The importance of democratic governance underlines why hybrid policies can only advance alongside political mobilisation. Liberalisation, however, has also eroded the power of the welfare state's traditional allies. The politics of welfare not only takes place in new spaces, it increasingly relies on new alliances and tactics.

Chapter 7

CHALLENGING LIBERALISED WELFARE

Liberalisation increases inequalities and weakens the allies of egalitarian social policy. The rise of the welfare state was led by powerful, industrial, trade unions and left political parties, often with middle-class or agrarian support (see Baldwin 1990; Manow 2009). It was the product of political-economic struggles, inspired by the possibility of moving beyond capitalism. Those driving the welfare state were organised around their role in the economy and particularly their role in industrial production.

The welfare state's origins do not lie directly in efforts to reorganise how we care and educate. They instead lie in efforts to protect workers and their families from the insecurities of an industrial economy. The organisation of the welfare state reflects strategies and 'statecraft' developed alongside ideas of macroeconomic management designed to 'democratise' industrial capitalism. This Keynesian welfare state, discussed in Chapter 1, distinguished between a private sector of market production regulated by competition and a public sector determined by democratic norms. Liberalisation weakens the welfare state by both extending competition to previously democratic, public spaces, and weakening the traditional political allies of the welfare state – industrial unions and socialist parties.

Of course, liberalisation in Australia has been uneven. The last chapter drew together examples of social policy expansion and renewal that took place alongside more conventional processes of residualisation, marketisation and financialisation. Exploring those examples, I argued policy success was associated with forms of hybridity, in which new proposals mimicked elements of liberalisation – advancing competition alongside redistribution and minimising (apparent) fiscal costs. Proposals did this by combining elements of state distribution and market exchange in ways that tended to socialise risk and appeal to universal principles of need and provisioning.

Hybridity is not straightforwardly egalitarian. All the examples outlined in the previous chapters opened space for erosion or complicated calls for further reform. But they successfully respond to the context of liberalisation, allowing egalitarian social provision to expand against the odds.

Well-designed policy, however, was not enough to constrain inequality. The boldest reforms were achieved when hybrid policy models combined with strong movement pressure. Unions struck in favour of Medicare and feminists organised behind family spending. If the traditional allies of the welfare state are becoming weaker, what does this mean for welfare state politics?

In this chapter, I look to connect the logic of hybridity to contentious politics. I draw on theories of social reproduction (Bhattacharya 2017) – the work of care and education associated with both social policy and unpaid work – to show how the centre of political conflict is shifting. Rather than imagining the welfare state as the by-product of broader class struggles in the commodity economy, I suggest that risk, distribution and value are increasingly contested within the realm of social reproduction itself.

Focusing on how we care for, raise, educate, organise and reproduce people and communities highlights different actors, alliances, struggles and tactics. Rather than focusing on the production and distribution of physical commodities, focusing on social reproduction places risk – organised either through the calculus of finance, or through socialisation of needs – at the centre of conflicts over distribution. It is precisely at the intersection of care and markets that hybridity emerges.

Of course, the wage labour relationship remains central, especially as the work of the welfare state moves from the informal to the formal economy. But it shifts the focus within the world of work – from emphasising the circuits of capital that produce things to emphasising the circuits of care that reproduce us. Political contests over the welfare state move to processes of social reproduction and to the workers, paid and unpaid, at the centre of these relationships.

This chapter explores alternative readings of liberalisation and the service transition. I begin with the 'death of class' thesis, which argues the rise of a knowledge economy and service industries challenge the fiscal and social bases of Keynesian social democracy. More recently, theorists identify a shift from emphasising the end of traditional class inequalities and politics to explaining the re-emergence of class inequalities alongside the demise of social democratic politics. Education plays a central role in these accounts by dividing the interests and solidarities of workers.

Analysing welfare state politics through the lens of social reproduction challenges this reading of liberalisation and the role of education. Higher education is not only human capital, it has also been an important strategy for challenging the gendered organisation of work and care. Universities are increasingly the training ground for the mass workforces of the welfare state. Particularly for younger generations, this presents competing models. Education as human capital fosters the winner-takes-all politics of the asset economy. Education as care and social reproduction instead offers possibilities to remake social policy by transforming gendered and generational solidarities.

I explore how these dynamics within the welfare state have shaped the politics of Australian inequality. Australia's dual welfare state has adapted to the pressures of a service economy, expanding the benefits of asset ownership to a broader constituency and disguising inequalities through opaque tax concessions. Liberalisation has reorganised welfare state services to provide steady streams of state-subsidised payments that facilitate the incorporation of social reproduction into financial markets.

Where egalitarian social policy has advanced, it has reflected the alliances built within the provision of education and care. The organisation of work within the welfare state differs from the work of commodity production. It is less centralised, and instead embedded in communities across the country. It directly ties producers to consumers, fostering broader coalitions and high trust relationships. Those coalitions potentially bring together some of the best organised allies of equality, through the unions that represent workers, and those claiming rights to social protection. Care and education are well suited to 'issue based' politics, while tying apparently different issues to a common ethic. It is exactly this kind of 'politics of care' that has driven egalitarian politics under liberalisation and has the potential to win a more egalitarian future.

Industrial Welfare States and the Death of Class

A long tradition in political sociology frames the welfare state as a strategic compromise (Offe 2018; Block 2008; Fraser and Jaeggi 2018). Capitalism and industrialisation generate social conflicts, which by the twentieth century saw socialism emerge as a credible alternative mode of production. For some this framed the welfare state as a sop to genuine social reform, designed to weaken radical impulses without delivering structural change in the underlying balance of power based on the ownership of resources (O'Connor 2017). To others the welfare state was a pathway to socialising risk within the parliamentary structures of bourgeois capitalism (Esping-Andersen 1999).

Across these accounts, however, the welfare state emerged in response to pressures within the industrial economy. Liberalisation and the rise of a service economy challenged this model. By weakening industrial working-class power and by disrupting the fiscal politics of Keynesian social democracy liberalisation replaces the welfare state compromise with a renewed focus on fiscal constraint.

Mass politics is central to explanations of the rise of the welfare state. Unions and mass left parties are the primary institutional actors. Where unions were strong, measured by membership density and strike action, and where left parties consistently held office, more egalitarian social policy developed (Korpi 1989). Reflecting Marxist theory and political experience, left power was understood to reside in industrial workforces.

Blue-collar workers embodied the mass experience of industrialisation, as their jobs and lives centralised around mines, factories and ports. Industrial labour centred on commodity production, which underpinned economic growth and profitability. This made the industries that produced surplus value, in a Marxist sense, or enabled its realisation, key to workers' industrial power. It was not only by winning elections but also by challenging economic profitability (Korpi 2006) that social democratic reforms advanced.

Even for those less sympathetic to class analysis, the organisation of mass politics was central to the operation of mid-century democracy. Parties created the mechanism that linked citizens to parliaments. Most pluralists acknowledge that economic interests are important to party formation and organisation, but also emphasise other identifies, seeing class antagonism as less central (Lipset 1981).

Across the developed world mass parties were demonstrably organised along class lines, and the relative strength of party blocks was understood to shape policy outcomes. Parliamentary systems created incentives to move beyond the left's industrial class base. In Scandinavia red-green alliances between urban workers and rural farmers proved central (Manow 2009), as did middle-class support in the United Kingdom (Baldwin 1990). Parties created a mechanism to represent different social interests, a space for citizens to engage in political debate and an institution to negotiate social compromise.

In all these debates, the welfare state remains a product of broader forces. Indeed, those most closely associated with social provision were more often caste as resisting, rather than advancing, social democratic reform. Doctors formed a powerful block *against* universal healthcare (Sax 1984). Nurses had strongly gendered professional commitments that militated against radicalisation (see Bessant 1992). Universities arose from social elites, training the better off for entry into professions protected from the intensity of competition applied to other workers. Women, often confined to unpaid caring roles in home and Church, consistently favoured conservatives over radicals at the ballot box (see De Vaus and McAllister 1989). Whether social policy advances in response to capitalist crisis, worker power or pluralist citizen engagement, social provision is the outcome, not the cause. Work, especially industrial work, drives the politics of welfare.

Neoliberalism, the political movement driving liberalisation, began with iconic battles against labour. In the United Kingdom, Thatcher's government confronted powerful mining unions, privatised mines and eventually dismantled the industry (Cahill and Konings 2017, 38–39). Reagan's administration was equally aggressive in taking on pilots, while inflation-first monetary policy, business friendly labour laws and deregulation hollowed out industrial employment (Moody 1987).

Australia's unions proved more resilient against efforts from the Fraser government to reign in wages. Instead, it was a Labor government, through the Accord, that 'moderated' wage growth (Humphrys 2018). Interpreting the trade-offs within the Accord is complicated. While it clearly did not facilitate a transition to socialism, it was associated with very significant social gains, particularly Medicare and family spending. Even so, by the late 1990s unions emerged from the Accord weaker than they had entered it, and Labor's primary vote has never recovered. While wages rose with the mining boom in the 2000s, the 2010s saw stagnation and then, post-Covid, a rapid decline (Stewart et al. 2022).

The decline of traditional labour institutions is not confined to Australia or to the Accord. Union membership has fallen across much of the industrialised world over the past 40 years (Sano and Williamson 2008). But the decline is particularly pronounced in Australia. Approximately half of the workforce were unionised in the early 1980s, compared to less than one in five today. The absolute number of union members declined by around a million over the same period (Gilfillan and McGann 2018, 2).

The decline is most pronounced in the private sector, where density has plummeted, even in former strongholds. But it also reflects a shift in the composition of employment, particularly in the private sector, away from factories, mines and ports and towards forms of service sector work, such as retail trade, accommodation and hospitality, that have very low density. Employment in the production industries has fallen significantly as a proportion of the economy, from almost half of all employment in the 1960s to around one in five jobs today (ABS 2011; ABS 2022a).

The decline in union membership parallels a decline in mass party politics. Party memberships have fallen even more dramatically than union membership, while voting patterns have become both more fragmented and volatile. Membership halved from the late 1960s to the late 1990s (Bean 1997, 110) and has more than halved again, to less than 1 per cent today (Davies 2020). When Hawke won office in 1983 Labor received 49.5 per cent of the primary vote. When Labor returned to office in 2007, its primary vote was only 43.4 per cent, and by 2022 it had fallen below 33 per cent (APEA 2020; AEC 2022). Labor's traditional voting block of blue-collar workers has become both less reliable and more conservative. The base has not swung to the Coalition as much as is sometimes claimed, but it is no longer the bedrock of progressive electoral politics it once was (see McAllister and Makkai 2019).

The shift in Labor's electoral fortunes and the weakness of industrial unionism are related. As Andrew Leigh shows, union membership is itself a strong predictor of voting intentions (2006). It was not only that blue-collar workers supported Labor, it was that *unionised* blue-collar workers supported Labor. Unions socialised and mobilised their members. That still happens, unionists remain much more likely to vote progressive, especially when the union movement commits resources to electorally mobilising its members, as it did most dramatically in 2007 (Wilson and Spies-Butcher 2011). But the collapse of union density means the impact is much more modest. Even when controlling for other changes, much of Labor's electoral weakness since the 1990s, Leigh argues, can be attributed to union decline (2006). If the welfare state is won by unions and mass parties, the prospect for resisting liberalisation seem bleak.

The political response to this challenge has centred on the role of education. Rising education levels have created new progressive constituencies, but also fragmented and realigned progressive priorities. Initially this was expressed through Inglehart's post-materialist thesis (1977, 1990), which emphasised a change in values associated with rising affluence. Post-materialism meant 'material' struggles over pay and redistribution increasingly gave way to new concerns about the environment, peace, democracy and identity. Movements developed around all these issues, mobilising different constituencies to those traditionally linked to social democratic politics. Gradually, tertiary educated voters in professional and managerial occupations shifted from stable conservative supporters to an increasingly progressive electorate, particularly via minor parties (see Goot and Watson 2007).

The hollowing out of union and party structures combined with new forms of civic participation. Parties increasingly moved from a mass party model to a catch-all (Kirchheimer 1966) or even cartel (see Katz and Mair 1995) model. Parties became increasingly professional, their connection to voters largely mediated by mass media, polling and advertising (Mair 2023).

Voter orientations increasingly fragmented, dividing not only between traditional left and right but also between cosmopolitan/libertarian attitudes and traditionalist/parochial attitudes. Changes in voter attitudes are increasingly reflected in a diversity of political parties (Kitschelt 1994), such as One Nation on the nationalist right and the Greens on the cosmopolitan left. Citizens have increasingly turned away from traditional forms of mass engagement, through unions, churches and parties, which foster broad collective identities (Putnam 2000). Instead, citizens, especially young people, engage in more diverse issue-specific forms of politics (see Vromen et al. 2015, 81–83).

The service transition not only eroded the industrial base of social democratic politics, it also complicated the economics of Keynesian-era policy. In Scandinavia, mass politics was supported by an economic model that connected solidarity to productivity and employment (Iversen and Wren 1998; Wren 2013). Wage compression made high-productivity export-orientated industries relatively competitive by holding down high-skilled wages, while reducing the competitive position of low-productivity industries reliant on low-wage labour. Social and economic policy supported retraining and adjustment, allowing a gradual shift in employment to higher wage, higher productivity industries.

The service transition challenges this Keynesian logic by concentrating employment growth in service industries, which typically see low productivity gains. The result is a 'trilemma' (Iversen and Wren 1998), where it is difficult to maintain relative wage equality and high employment without expanding social spending against the fiscal constraints imposed by neoliberalism.

Taken together, the rise of new issues, the changing nature of social movements and the fragmentation of parties suggest to many the 'death' of traditional class politics focused on work and distribution (see Pakulski and Waters 1996). The distinction between 'identity' and 'class' politics has always been somewhat overdrawn. In Australia key activists in feminist, ecological, Indigenous rights and gay liberation struggles were members of the Communist Party (MacIntyre 2022). Internationally, the integration of radical student movements into broader worker movements and the internationalisation of progressive politics against colonialism posed a significant challenge to capitalism. As Nancy Fraser (1995) influentially argues, all social movements involve a mixture of claims for both 'redistribution' of material resources and 'recognition' of diverse identities.

However, there has been a significant realignment of political orientations. Those on low incomes and in manual work are less likely to support the parties of the left than they once were. Those with university qualifications and, particularly, professional employment are more progressive. Just as Whitlam appealed to women, students and migrants and Hawke to environmental concerns to broaden Labor's appeal, so Howard successfully appealed to many, particularly male and retired, workers. That realignment potentially shifts the dynamics within and between progressive and conservative politics, and thus broader struggles over welfare.

A New Elite Politics?

Provocatively, Thomas Piketty (2018, 2020) suggests the weakening of traditional class indicators of income and occupation on voting patterns might mark a return to an older politics. Prior to the expansion of the franchise, most democracies were structured around inter-elite conflicts that rarely centred the experience of the mass of workers. The right, Piketty claims, remains a party of capital, but is increasingly supported by voters with less formal education through appeals to nationalism that promise to shield their jobs from international competition. The left increasingly reflects the interests of higher paid educated voters, whose attitudes and interests align with cosmopolitanism.

Piketty's analysis is most closely based on the United States, Britain and France. Similar trends appear to be emerging in Australia, with education constituting an important new axis of partisan cleavage and progressive politics making gains in the inner cities (Cameron et al. 2022). However, our case studies also point to a different dynamic and reading of the changing role of education. Rather than education as 'human capital' stratifying people in a global asset economy, education might also be organised as a democratic and social resource into a politics of care.

Piketty's account of the 'merchant right' and 'Brahman left' builds on his earlier analysis of rising inequalities. In *Capital in the Twenty-first Century* (2014) he argued that slowing growth rates, linked to the service transition, meant existing wealth became relatively more economically important. Returns on capital (r) had begun to outstrip aggregate economic growth (g). If $r > g$, then returns to all those without significant capital must be rising more slowly than the average. Asset ownership is also much less equal than wage income, and is strongly concentrated at the very top. Piketty's formula helps explain not only rising inequality, but a super-charged form of inequality that only benefited the 1 per cent.

Piketty argues class increasingly intersects with global competition to undermine egalitarianism. The changing structure of jobs has meant many low-skill workers lose out from international competition, or at least see themselves losing out, while high-skilled (read highly educated) voters benefit (2018). That combination facilitates forms of right-wing populism that appeal to much of the left's traditional base, while in practice advancing the interests of the ultra-rich merchant right. The same dynamics fuel racial divisions within countries, not so much amongst migrants and native voters in general, but through an aggressive nationalist politics targeting specific and visible minorities – black Americans or French Muslims – who in turn vote overwhelmingly for the left, seemingly reinforcing 'identity' politics over class (*Ibid*).

There is some evidence for this thesis in Australia. Spatial inequalities in Australia are rising, including a rise in the social gradient of health – the degree to which income and wealth inequalities translate into different health outcomes for those in affluent and poor regions (Favel et al. 2022). The

2019 and 2022 elections saw educated inner-metropolitan electorates shift from right to left. Some in the Coalition look to a US Republican-like strategy based on appeals to blue-collar workers in 'left-behind' regions, especially those dependent on resource extraction. Australia's brand of 'wedge politics' reflects a similar targeting of visible minorities.

So far, however, these appeals have been less effective. Traditional measures of class voting remain stronger in Australia, at least within the cities, which in turn dominate Australia's highly urbanised demography. Even in 2019, when Labor's vote grew amongst the educated and fell in the regions, Labor continued to lead the Coalition amongst voters identifying as working class, Labor's vote steadily declines as income rises, while voting based on asset ownership, especially housing, marks clear partisan divides (Cameron and Macallister 2019, 19–20).

Education is often understood in these debates as a form of 'human capital'. Australia's early debates over the expansion of universities, where some in Labor saw university funding as 'middle class welfare' and economists encouraged fees to reflect education's 'private returns', reinforce that frame. But education now intersects with other demographic cleavages that are also transforming politics – particularly age and gender.

For those leaving high school today, university is not only the bastion of elitism, but a mass institution catering to around half the population, a very different reality to the experience of those now entering retirement. The risks these groups face are likewise starkly different. An overwhelming majority of older Australians continue to own their home and have access to a guaranteed income through the pension. Even for younger people on reasonable incomes, work is often insecure and housing expensive. The streams of income they pay on childcare, rent and health insurance feed a financialised asset economy.

Education has also been key to the expansion of egalitarian social policy. Access to education is not only an individual pathway to better pay and higher status. Professionalisation has also been used in combination with industrial strategies to collectively advance pay and conditions and to revalue feminised labour. Union campaigns have tied professional qualifications to quality provision and higher pay, creating opportunities to unite the interests of workers and service users. Professional care labour can be potentially transformed from a model imposing distant bureaucratic control to one that reflects egalitarian rather than elite values and knowledge (see Carey et al. 2009). Struggles within professions, and universities, contest how knowledge and skills are constructed and valued. Those struggles challenge the epistemological supremacy of the elite knowledge traditionally privileged by powerful professional communities.

Feminist critiques of the male bias within medicine (Hamberg 2008) and the undervaluation of care labour reshape professional norms and expand access to better paid and respected work. Those subject to professional control have increasingly asserted their interests not only as 'lived experience', but increasingly as 'lived expertise' (Clifton et al. 2020; APC nd), highlighting the knowledge and skill that come from being forced to navigate complex bureaucracies and directly manage exclusion and disadvantage. Likewise, Indigenous data sovereignty challenges the definition, control and use of data by non-Indigenous bureaucracies (Walter et al. 2021). The pluralisation of knowledge creates challenges to traditional professional authority, but also has the potential to reinforce opportunities for worker-consumer coalitions that reflect the relational and reciprocal nature of care provision (Williams 2001; Fine 2018).

The welfare state is central to both these readings. The gradual erosion of security facilitated by the asset economy and the incorporation of care labour into paid work sit at the centre of politics and the future of the welfare state. Such a reading echoes scholarship on the importance of social reproduction to political economic analysis, a topic often marginalised in discussion of class, but which is increasingly central to welfare politics post-liberalisation.

As Nancy Fraser argues, Keynesian social democracy gave way to liberalisation due to the 'one-two punch' of New Left social movements and neoliberalism, which each challenged the valorisation of the breadwinner model (Fraser and Jaeggi 2018, 77). That challenge has made social reproduction central to the paid economy. Fraser argues we should broaden our analysis, rejecting the 'view that class alone is structural' (*ibid*, 98). Instead, social reproduction is also the site of 'boundary struggles' to challenge the categories that organise market economies.

The idea of 'boundary struggles' fits neatly with the conception of hybridity. The strategies of hybrid policy target the boundaries between public and private finance. They do so not only by asserting symmetry in accounting terms, but by redefining value in social, rather than profit, terms. Asserting social spending as investment challenges the boundary between the 'productive' commodity economy of class and the gendered 'service' work of social reproduction.

Together with liberalisation, social movements have increasingly moved the site of contestation from the traditional politics of industrial class conflict to within the welfare state itself. That cuts both ways. Dual welfare incorporates social reproduction into circuits of finance and the asset economy. Hybridity potentially offers space within liberalised welfare states to socialise risk and reconnect care to social need.

Age, Assets and the Endurance of the Dual Welfare State

The dual welfare state complicates the politics of asset ownership in Australia. Even as home ownership rates decline, most Australians continue to benefit from rising house prices. Generous tax concessions are built into the foundations of home ownership. Many anticipate benefiting from tax concessions, while the structure of those arrangements conceals just how unevenly the benefits are divided. As a result, Australia's wealth inequality appears low by international standards (Bryant et al. 2024, 8).

The asset economy can foster a broad coalition of supporters, extending beyond the genuinely asset rich to include many older Australians. Home ownership continues to protect older generations from some of the most pernicious elements of liberalisation by ensuring tenure security and insulating people from cost-of-living pressures. As the older retirement income policy model erodes, insecurities of tenure and income steadily increase for each new generation. Growing differences in voting patterns by age do not only reflect changes in social attitudes, but increasingly reflect the very different welfare states, economies and risks confronting different generations.

The patterns and dynamics of the asset economy differ from those of income distribution upon which most welfare state theory is centred. Despite liberalisation, international comparisons of income inequality continue to follow the contours of Esping-Andersen's worlds of welfare (see Bryant et al. 2024); Scandinavian countries are significantly more egalitarian, the liberal Anglophone world much less so. Indeed, the unwinding of Australia's older wage-earner model has intensified these trends by moving Australia back towards other liberal nations. This is not true of wealth.

Wealth inequalities are far wider than income inequalities in all countries; however, Scandinavian countries are amongst the least equal in terms of wealth. Australia and other countries with high levels of home ownership stand close to the bottom of the OECD league table on wealth inequality. Figure 7.1 reports the proportion of wealth held by the wealthiest and least wealthy households. Australians at the top own relatively less, and those at the bottom relatively more, than in similar high-income economies. Home ownership explains much of the difference, and is also associated with higher average wealth (Bryant et al. 2024). Wealth inequalities are more closely connected to housing than the welfare state (Pfeffer and Waitkus 2021), although both are complicated by hybridity (Bryant et al. 2024).

Both superannuation and housing inflate per capita wealth measures in Australia. It makes for difficult comparisons. Many European workers, for example, will enjoy more generous pension entitlements than many Australian workers, even when super and pension entitlements are

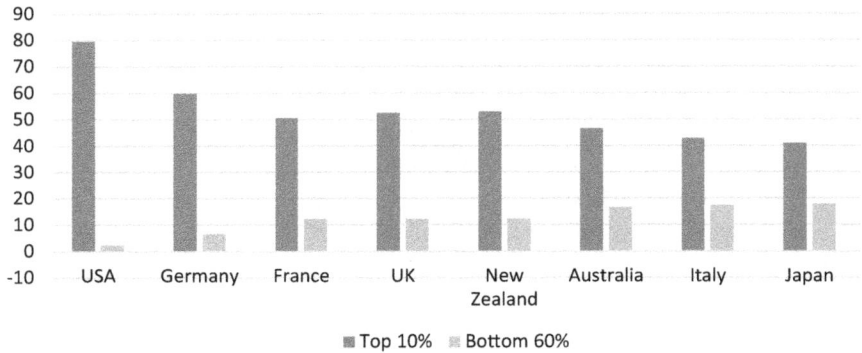

Figure 7.1 Proportion of wealth held by top 10 per cent and bottom 60 per cent of wealth holders, selected OECD countries.

combined. Yet, because European pension entitlements are not tradable (you can't sell someone your pension rights, and payments end when you die), they do not count as wealth (a measure of tradable property). Similarly, despite liberalisation, many in Berlin and Vienna continue to enjoy secure, well-maintained and centrally located accommodation through social housing (see Kadi et al. 2021).

Super and housing give Australians access to (property) rights that citizens gain through public entitlements elsewhere. But structured as tradable property, these rights are also tied to the asset economy and the prospect of capital gains. Housing and super might make Australians richer, but it does not necessarily increase their standard of living.

It does expand the constituency in favour of policies that inflate asset prices. Asset prices, however, tend to rise as the rights of property owners expand and those of everyone else decline. Overseas examples suggest that as tenure rights for renters have weakened, house prices have risen, reflecting the monetary value that comes with changing property rights (Christophers 2021). For Australia, changing home ownership patterns, combined with weak tenancy laws, potentially divide the political interests of generations.

The relationship between age and home ownership is central to understanding housing. Many younger people with little wealth now will acquire wealth later. The relationship between age, risk and wealth, however, is changing as the retirement income system is gradually reworked. Examining the distribution of wealth by *income* group helps to see both trends. Figure 7.2 reports the distribution of different kinds of wealth according to household income (not wealth).

Organised according to income, ownership suddenly appears more equitable. Many low-income retirees have savings while many young workers do not. Even so, the top of the wealth distribution is more concentrated than

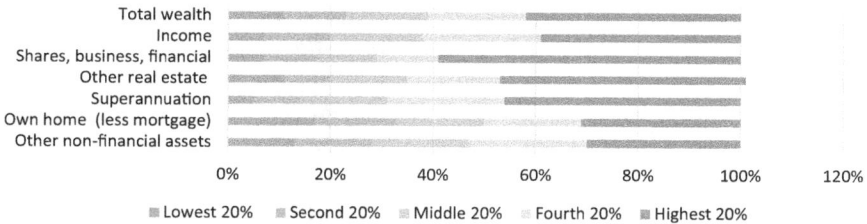

Figure 7.2 Distribution of wealth and income by income quintile and asset type, Australia, 2017/18. *Source*: ACOSS, nd, 'Wealth distribution among income groups' in Poverty and Inequality in Australia, https://povertyandinequality.acoss.org.au/inequality/shares-of-wealth-across-income-groups-by-asset-type-2016/.

for income, driven by the very unequal distribution of financial and business assets, which are more strongly correlated with class than age.

Focusing on different asset categories there is a clear divide in Australia's asset-based welfare. The most recent additions – compulsory superannuation and the significant expansion in the number of households owning investment properties (other real estate) – are not egalitarian, even by the unequal standards of asset ownership. These inequalities, however, are balanced by home ownership, which remains an enduring source of relative wealth equality – albeit for an increasingly older demographic.

For those already past retirement age, home ownership continues to play its established role in the retirement income system, reflected in the relatively high proportion of low-income households with wealth in their own home. As the established model of housing in the retirement income system erodes so wealth inequality will rise. Far from acting as a countervailing force, the rise of superannuation and investment properties are eroding wealth equality.

The slow transition facilitated by Australia's dual welfare state threatens to significantly widen the lived experience of inequality, towards something like Piketty's vision of pre-democratic Europe. Yet, in the short run it limits the electoral base for egalitarian alternatives. Amongst older Australians, the dual welfare state has somewhat frozen class relations, especially for those retired from paid work.

For most, the aged pension creates a guaranteed minimum income and home ownership ensures secure tenure. Changes to health insurance to forcibly enrol the young through lifetime cover cross-subsidise the old and help insulate a larger pool of older voters from concerns over the erosion of Medicare. In contrast, those entering the labour market face ever greater precarity. The growing divide in voting patterns by age is matched by a growing wealth divide between generations (Daley and Woods 2014).

It is a supreme irony that the dual welfare state, which produced this generational divide of social protection, did so in the name of generational equality. As discussed in Chapter 5, it was to save future generations of tax payers that a new privatised model of retirement incomes was so vigorously promoted. The prospect of any real generational conflict based on expanding social spending was always overblown by the distortions of Generational Accounting. Unsurprisingly, cutting taxes primarily benefits those who would otherwise pay more tax, and in Australia that is overwhelmingly the rich.

The rise of dual welfare associated with an asset economy has fostered widening differences in voting patterns, but it has not led to the kind of 'generational war' some anticipated. Young people are not clamouring to cut pensions and aged care. Instead, the dual welfare state creates political opportunities for generational solidarity. The most obvious response is not to mobilise the young to tear down the social protections enjoyed by the old, but to universalise those protections for all.

Labor's 2019 election loss was seen by many as ruling out the possibilities for reforming the generous tax concessions built into Australia's retirement system. However, analysis of the results suggest those positions were far less influential than initially claimed (see McAllister and Makkai 2019). Labor's plan also failed to clearly connect changes to tax concessions and new social entitlements. Instead, the changes were proposed as a generic funding measure to balance Labor's overall policy platform. Looking to the successful examples of welfare reform, a more explicit link, which sought to remake the generational contract, is likely to enjoy more success.

The last chapter discussed how a proposal that emphasises generational solidarity might work. The key to any reform is to address the very unequal impacts of the retirement income system for *older* Australians as well as across generations. Not only do many retirees rely almost exclusively on the pension, part-pensioners face punitive means-tests. The pension means-test effectively taxes the super savings of middle-income workers at very high rates, while tax concessions provide windfall gains to the very rich.

The pension means-tests also undermine housing affordability, by creating exemptions for the family home. Middle-income workers are effectively paid by the government to *upgrade* their housing when they retire. A more systematic reform could change both sides of retirement income, eliminating tax concessions and universalising the pension. The combination would leave most older people better off, reduce inequality and improve work and housing incentives. The size of the concessions should allow changes to other benefits, reducing conditionality and improving adequacy for younger people too.

A separate set of reforms might be considered for housing concessions, especially those benefiting investors. Australia's asset economy model creates a political challenge, given a majority of households benefit from rising prices, and the macro-economy is increasingly tied to mortgage lending.

Rather than simply deflating house prices, unwinding concessions could allow governments to expand their role as creditor, underwriter and investor. And instead of tying those roles to stock market investments, as the Albanese government's social housing policy does, the state could explicitly link its housing policy to house prices. As concessions are withdrawn and tenant rights strengthened, the state could offer to buy out investors (and over indebted home owners). It might even shape a policy that allowed specific interventions to manage house price movements, simplifying the operation of monetary policy.

Converting the huge concessions of the dual welfare state has the potential to build a coalition across generational lines to counter the aspirational politics of the asset economy. The rise of the asset economy opens new strategies for resisting rising inequality, for example by withholding rents or opposing evictions (Bryan and Rafferty 2018). Campaigns for tenant rights and more secure working age income support have also gained growing energy. However, it is easier to connect both to electoral strategies than broader political mobilisation. Transforming the asset economy is likely to require broader coalitions that combine more radical support for secure income and tenure with a larger transformation of social reproduction, framed less around generations than care.

The Material Politics of Social Reproduction

The care labour involved in social reproduction has gained significantly more attention in recent decades. The rise of social movements critical of the white, breadwinner model at the core of Australia's older welfare state not only challenges traditional welfare state alliances, but also opens new opportunities to rethink economic debates over class, value and inequality. Through the service transition care labour has simultaneously become a significant source of income, employment and profit.

The values of care and the logic of care relationships confound traditional economic approaches, challenging economic orthodoxy. Proposals to centre and expand the 'care economy' also speak to ecological challenges and to post-colonial questions around caring for country. Those themes are increasingly brought together in political platforms and proposals, such as the Care Manifesto (Chatzidakis et al. 2020a) and calls to invest in 'soft' infrastructure, such as care services, within a Green New Deal. Here I focus on how the care economy potentially reshapes the politics of mobilisation within the welfare state.

The incorporation of social reproduction into the paid, formal economy has meant an expansion of the welfare state and made the politics and ethics of care public issues (Fine 2018). That shift provides new strategic opportunities for what Nancy Folbre (2006) calls a 'high-road' of quality, well-paid care employment. Folbre's strategy highlights an alternative politics, which is well suited to contesting liberalised welfare.

The workforce associated with the provision of social policy, in education, health and care services, is now both large and the fastest growing section of the workforce (see Figure 7.3), although marketisation means this is not synonymous with an expansion of public sector employment. These sectors are often the best organised industrially, and their workers are amongst the most trusted. Reflecting the gendered organisation of Australia's wage-earner model, the work of the welfare state remains feminised, informing distinct industrial and political strategies, in which education plays a key role. Not only have tertiary qualifications supported campaigns for pay and conditions, they also inform efforts to assert normative principles within social provision.

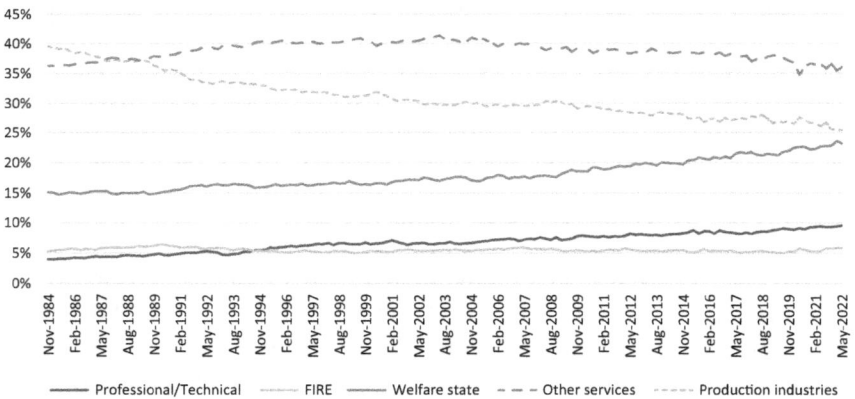

Figure 7.3 Workforce by selected industry groupings, Australia, 1984–2022. *Source*: Author calculations based on ABS, 6291.0.55.001 Labour Force, Australia, Detailed Table 04. Employed persons by Industry division of main job (ANZSIC) – Trend, Seasonally adjusted and Original.[1]

1 Categories in Figure 7.3 aggregate those used by the ABS. Professional and Technical remains as per ABS category. FIRE industries includes 'Financial and Insurance Services' and 'Rental, Hiring and Real Estate Services'. Welfare state industries includes 'Education and Training' and 'Health Care and Social Assistance'. Production industries includes 'Agriculture, Forestry and Fishing', 'Mining', 'Manufacturing', 'Electricity, Gas, Water and Waste Service' and 'Construction'. Other industries includes all remaining categories.

Within the welfare state, tertiary education is less the preserve of a high paid elite, creating the new class cleavage Piketty fears, and is instead a political strategy for asserting the value of and control over care labour by a mass care labour force. The section begins by focusing on care, work and education. I then analyse the potential for those working within welfare to mobilise politically. And finally, I reflect on opportunities to connect movements and 'economic technicians' to build new egalitarian social policy.

Work, Women and Education

Our imaginary for thinking about work and industrial contestation remains anchored in the twentieth century. The legacy of the wage-earner model built around white, male blue-collar workers continues to weigh upon the politics of today. However, as an important group of industrial relations scholars have shown, that image is increasingly misleading (see Hill et al. 2018). An alternative vision of work may now be emerging around the care economy (see PM&C 2023).

Not only have women moved on mass into the paid labour market, increasingly they are also the face of many of the best organised and most powerful campaigns. Unions, of course, were also 'central agents' advancing the male breadwinner model (Ellem and Cooper 2019, 100). However, women's efforts to challenge gendered inequalities have often worked through the same institutions. Rather than focusing on service work per se, it is the reorganisation of social reproduction within the paid economy that is changing the face of the workforce, and with it the face of unions and the role of education.

The service transition has significantly shifted the composition of employment towards the care economy (see Figure 7.3). Figure 7.3 traces changes in the proportion of workers employed in different industries. It combines a number of ABS categories to focus on how different types of work associated with industrial and care economies have changed. The categories include Production industries built around physical outputs, the work associated with the financial sector in FIRE industries, Professional and Technical employment associated with a high-wage knowledge economy, the paid work of social reproduction in Welfare State industries (both public and private) and finally Other Services, notably hospitality and retail.

The conventional story of deindustrialisation and a shift to service sector employment is clear. Automation of physical commodity production, alongside Australia's relative absence of industry policy, has seen a steady decline in production work associated with the commodity economy (manufacturing, agriculture, mining, energy and transport).

Growth within the service economy, however, is uneven. The FIRE industries – finance, insurance and real estate – that drive financialisation have been far more successful at producing profits than jobs (see Foster 2008). There has been significant growth in professional, scientific and technical jobs, which exemplify the imaginary of the Brahman left; however, these remain a relatively small segment of the total workforce.

The biggest increase in employment, particularly in the last decade, is in health and care. Combined with education, the core workforce of the welfare state now accounts for more than one in five jobs across the economy. Even before the pandemic, health and care jobs were growing more rapidly than any other section of the workforce. These sectors can be understood as the centre of paid social reproductive labour, and the core of both the welfare state workforce and a care economy. The rise in care labour dominates the 'service transition'. 'Other services', while always a significant employer, show little evidence of increasing further.

Changing patterns of employment have developed alongside a significant shift in the face of unionism. While the dominant trend across the workforce is a stark decline in density, the care economy has proved relatively resilient. As Ray Cooper has documented, women have been steadily rising as a proportion of all union members for several decades, and recently became a majority (Cooper 2012, Foley and Cooper 2021, 470).

Density for woman workers is not rising, rather the collapse of female union membership is far less steep. Male union density fell almost 70 per cent between 1992 and 2016, from 43 to 13 per cent, while female density fell by about half, from 35 to 16 per cent (Gilfillan and McGann 2018). Not only are there more women unionists than men, women workers are more likely to be unionists than their male counterparts. The union movement's national leadership increasingly reflects this transformation.

The relative resilience of unionism amongst women is potentially surprising given the structure of the labour market. Women are more likely to work part-time and casually, both groups with significantly lower union densities. Women's participation rates fall more dramatically with age than for men, and young people are also much less likely to join unions (Esders et al. 2011). Likewise, the relative rise in female versus male unionisation rates is not matched across all industries. Retail trade, for example, is both female dominated and less unionised than the broader workforce (ABS 2022b).

The relative resilience of women's unionisation is best explained through the rise and organisation of paid work in social reproduction. The correlation between the feminisation of work and union density is concentrated within the industries of the welfare state, reflecting the work of social reproduction and care. Despite marketisation, which often pushes jobs outside the public sector, employment associated with the welfare state is rising and represents one of the few sources of sustained industrial strength.

The industrial organisation of care work was not inevitable. Many of the strongest unions in these sectors have only become industrially active relatively recently. Through the rise of the wage-earners' welfare state, those working in health, education and care were rarely organised along industrial lines, reflecting the dominance of religious and professional cultures. It took sustained organising efforts to transform these industries (see Tierney and Cregan 2013).

Efforts to organise transformed cultures, work practices and identities and created some of the most important unions in the country. The Australian Nurses and Midwifery Federation gained more members than any other union since 2003, and is now the largest union in the country. The health and education unions now represent 40 per cent of all unionists (Gilfillan and McGann 2018).[1]

The shift is not unique to Australia, but it has been central to reshaping the politics of welfare, and as professional work has been unionised and massified, so it has reshaped the role of education. Even so, some of the most rapidly growing care sectors are dominated by precarious work and are poorly organised (Macdonald and Charlesworth 2021), reflecting not only the possibilities but also the contingency of organising efforts.

The organisation of professional care workers mirrors a shift in the nature and role of professionalisation. Social movements have often had an antagonistic relationship to professional 'care'. Second-wave feminism sought to democratise childcare against champions of professionally orientated preschool (Brennan 1998). The disability rights movement has critiqued an 'oppressive' history of professionally provided care (Williams 2001, 478). Likewise, the professionalisation of nursing was associated with the assertion of Victorian-era femininity that reinforced gender roles and mitigated against industrial organisation (see Lingel et al. 2022).

However, professional accreditation has increasingly been associated with industrial strategies. The massification of these professions, alongside efforts to democratise care provision, suggest professionalisation and the role of higher education contain alternative political potentials.

Nurses, teachers and care workers have all pursued professionalisation as an industrial strategy. University qualifications are now widely required

---

1 This calculation includes the Australian Nurses and Midwives Federation, Health Services Union, Independent Education Union, National Teachers Federation and National Tertiary Education Union.

in hospitals and schools. Qualifications are directly tied to pay levels and to campaigns for adequate staffing. Campaigns are built around notions of adequacy grounded in professional qualifications, such as the number of registered nurse in aged care (see NSWNMA nd) or tertiary qualified EEC workers (Cook et al. 2017).

Professionalisation not only facilitates claims to improve pay, as trade qualifications have traditionally done in blue-collar industries, it lays the basis for an assertion of worker control over the conditions of work. It is as professionals that teachers and nurses can make claims about the *quality* and nature of their work, and assert an ethic of care (see Williams 2001). Professional ethics are intrinsically normative. Through unions, the norms of care are linked to mass organisation and democratic claim making.

The professionalisation and massification of the welfare state workforce rarely features in discussions of education and politics. Instead, the expansion of tertiary education is usually framed as a product of the knowledge economy. During the peak of liberalisation, Third Way administrations in the Anglo world saw education as a means to help workers compete globally (Giddens 2013). By equipping their citizens with 'human capital', Australian workers could take the high-road of globalisation, gaining better paid jobs and avoiding the 'race to the bottom'.

Framing education as human capital connects education to cosmopolitan values through global competition. There is, of course, some truth to this. And despite efforts to expand educational opportunities, education remains an important site for reproducing class privilege across generations (Hancock et al. 2016).

When it is framed as a resource to win the competition of globalisation, education has a clear potential to fragment class solidarities, as Piketty identifies. However, this framing presents a misleading picture of the possibilities for a progressive welfare state politics. The expansion of higher education also reflects the expansion of an educated welfare state labour force grounded not in global markets, but in local communities.

The varied sources of growth amongst Australian students are obscured by the marketisation of universities themselves, which have made them far more reliant on fee-paying students. Walking around campuses or analysing aggregate enrolment and graduation data, it can be hard to see the rise of the welfare state within education. The biggest growth in university course enrolments has been within management and commerce, which now account for roughly a quarter of all enrolments.

These figures partly reflect the university as exporter. A similar proportion, just under a quarter, of domestic students are enrolled in health and education degrees. That proportion rises to half if society and culture degrees are included (DESE 2022, Table 2.9). Even amongst international students, care and education qualifications are much more likely to attract students plan-ning to permanently migrate (QILT 2022). If those planning to play similar roles in local communities outside Australia were included, the figure would rise further. That is, professional training within social reproduction is more tightly tied to community connection than global markets.

Work and education are changing as the work of social reproduction moves into the paid economy. This is not to suggest that other forms of work are politically unimportant, nor to deny education's potentially stratifying implications. Rather it is to identify a significant shift in the centre of gravity of contestation over welfare; to acknowledge workers within the welfare state as an increasingly significant mass workforce who are both relatively well organised and who have used education as a political strategy.

Care work is not intrinsically gendered. Rather the gendered patterns of 'feminised' care labour reflect the strongly gendered organisation of the ear-lier wage-earner model, while efforts to assert the value of care challenge that gender order. The strategies of organised care workers not only advance pay and conditions but also help to assert workers as experts and advance care as an ethic. Those strategies, however, are not grounded in structural shifts alone, but in campaigns, which despite a period of liberalisation, have proved surprisingly successful.

Political Campaigning and Coalition Building

The decline in traditional forms of mass politics coincides with a shift to issue-based campaigning. Hemmed in by legal restraints and low density, unions have also shifted to forms of political, rather than industrial, organising (Buchanan et al. 2014; Wilson and Spies-Butcher 2011). The recent history of successful campaigns to expand social protection, however, suggests potential models that combine elements of industrial and political organising.

Early education and care workers, teachers and nurses have each won important advances by building coalitions that combine political and indus-trial campaigns with issue-based politics. These campaigns reinforce efforts to revalue the labour of social reproduction alongside claims to expand high-quality and universal provision (Folbre 2006). The strategies build on the common interests of workers and citizens needing care, and assert the exper-tise of those directly connected to care provision, most obviously through professional accreditation of workers, but increasingly also through the acknowledgement and incorporation of lived expertise of those relying on, receiving and co-producing care.

The repertoire of traditional mass mobilisation suffered significant set-backs in the early 2000s. The largest mass mobilisation in history, against the second Iraq War, failed to stop the invasion or Australia's participation (Hil 2008). Rather than being punished at the ballot box, the Coalition triumphed at the subsequent election, gaining a Senate majority.

In response, progressive movements embraced issue-based, data-informed and communication focused strategies (Bowyer-Pont 2023). GetUp!, following the US organisation MoveOn, developed a mass email subscription model to respond quickly as issues arose, and to maintain contact with its mass audience (*Ibid*). The union movement's Your Rights at Work campaign drew on framing, TV advertising and marginal seat campaigning to oppose draconian new industrial relations laws, and support a change of government (Muir 2008). While union members were organised and mobilised on mass, the campaign carefully avoided industrial disruption, prioritising political strategies (Buchanan, Oliver and Briggs 2014).

The success of GetUp and YR@W reflect the shift away from the mass politics that built the welfare state towards a professionalisation of politics. However, similar campaigns within the welfare state have tended to combine elements of political and industrial organising. The strategies of early education and care workers to expand equitable funding discussed in Chapter 5 are mirrored in campaigns for nurse: patient ratios in hospitals and smaller class sizes in public schools.

Each of these campaigns combined political and industrial organising and built local grassroots campaign structures alongside broader state or national campaigns (see Tattersall 2013). Campaigners drew on the experience of workers to build their own evidence base. Campaigns mobilised around issues of access and quality where the interests of workers and those accessing services aligned. Parents wanted access to high-quality care, which in turn required an expansion of provision and an increase in quality assurance, training and pay for workers. Brennan (1998) has explored how unions played a key role bringing these groups together, while femocrats played a strategic role negotiating funding through government.

Amanda Tattersall (2013) has studied this kind of coalition building more broadly. Drawing on campaigns in the United States and Australia, her analysis highlights the social purpose of work and grassroots priorities. It is unsurprising her case studies – in education, health and minimum wages – overlap the core elements of the welfare state. The campaigns built coalitions by framing concerns around universal social needs, rather than primarily framing them as industrial issues. Framed as issues of needs and rights, the claims are implicitly political, requiring political action to set minimum standards even for those workers employed outside the public sector.

The model unions developed and Tattersall theorises is clearly well suited to contesting the welfare state. The NSW Teachers Federation, for example, linked smaller class sizes to better educational outcomes. The campaigns drew on the expertise of teachers and parents, facilitated by a union-funded research project, the Vinson Report (2002), to identify an issue that at once shaped work intensification, access and equity.

The strategies are not unique to the Anglosphere, although the relative lack of industrial strength in the United States has made community coalitions particularly important (Moody 1997). An even more successful politics emerged in Sweden in the 1980s. Winton Higgins, looking to Sweden to inform unions strategy in Australia, highlighted the role of the Municipal Workers' Union (Svenska Kommunalarbetare-forbundet or Kommunal) in resisting liberalisation of care services and advancing gender equity (1996). Kommunal, a large public sector union, drew on the insights of workers to develop industrial strategies and built coalitions between workers and services users to make claims (1996, 181).

Rather than reflecting a turn away from industrial organising, these campaigns might be better understood as adapting industrial organising to the context of the care economy. Many industrial campaigns typically targeted the production and sale of physical commodities. Strike action denies the realisation of profits, and campaigns often focused on key points in the production cycle around energy and transportation.

The welfare state is based on social services, which are inherently relational (see Folbre 2006) and which are more directly orientated to social needs and rights. Thus, they are better suited to coalition building between care providers and recipients, and to normative claims around universal access to quality provision. By contesting and prioritising the labour of the welfare state, these campaigns also tend to contest the gendered organisation of knowledge and value, elevating the expertise of those directly engaged in care provision.

The relational nature of social services creates three important advantages that adapt industrial strength to broader changes in politics. First, workers within the welfare state are trusted. Social research on attitudes to different occupations consistently rates nurses as one of the most trusted professions, with teachers and other welfare state workers also enjoying high trust (Roy Morgan 2021). The professional ethics associated with most work in social provision, alongside the care ethic that underpins provision, reinforce trust.

Their trusted position makes nurses, teachers and care workers ideal faces to tell political stories, which have become central to campaigning (Ganz 2010). Australian political campaigns are increasingly narrative based. Ariadne Vromen has detailed how a framework connecting people to issues via personal stories has become a central part of GetUp's tactics (Vromen and Coleman 2013; Vromen 2015), including stories of professional care workers advocating for policy reform (GetUp 2021). Similar tools have been used by the 'Voices' campaigns and the Climate 200 supported independents.

Unions are well placed to gather and organise stories, gaining media attention and helping communicate campaign messages. The personal experiences of workers are not only useful for informing centralised media messaging, they can also support grassroots strategies, where individual workers and those accessing services are able to directly share stories with others in their own communities.

Second, welfare service provision is decentralised. Unlike industrial production organised around ports, mines and factories, hospitals, schools and care facilities are located in every community. The geography of the welfare state significantly changes the politics of these campaigns. Industrial centres are traditional bastions of left party power. The organisation of mass party politics allowed local concerns and campaigns to influence left party politics.

The concentration of industrial communities came to be seen as a liability by a newly professionalised 'Third Way' politics, because it clustered progressive voters in safe seats, rather than suburban marginals (Pierson and Castles 2002). Labour's loss of electoral support in Northern England, and the potential loss of support in regions like the Hunter Valley, demonstrate the risks of ignoring these communities. However, the decentralisation of the care and education workforce brings strategic opportunities. Nurses and teachers live in every community, and it is unsurprising many successful progressive candidates in traditionally conservative areas work in social provision.

Finally, the welfare state reflects a set of concerns that are both electorally salient and favourable to progressive politics. Jobs, pay and conditions are, of course, also electorally salient. However, both the solutions to these concerns and the industrial tactics used to disrupt profitability are often framed through the lens of economic management. The rise of neoliberal politics is evidence of the challenges progressive politics faces contesting the 'economic', where conservatives consistently enjoy greater public support as economic managers, and progressives often respond to adopting and reaffirming fiscal limits. Alternatively, health, education and care all consistently rank as significant voter concerns, with progressive positions and parties generally favoured to expand the welfare state (see Budge 2015). Combined, this positions welfare state workers as key industrial and political actors, both in advancing the welfare state and in broader political contestation.

Institutions of Political Contest

Contentious politics advances through collective interests and institutions. However, articulating worker concerns into parliamentary politics and the party system is complex, particularly as partisan politics fragments. The relational nature of social provision positions workers as important political, as well as economic, agents. Unions played important roles in the successful campaigns Tattersall and Brennan identify, alongside collective institutions representing those accessing services, such as Parents and Citizens Associations. The historic role of unions in Australian politics, alongside their ability to generate significant ongoing income from their members, gives them a unique strategic role supporting coalition building and resourcing campaigns. Unions also have a strategic role connecting workers to the policy system, as institutionally privileged and well organised actors.

Liberalisation has wound back the power of arbitration. However, unions continue to occupy a strategic position within industrial relations, which has been important in contesting social provision. Feminists within the union movement have used the older wage-earner institutions to contest gendered pay, and increasingly, the gendered organisation of work. This not only includes access to care leave and non-discrimination, increasingly unions have contested gendered understandings of value.

Care unions have been at the centre of successful cases to advance equal pay by recognising the value of care labour. The 2010 test case brought by the Australian Services Union successfully established that the undervaluation of care labour is a key factor in the gender pay gap, and thus requires an institutional response (Cortis and Meagher 2012). Progress in the 2010s was slower than hoped but has recently been affirmed through both new legal changes and decisions to fund care worker pay increases under Labor. These legal strategies reinforce and complement political and industrial campaigns that seek to advance social provision by simultaneously improving service quality and worker recognition.

By contesting gendered pay and safe work, unions connect worker experience to technocratic modes of governance that enable claims to be advanced and entrenched. Equal pay cases relied on expertise from feminist economists working closely with workers to reveal the complexity and skill involved in care labour (*Ibid*). Professionalisation has advanced through processes of accreditation that codify those skills and assert professional ethics and standards in the provision of services. OH&S laws play a similar role in limiting managerial prerogatives and disciplining the organisation of work according to social principles.

While these strategies are not unique to welfare state work, because social provision so clearly involves normative principles of need and equity, it allows greater scope for these strategies. In Sweden Kommunal drew on worker experience to challenge managerial prerogative. Workers used their experience to develop alternative delivery and funding models, which often proved more efficient and effective than those developed by pro-market managements (Higgins 1996). Recent efforts by university staff to challenge university governance and assert the expertise of staff and students as the source of managerial direction reflect a similar logic (see Hil et al. 2022).

Where unions play a marginal role, less universal models of provision tend to emerge. In disability and aged care, for instance, consumer groups and financial consultants were at the forefront of reform efforts (Galbally 2016; COTA 2020). Consumer agency is particularly important in disability care, where the agency of people with disability has often been denied. The historic organisation of institutional care also creates challenges for developing solidarities across care relationships.

The disability rights movement has been effective at expanding resources; however, the politics of the NDIS has tended to entrench marketisation as a means to facilitate consumer choice (O'Keeffe and David 2022). By emphasising choice in the market, these models not only allow forms of dual welfare that subsidise private purchase, they also re-frame the relationship between provider and consumer, emphasising market contract. Building genuine solidarities around care is central to challenging more privatised models of care and growing austerity towards disability spending.

Finally, the reorganisation of party politics requires some rethinking of the relationship between work, welfare and parliament. The rise of the Greens on Labor's left flank, and most recently in the success of 'Teal' independents demonstrates a fragmentation of party politics. Professional women sit at the centre of the Teal wave, while younger women are increasingly central to the Greens base. The gendered and generational inequalities of the welfare state may offer an important common ground to advance new alliances. Reforms to expand access to paid care and de-gender work have strong support across these groupings.

Fragmentation also brings challenges. The Greens have consolidated their position as ideological champions of the welfare state, while Australia's electoral institutions position Labor as the only viable progressive party of government. Electoral institutions create incentives for both parties to compete as much as cooperate. Given these conflicting imperatives it is notable that the broader progressive landscape has become less partisan. Unlike its American counterpart MoveOn, for example, GetUp! is non-partisan (Bowyer-Pont 2023), while clearly progressive. Many welfare state unions also remain unaffiliated to Labor, and there is a significant overlap of Labor and Green support within some, particularly education, unions. The pluralisation of progressive politics reinforces the advantages of issue-based campaigns that can facilitate cooperation.

Beyond Liberalisation

Workers within the welfare state increasingly play a strategic role in advancing egalitarian social provision. This implies a shift in the politics of the welfare state, from a model of mass politics where organised labour outside the welfare state advances social policy as a strategy to insulate labour from market risk, to one where policy advances through the dynamics of social provision itself. Care as a social relation opens opportunities for broad coalitions that can navigate a more fragmented and issues-based politics. Professionalisation within the welfare state does not necessarily foster political elitism or fracture progressive constituencies. Instead, professionalisation can be a vehicle to challenge the gendered relations of social reproduction, to revalue care and to connect technical statecraft to the experiences and expertise of paid and unpaid workers and those accessing services.

Asserting the power of workers to determine the socially useful purpose of their labour has a long lineage not confined to the welfare state. In relatively recent times it was exemplified by blue-collar workers in the construction industry. The Builders Labours Federation mobilised a very similar logic to pursue the Green Bans (Burgmann and Burgmann 1998). Workers, Jack Mundey argued, should have a say over the nature and social purpose of their labour, over the cities they build and the communities they support (*Ibid*). When dock workers refused to supply pig iron to an imperialist Japan prior to the Second World War, or more recently, when Fire Fighters work for climate justice, they reflect a similar politics. The logic of alliance building, solidarity and asserting worker control over the purpose, not just the conditions, of production are not confined to the welfare state.

Likewise, the politics of care and the techniques of hybridity extend beyond the welfare state. Francis Flanagan (2019) has powerfully described a politics of care that embraces both social and ecological provision. Campaigns for 'justice reinvestment' advance a similar hybrid logic to social investment. By centring local control and community building, justice reinvestment potentially connects hybrid policy models to movements for self-determination. Rather than returning to an older conception of class or the Keynesian welfare state, it is useful to acknowledge how these varied 'boundary struggles' seek to make a different 'structural' challenge to liberalised economies.

The Covid-19 crisis created a brief window where the political dynamics I have discussed seemed more possible and the fiscal constraints that I have taken to define neoliberal politics appeared to crumble. Sadly, fiscal constraints have re-emerged. Even so, the brief priority afforded human health and enormous fiscal resources mobilised to manage interdependent social and financial risks suggests hope. The crisis revealed the very real dependence of 'economic' relations on human beings, care and communities (see Chatzidakis et al. 2020b). It is our interdepence, best expressed in the relations of care, that offers a politics to transcend liberalisation, challenging the financialisation of risk for profit by forging new hybrid solidarities.

REFERENCES

ACTU/TDC Mission to Western Europe. 1987. *Australia Reconstructed: ACTU/TDC Mission to Western Europe: A Report.* Australian Government Publishing Service.

Adereth, M. 2020. The postindustrial welfare state. Interview with Gosta Esping-Andersen, *Phenomenalworld.org,* May 14. https://phenomenalworld.org/interviews/gosta- esping-andersen.

Adkins, L., Cooper, M. and Konings, M. 2020. *The Asset Economy.* John Wiley & Sons.

Adkins, L., Bryant, G. and Konings, M. 2021. The asset economy during and after the Covid-19 crisis. *IPPR Progressive Review,* 28(3), pp. 242–252.

Altman, J. 2018. The Howard Government's northern territory intervention: Are neo-paternalism and indigenous development compatible? Keynote address, Australian Institute of Aboriginal and Torres Strait Islander Studies Conference. Available at: https://openresearch-repository.anu.edu.au/bitstream/1885/148959/1/Altman _AIATSIS_0%20(1).pdf.

Altman, J. and Hinkson, M. eds. 2007. *Coercive Reconciliation: Stabilise, Normalise, Exit Aboriginal Australia.* Melbourne: Arena Publications Association.

Altman, J. and Sanders, W. 2018. *From Exclusion to Dependence: Aborigines and the Welfare State in Australia.* Canberra, ACT: Centre for Aboriginal Economic Policy Research (CAEPR), The Australian National University.

Ando, A. and Modigliani, F. 1963. The life cycle hypothesis of saving. *American Economic Review,* 53(1), pp. 55–74.

Antipoverty Centre (APC). n.d. Social policy on out terms. Available at: https:// antipovertycentre.org/about/ (Accessed 9 August 2022).

Apps, P. and Rees, R. 2010. Australian family tax reform and the targeting fallacy. *Australian Economic Review,* 43(2), pp. 153–175.

Auerbach, A.J., Gokhale, J. and Kotlikoff, L.J. 1994. Generational accounting: A meaningful way to evaluate fiscal policy. *Journal of Economic Perspectives,* 8(1), pp. 73–94.

Austen, S., Sharp, R. and Hodgson, H. 2015. Gender impact analysis and the taxation of retirement savings in Australia. *Australian Tax Forum,* 30(4), pp. 763–781.

Australian Bureau of Statistics (ABS). 2011. Australian social trends, December 2011. Available at: https://www.abs.gov.au/AUSSTATS/abs@.nsf/Lookup/4102.0Main +Features30Dec+2011.

Australian Bureau of Statistics (ABS). 2022a. Labour force, Australia: Table 04. Employed persons by Industry division of main job (ANZSIC) – Trend, Seasonally adjusted, and Original. Available at: https://www.abs.gov.au/statistics/labour/employment-and -unemployment/labour-force-australia-detailed/latest-release#industry-occupation -and-sector.

Australian Bureau of Statistics (ABS). 2022b. Trade union membership, August. Available at: https://www.abs.gov.au/statistics/labour/earnings-and-working-conditions/trade-union-membership/latest-release#industry.

Australian Electoral Commission (AEC). 2022. First preferences by party, 2022 Federal Election. Available at: https://results.aec.gov.au/27966/Website/HouseStateFirstPrefsByParty-27966-NAT.htm.

Australian Government. 2008. Budget measures, budget paper No.2 2008-09.

Australian Labor Party (ALP). 1988. Report of the working party on child care to the Caucus Committee on welfare and community services, Canberra.

Australian Labor Party (ALP). 2022a. Helping more Australians into home ownership. ALP website. Available at: https://www.alp.org.au/policies/helping-more-australians-into-home-ownership.

Australian Labor Party (ALP). 2022b. Justice reinvestment: Turning the tide on incarceration and deaths in custody. ALP website. Available at: https://www.alp.org.au/policies/justice-reinvestment.

Australian Politics and Elections Archive (APEA). 1856–2018. University of Western Australia. Available at: https://elections.uwa.edu.au/.

Australian Super. 2022. The gender super gap: How gender inequality affects superannuation. June 24. Available at: https://www.australiansuper.com/superannuation/superannuation-articles/2020/02/gender-equality-and-your-super.

Baird, M., Hamilton, M. and Constantin, A. 2021. Gender equality and paid parental leave in Australia: A decade of giant leaps or baby steps?. *Journal of Industrial Relations*, 63(4), pp. 546–567.

Baird, M. and Whitehouse, G. 2012. Paid parental leave: First birthday policy review. *Australian Bulletin of Labour*, 38(3), pp. 184–198.

Baker, T. and Evans, J. 2016. 'Housing First' and the changing terrains of homeless governance. *Geography Compass*, 10(1), pp. 25–41.

Baker, T., Evans, J. and Hennigan, B. 2020. Investable poverty: Social investment states and the geographies of poverty management. *Progress in Human Geography*, 44(3), pp. 534–554. https://doi.org/10.1177/0309132519849288.

Baldwin, P. 1990. *The Politics of Social Solidarity: Class Bases of the European Welfare State, 1875–1975*. Cambridge: Cambridge University Press.

Banks, G. 2003. Australia's economic 'miracle'. Productivity Commission, speech. Available at: https://www.pc.gov.au/news-media/speeches/cs20030801/cs20030801.pdf.

Barber, W.J. 1996. *Designs within Disorder: Franklin D. Roosevelt, the Economists, and the Shaping of American Economic Policy, 1933–1945*. Cambridge: Cambridge University Press.

Barr, N. 2001. *The Welfare State as Piggy Bank: Information, Risk, Uncertainty, and the Role of the State*. Oxford: Oxford University Press. https://doi.org/10.1093/0199246599.001.0001, accessed 24 May 2023.

Barr, N. 2016. Milton Friedman and the finance of higher education. In Robert A. Cord, and J. Daniel Hammond (eds.), *Milton Friedman: Contributions to Economics and Public Policy*. New York, pp. 436–463. https://doi.org/10.1093/acprof:oso/9780198704324.003.0024, accessed 26 May 2023.

Barton, A. 2005. Professional accounting standards and the public sector—A mismatch. *Abacus*, 41(2), pp. 138–158. https://doi.org/10.1111/j.1467-6281.2005.00173.x.

Barton, A. 2007. Accrual accounting and budgeting systems issues in Australian governments. *Australian Accounting Review*, 17(41), pp. 38–50. https://doi.org/10.1111/j.1835-2561.2007.tb00452.x.

Bean, C. 1997. Parties and elections. In B. Galligan, I. McAllister and J. Ravenhill (eds.), *New Developments in Australian Politics*. Melbourne: Macmillan.

Bean, C. 2000, July. The Australian economic 'miracle': A view from the north. In *The Australian Economy in the 1990s, Proceedings of a Conference* (pp. 73–114). Sydney: Reserve Bank of Australia.

Cameron, S., McAllister, I., Jackman, S. and Sheppard, J. 2022. *The 2022 Australian federal election: Results from the Australian Election Study*. Canberra: ANU Press.

Becker, G.S. 1964. *Human Capital: A Theoretical and Empirical Analysis, with Special Reference to Education*. New York: National Bureau of Economic Research.

Beer, G. 2003. Work incentives under a new tax system: The distribution of effective marginal tax rates in 2002. *Economic Record*, 79(Special Issue), pp. S14–S25.

Beggs, M. 2015. *Inflation and the Making of Australian Macroeconomic Policy, 1945–85*. Springer.

Beilharz, P. 1994. *Transforming Labor: Labor Tradition and the Labor Decade in Australia*. Melbourne: Cambridge University Press.

Beilharz, P. and Cox, L. 2007. Review essay: Settler capitalism revisited. *Thesis Eleven*, 88(1), pp. 112–124.

Bessant, J. 1992. 'Good women and good nurses': Conflicting identities in the Victorian nurses strikes, 1985/86. *Labour History*, (63), pp. 155–173.

Bhattacharya, T. 2017. *Social Reproduction Theory: Remapping Class, Recentering Oppression*. Pluto Press.

Biggs, A. 2011. Legislation to means test the private health insurance rebate re-introduced—debate continues. *Flagpost*, Parliament of Australia. Available at: https://www.aph.gov.au/About_Parliament/Parliamentary_Departments/Parliamentary_Library/FlagPost/2011/July/Legislation_to_means_test_the_private_health_insurance_rebate_re-introduceddebate_continues.

Bitler, M., Hoynes, H. and Kuka, E. 2017. Do in-work tax credits serve as a safety net?. *Journal of Human Resources*, 52(2), pp. 319–350.

Block, F. 2008. Polanyi's double movement and the reconstruction of critical theory. *Revue interventions économiques. Papers in political economy*, (38). http://journals.openedition.org/interventionseconomiques/274

Block, F. 2019. Problems with the concept of capitalism in the social sciences. *Economy and Space* A, 51(5), pp. 1166–1177.

Borowski, A. 2013. Risky by design: The mandatory private pillar of Australia's retirement income system. *Social Policy & Administration*, 47(6), pp. 749–764.

Bowyer-Pont, P. 2023. *GetUp! Understanding Australia's Largest Internet-mediated Political Campaigning and Advocacy Organisation*. Doctoral Thesis. Macquarie University, Australia.

Boxall, A.M. and Gillespie, J. 2013. *Making Medicare: The Politics of Universal Health Care in Australia*. Sydney: UNSW Press.

Braithwaite, J. 1999. Accountability and governance under the new regulatory state. *Australian Journal of Public Administration*, 58(1), pp. 90–94.

Bramble, T. and Kuhn, R. 2010. *Labor's Conflict: Big Business, Workers and the Politics of Class*. Melbourne: Cambridge University Press.

Brennan, D. 1998. *The Politics of Australian Child Care: Philanthropy to Feminism and Beyond*. Cambridge: Cambridge University Press.

Brennan, D. 2007. The ABC of child care politics. *Australian Journal of Social Issues*, 42(2), pp. 213–225.

Brennan, D. 2009a. Australia: The difficult birth of paid maternity leave. In Kammerman and Moss (eds.), *The Politics of Parental Leave Policies: Children, Parenting, Gender and the Labour Market* (pp. 15–32). Policy Press.

Brennan, D. 2009b. Child care and Australian social policy. In J. Bowes & R. Grace (eds.), *Children, Families & Communities: Contexts and Consequences* (pp. 205–218). Melbourne: Oxford University Press.

Brennan, D., Cass, B., Himmelweit, S. and Szebehely, M. 2012. The marketisation of care: Rationales and consequences in Nordic and liberal care regimes. *Journal of European Social Policy*, 22(4), pp. 377–391.

Brennan, D. and Mahon, R. 2011. State structures and the politics of child care. *Politics & Gender*, 7(2), pp. 286–293.

Brenton, S. 2016. *The Politics of Budgetary Surplus*. London: Springer.

Brett, J. 2004. Comment: The country and the city. *Australian Journal of Political Science*, 39(1), pp. 27–29.

Briggs, C. and Buchanan, J. 2000. Australian labour market deregulation: A critical assessment, Research Paper No. 21 1999–2000, Australian Parliamentary Information and Research Service, Canberra.

Brittle, S.A. 2009. *Fiscal Policy and Private Saving in Australia: Ricardian Equivalence, Twin Deficits and Broader Policy Inferences*. PhD thesis, University of Wollongong.

Broomhill, R., Costa, M., Austen, S. and Sharp, R. 2021. What went wrong with super?: Financialisation and Australia's retirement income system. *Journal of Australian Political Economy*, (87), pp. 71–94.

Bryan, D. and Rafferty, M. 2014. Financial derivatives as social policy beyond crisis. *Sociology*, 48(5), pp. 887–903.

Bryan, D. and Rafferty, M. 2018. *Risking Together: How Finance is Dominating Everyday Life in Australia*. Sydney: Sydney University Press.

Bryant, G. 2022. Who should pay for university? Eight logics of higher education funding in Australia. In J. Horne and M. Thomas (eds.), *Australian Universities: A Conversation about Public Good*. Sydney: Sydney University Press.

Bryant, G. and Spies-Butcher, B. 2020. Bringing finance inside the state: How income-contingent loans blur the boundaries between debt and tax. *Environment and Planning A*, 52(1), pp. 111–129.

Bryant, G. and Spies-Butcher, B. 2024. From marketisation to self-determination: Contesting state and market through 'justice reinvestment'. *Environment and Planning A*. https://doi.org/10.1177/0308518X221125797.

Bryant, G., Spies-Butcher, B. and Stebbing, A. 2024. Comparing asset- based welfare capitalism: Wealth inequality, housing finance and household risk. *Housing Studies*, pp. 1–22. https://doi.org/10.1080/02673037.2022.2056150.

Bryson, L. and Verity, F. 2009. Australia: From wage-earners to neo-liberal welfare state. In P. Alcock and G. Craig (eds.), *International Social Policy: Welfare Regimes in the Developed World*. Basingstoke: Palgrave Macmillan.

Buchanan, J., Oliver, D. and Briggs, C. 2014. Solidarity reconstructed: The impact of the Accord on relations within the Australian union movement. *Journal of Industrial Relations*, 56(2), pp. 288–307.

Budge, I. 2015. Issue emphases, saliency theory and issue ownership: A historical and conceptual analysis. *West European Politics*, 38(4), pp. 761–777.

Bueskens, P. 2019. Gillard's dilemma. The sexual contract and maternal citizenship: The case of Australian single mothers. In C. Pascoe Leahy and P. Bueskens (eds.), *Australian Mothering*. Cham: Palgrave Macmillan.

Burgmann, M. and Burgmann, V. 1998. *Green Bans, Red Union: Environmental Activism and the New South Wales Builders Labourers' Federation*. UNSW Press.

Butler, J.R. 2002. Policy change and private health insurance: Did the cheapest policy do the trick?. *Australian Health Review*, 25(6), pp. 33–41.

Cahill, D. 2004. *The Radical Neo-liberal Movement as a Hegemonic Force in Australia, 1976–1996*. Doctoral thesis, University of Wollongong.

Cahill, D. 2010. 'Actually existing neoliberalism' and the global economic crisis. *Labour & Industry: A Journal of the Social and Economic Relations of Work*, 20(3), pp. 298–316.

Cahill, D. 2014. *The End of Laissez-Faire?: On the Durability of Embedded Neoliberalism*. Cheltenham: Edward Elgar.

Cahill, D. and Beder, S. 2005. Neo-liberal think tanks and neo-liberal restructuring: Learning the lessons from Project Victoria and the privatisation of Victoria's electricity industry. *Social Alternatives*, 24(1), pp. 43–48.

Cahill, D. and Konings, M. 2017. *Neoliberalism*. Cambridge: Polity Press.

Cameron, S. and McAllister, I. 2019. *Trends in Australian Political Opinion, 1987–2019*. Canberra: ANU. https://australianelectionstudy.org/.

Carey, G., Braunack-Mayer, A. and Barraket, J. 2009. Spaces of care in the third sector: Understanding the effects of professionalization. *Health*, 13(6), pp. 629–646. https://doi.org/10.1177/1363459308341866.

Carey, G., Dickinson, H., Malbon, E. and Reeders, D. 2018. The vexed question of market stewardship in the public sector: Examining equity and the social contract through the Australian National Disability Insurance Scheme. *Social Policy & Administration*, 52(1), pp. 387–407.

Carling, R. 2016. The case against levying CGT on the family home. *The Australian*, January 11.

Carson, A., Martin, A.J. and Ratcliff, S. 2020. Negative campaigning, issue salience and vote choice: Assessing the effects of the Australian Labor party's 2016 "Mediscare" campaign. *Journal of Elections, Public Opinion and Parties*, 30(1), pp. 83–104.

Casey, S. 2020. Mutual obligation after COVID-19: The work for the dole time bomb. Per Capita Discussion Paper.

Cass, B. 1986. Income support for families with children (Issue Paper No 1, Department of Social Security).

Cass, B. 1990. Reforming family income support; Reforming labour markets: Pursuing social justice in Australia in the 1980s. In Manning and Ugers (eds.), *Social Policy Review 1989–90* (pp. 187–213). Melbourne: Longman.

Cass, B. and Brennan, D. 2002. Communities of support or communities of surveillance and enforcement in welfare reform debates. *Australian Journal of Social Issues*, 37(3), pp. 247–262.

Cass, B. and Brennan, D. 2003. Taxing women: The politics of gender in the tax/transfer system. *eJournal of Tax Research*, 1, pp. 37–63.

Cass, B. and Freeland, J. 1994. Social security and full employment in Australia: The rise and fall of the Keynesian welfare state and the search for a Post-Keynesian consensus. In J. Hills, et al. (eds.), *Beveridge and Social Security*. Oxford: Clarendon Press.

Castles, F. 1985. *The Working Class and Welfare: Reflections on the Political Development of Welfare State in Australia and New Zealand, 1890–1980*. Sydney: Allen and Unwin.

Castles, F. 1989. Social protection by other means: Australia's strategy of coping with external vulnerability. In F.G. Castles (ed.), *The Comparative History of Public Policy Cambridge* (pp. 73–77). Polity Press.

Castles, F. 1994. The wage earners' welfare state revisited: Refurbishing the established model of Australian social protection, 1983–93. *Australian Journal of Social Issues*, 29(2), pp. 120–145.

Castles, F. 1997a. The institutional design of the Australian Welfare State. *International Social Security Review*, 50(2), pp. 25–34.

Castles, F.G. 1997b. Leaving the Australian labor force: An extended encounter with the state. *Governance*, 10(2), pp. 97–121.

Castles, F. 1998. The really big trade-off: Homeownership and the welfare state in the new world and old. *Acta Politica*, 33(1), pp. 5–19.

Castles, F.G. 2001. A farewell to the Australian welfare state. *Eureka Street*, 11(1), pp. 29–31.

Castles, F.G. 2004. *The Future of the Welfare State: Crisis Myths and Crisis Realities*. Cambridge: Cambridge University Press.

Castles, F.G. and Mitchell, D. 1990. *Three Worlds of Welfare Capitalism or Four?* Discussion paper 21, Canberra: Graduate Program in Public Policy, Australian National University.

Causa, O. and Hermansen, M. 2017. Income redistribution through taxes and transfers across OECD countries, OECD Economics Department Working Paper No. 1453.

Chalmers, J. 2022. Economic challenges, opportunities and wellbeing on both sides of the Tasman. Address to the Australia New Zealand Leadership Forum, Sydney. July 8. Available at: https://ministers.treasury.gov.au/ministers/jim-chalmers-2022/speeches/address-australia-new-zealand-leadership-forum-sydney.

Chapman, B. 2014. Income contingent loans: Background. In B. Chapman, T. Higgins and J.E. Stiglitz (eds.), *Income Contingent Loans: Theory, Practice, Prospects* (pp. 12–28). Basingstoke: Palgrave Macmillan.

Chapman, B., Higgins, T. and Stiglitz, J., eds. 2014. *Income Contingent Loans: Theory, Practice, Prospects*. Basingstoke: Palgrave Macmillan.

Chapman, B. and Pope, D. 1992. Government, human capital formation and higher education. *Australian Quarterly*, 64(3), pp. 275–292.

Chatzidakis, A., Hakim, J., Litter, J. and Rottenberg, C. 2020a. *The Care Manifesto: The Politics of Interdependence*. London: Verso Books.

Chatzidakis, A., Hakim, J., Littler, J., Rottenberg, C. and Segal, L. 2020b. From carewashing to radical care: The discursive explosions of care during Covid-19. *Feminist Media Studies*, 20(6), pp. 889–895.

Christophers, B. 2021. A tale of two inequalities: Housing-wealth inequality and tenure inequality. *Environment and Planning A: Economy and Space*, 53(3), pp. 573–594.

Clifton, S., Fortune, N., Llewellyn, G., Stancliffe, R.J. and Williamson, P. 2020. Lived expertise and the development of a framework for tracking the social determinants, health, and wellbeing of Australians with disability. *Scandinavian Journal of Disability Research*, 22(1). pp. 137–146.

Coates, N. and Vidler, S. 2004. Superannuation policy: Commentary on an interview with Paul Keating, former Prime Minister. *Journal of Australian Political Economy*, (53), pp. 9–16.

Colombo, F. and N. Tapay (2003), Private health insurance in Australia: A case study. OECD Health Working Papers, No. 8, OECD Publishing, Paris, https://doi.org/10.1787/478608584171.

Collyer, F. and White, K. 2001. Corporate control of Healthcare in Australia. Discussion paper no.42, The Australia Institute, Canberra.

Considine, M., Lewis, J.M. and O'Sullivan, S. 2011. Quasi-markets and service delivery flexibility following a decade of employment assistance reform in Australia. *Journal of Social Policy*, 40(4), pp. 811–833.

Cook, K., Corr, L. and Breitkreuz, R. 2017. The framing of Australian childcare policy problems and their solutions. *Critical Social Policy*, 37(1), pp. 42–63.

Cooper, R. 2012. The gender gap in union leadership in Australia: A qualitative study. *Journal of Industrial Relations*, 54(2), pp. 131–146.

Corr, L. and Carey, G. 2017. Investigating the institutional norms and values of the productivity commission: The 2011 and 2015 childcare inquiries. *Australian Journal of Public Administration*, 76(2), pp. 147–159.

Cortis, N. and Meagher, G. 2009. Women, work and welfare in the activation state: An agenda for Australian research. *Australian Bulletin of Labour*, 35(4), pp. 629–651.

Cortis, N. and Meagher, G. 2012. Recognition at last: Care work and the equal remuneration case. *Journal of Industrial Relations*, 54(3), pp. 377–385.

Council on the Aged (COTA). 2020. Submission to the royal commission into aged care quality and safety, aged care program redesign: Services for the future. Available at: https://www.cota.org.au/information/resources/submission/cota-response-to-royal -commission-program-redesign-consultation-paper/.

Crozier, M., Huntington, S.P. and Watanuki, J. 1975. *The Crisis of Democracy*. Report on the governability of democracies to the Trilateral Commission. New York: New York University Press.

Curtin, J. and Higgins, W. 1998. Feminism and unionism in Sweden. *Politics & Society*, 26(1), pp. 69–93.

Daley, J. and Woods, D. 2014. The wealth of generations. Grattan Institute, Melbourne.

Daley, J., Coates, B. and Wood, D. 2015. Super tax targeting. Grattan Institute, Melbourne.

Davidson, P. and Bradbury, B. 2022. The wealth inequality pandemic: COVID and wealth inequality ACOSS/UNSW Sydney Poverty and Inequality Partnership, Build Back Fairer Series Report No. 4, Sydney.

Davies, A. 2020. Party hardly: Why Australia's big political parties are struggling to compete with grassroots campaigns. *Guardian*, December 13.

De Vaus, D. and McAllister, I. 1989. The changing politics of women: Gender and political alignment in 11 nations. *European Journal of Political Research*, 17, pp. 241–262.

Deeble, J. 1982. Financing health care in a static economy. *Social Science & Medicine*, 16(6), pp. 713–724.

Deeming, C. 2014. Social democracy and social policy in neoliberal times. *Journal of Sociology*, 50(4), pp. 577–600.

Deeming, C. and Smyth, P. 2015. Social investment after neoliberalism: Policy paradigms and political platforms. *Journal of Social Policy*, 44(2), pp. 297–318.

Department of Education, Skills and Employment (DESE). 2022. Higher education statistics 2020, all students. Available at: https://www.dese.gov.au/higher-education -statistics/resources/2020-section-2-all-students.

Dowrick, S. and Nguyen, D.T. 1988. A re-assessment of Australian Economic Growth in the light of the convergence hypothesis. *Australian Economic Papers*, 27(51), pp. 196–212.

Dunleavy, P. and Hood, C. 1994. From old public administration to new public management. *Public Money & Management*, 14(3), pp. 9–16.

Eardley, T., Saunders, P. and Evans, C. 2000. *Community Attitudes Towards Unemployment, Activity Testing and Mutual Obligation.* Sydney: Social Policy Research Centre, University of NSW.

Economic Planning Advisory Council [EPAC]. 1986. Tax expenditures in Australia. Council. Paper No. 13, Commonwealth of Australia, Canberra.

Economic Planning Advisory Council (EPAC). 1994. Australia's ageing society. Background Paper 37, Commonwealth of Australia, Canberra.

Eisenstein, H. 1992. *Gender Shock: How Australian Feminists Make the System Work and What American Women Can Learn from Them.* Boston: Beacon Press.

Ellem, B. and Cooper, R. 2019. What have they ever done for us?: Unions in Australia. In R. Lansbury, A. Johnson, D. van den Broek (eds.), *Contemporary Issues in Work and Organisations* (pp. 95–109). London: Routledge.

Elliot, A. 2006. 'The best friend Medicare ever had'? Policy narratives and changes in Coalition health policy. *Health Sociology Review,* 15(2), pp. 132–143.

Ellwood, S. and Newberry, S. 2007. Public sector accrual accounting: Institutionalising neo-liberal principles? *Accounting, Auditing & Accountability Journal,* 20(4), pp. 549–573. https://doi.org/10.1108/09513570710762584.

England, P., Budig, M. and Folbre, N. 2002. Wages of virtue: The relative pay of care work. *Social Problems,* 49(4), pp. 455–473.

Esders, L., Bailey, J. and McDonald, P. 2011. Declining youth membership: The views of union officials. In Price, McDonald and Pini (eds.), *Young People and Work* (pp. 281–300). London: Routledge.

Esping-Andersen, G. 1990. *The Three Worlds of Welfare Capitalism.* Padstow: Polity Press.

Esping-Andersen, G. 1999. *Social Foundations of Postindustrial Economies.* Oxford: OUP.

Esping-Andersen, G. 2002. A child-centred social investment strategy. In G. Esping-Andersen, D. Gallie, A. Hemerijck and J. Myles (eds.), *Why We Need a New Welfare State* (pp. 26–68). Oxford: Oxford University Press.

Esping-Andersen, G. 2015. Welfare regimes and social stratification. *Journal of European Social Policy,* 25(1), pp. 124–134.

Evans, M. 2010. Some big donors refuse to give, others unable to. *Sydney Morning Herald,* February 3.

Fabian, M. and Breunig, R. eds. 2018. *Hybrid Public Policy Innovations: Contemporary Policy Beyond Ideology.* London: Routledge.

Favel, J., McKee, M., Tesfay, F., Musolino, C., Freeman, T., van Eyk, H. and Baum, F. 2022. Explaining health inequalities in Australia: The contribution of income, wealth and employment. *Australian Journal of Primary Health.* Available at: https://www.publish.csiro.au/PY/justaccepted/PY21285.

Fenna, A. 2010. The Return of Keynesianism in Australia: The Rudd government and the lessons of recessions past. *Australian Journal of Political Science,* 45(3), pp. 353–369.

Fenna, A. 2012. Putting the 'Australian settlement' in perspective. *Labour History,* 102(1), pp. 99–119.

Fenna, A. and t Hart, P. 2019. The 53 billion dollar question: Was Australia's 2009–10 fiscal stimulus a good thing? In J. Luetjens, M. Mintrom and P. t Hart (eds.), *Successful Public Policy: Lessons from Australia and New Zealand.* ANU Press.

Fenna, A. and Tapper, A. 2012. The Australian welfare state and the neoliberalism thesis. *Australian Journal of Political Science,* 47(2), pp. 155–172.

Ferguson, P. 2016. The politics of productivity growth in Australia. *Australian Journal of Political Science,* 51(1), pp. 17–33.

Fernandez, R., Adriaans, I., Klinge, T.J. and Hendrikse, R. 2020. *The Financialisation of Big Tech*. SOMO (Stichting Onderzoek Multinationale Ondernemingen).

Fine, M.D. 2018. *A Caring Society? Care and the Dilemmas of Human Services in the 21st Century*. Bloomsbury Publishing.

Fine, M. and Davidson, B. 2018. The marketization of care: Global challenges and national responses in Australia. *Current Sociology*, 66(4), pp. 503–516.

Flanagan, F. 2019. Climate change and the new work order. *Inside Story*, February 28. https://insidestory.org.au/climate-change-and-the-new-work-order/.

Folbre, N. 2006. Demanding quality: Worker/consumer coalitions and "high road" strategies in the care sector. *Politics & Society*, 34(1), pp. 11–32.

Folbre, N. 2008. Reforming care. *Politics & Society*, 36(3), pp. 373–387.

Foley, M. and Cooper, R. 2021. Workplace gender equality in the post-pandemic era: Where to next?. *Journal of Industrial Relations*, 63(4), pp. 463–476.

Forrest, R. and Hirayama, Y. 2015. The financialisation of the social project: Embedded liberalism, neoliberalism and home ownership. *Urban Studies*, 52(2), pp. 233–244.

Foster, C. 1988. Towards a national retirement incomes policy. Social Security Review Issues Paper 6, Department of Social Security, Canberra.

Foster, G. and Frijters, P. 2022. Hiding the elephant: The tragedy of COVID policy and its economist apologists, IZA DP No. 15294, IZA Institute of Labour Economics.

Foster, J.B. 2008. The financialization of capital and the crisis. *Monthly Review*, 59(11) pp. 1–15.

Foucault, M. 2008 [1978/9]. *The Birth of Biopolitics*, Lectures at the College de France, M. Senellart (ed.), trans. G. Burchell. New York: Martin's Press.

Fraser, N. 1995. From redistribution to recognition? Dilemmas of justice in a "postsocialist" age. *New Left Review*, 212, pp. 68–93.

Fraser, N. and Jaeggi, R. 2018. *Capitalism: A Conversation in Critical Theory*. Cambridge: Polity Press.

Friedman, M. 1962. The alleviation of poverty. In *Capitalism and Freedom*. Chicago: University of Chicago Press.

Fukuyama, F. 1989. The end of history? *The National Interest*, (16), pp. 3–18. https://www.jstor.org/stable/24027184

Galbally, R. 2016. The genesis of the NDIS: Bringing competing agendas together. Sambell Oration, Brotherhood of St Laurence, Melbourne.

Gallagher, P., Rothman, G. and Brown, C. 1993. Saving for retirement: The benefits of superannuation for the individual and the nation. RIM: Taskforce, Conference Paper – 9312.

Ganz, M. 2010. Leading change: Leadership, organization, and social movements. In Nohria and Khurana (eds.), *Handbook of Leadership Theory and Practice* (pp. 527–568). Brighton: Harvard Business Press.

Gardner, H. 2008. Population health, the health system and policy. In Barraclough and Gardner (eds.), *Analysing Health Policy a Problem-oriented Approach* (pp. 41–54). Sydney: Elsevier.

Garnaut, R. 2005. Breaking the Australian great complacency of the early twenty first century. Paper presented at the 2005 Economic and Social Outlook Conference, Melbourne Institute and The Australian, 31 March.

Garnaut, R. 2008. The climate change review. Australian Government Printing Service, Canberra.

Garnaut, R. 2011. *The Garnaut Review 2011: Australia in the Global Response to Climate Change*. Melbourne: Cambridge University Press.

Garritzmann, J.L., Häusermann, S. and Palier, B. eds. 2022. *The World Politics of Social Investment: Volume I: Welfare States in the Knowledge Economy.* Oxford: Oxford University Press.

Gatens, M., Braithwaite, V. and Mitchell, D. 2002. If mutual obligation is the answer, what is the question? *Australian Journal of Social Issues,* 37(3), pp. 225–245.

Gee, E.M. 2002. Misconceptions and misapprehensions about population ageing. *International Journal of Epidemiology,* 31(4), pp. 750–753.

GetUp. 2021. Aged care royal commission explained by a registered nurse. GetUp website. Available at: https://www.getup.org.au/campaigns/aged-care/explainer -video/aged-care-royal-commission-explained-by-a-registered-nurse.

Giddens, A. 2013. *The Third Way: The Renewal of Social Democracy.* New Jersey: John Wiley & Sons.

Gilfillan, G. and McGann, C. 2018. Trends in union membership in Australia, Parliamentary Library Research Paper Series, October. Available at: https://apo.org .au/sites/default/files/resource-files/2018-10/apo-nid197221.pdf.

Gillespie, J. 1991. *The Price of Health: Australian Governments and Medical Politics 1910–1960.* Melbourne: Cambridge University Press.

Gillespie, J. 1988. Medical markets and Australian medical politics, 1920–45. *Labour History,* (54), pp. 30–46.

Gilmore, R.W. 2007. *Golden Gulag: Prisons, Surplus, Crisis, and Opposition in Globalizing California.* Berkley: University of California Press.

Gilmour, T. 2018. *Champions of Change: Shelter NSW, Community Activism and Transforming NSW's Housing System.* Sydney: Shelter NSW.

Gingrich, J. 2011. *Making Markets in the Welfare State: The Politics of Varying Market Reforms.* Cambridge: Cambridge University Press.

Goot, M. and Watson, I. 2007. Explaining Howard's success: Social structure, issue agendas and party support, 1993–2004. *Australian Journal of Political Science,* 42(2), pp. 253–276.

Gordon, L. 1988. What does welfare regulate? *Social Research,* 55(4), pp. 609–630.

Grattan, M. 2022. For new government, consensus is the word. *Sydney Morning Herald,* July 8.

Gray, G. 1991. *Federalism and Health Policy: The Development of Health Systems in Canada and Australia.* Toronto: University of Toronto Press.

Gregory, R. 1995. The peculiar tasks of public management: Toward conceptual discrimination. *Australian Journal of Public Administration,* 54(2), pp. 171–183.

Gregory, R. 2012. Living standards, terms of trade and foreign ownership: Reflections on the Australian mining boom. *Australian Journal of Agricultural and Resource Economics,* 56(2), pp. 171–200.

Grout, P. 1983. Education finance and imperfections in information. *Economic and Social Review,* 15(1), pp. 25–33.

Gruen, F.H. 1986. How bad is Australia's economic performance and why? *Economic Record,* 62(2), pp. 180–193.

Grundoff, M. 2021. Unemployment payments and work incentives: An international comparison. Australia Institute, Canberra.

Grundoff, M. and Littleton, E. 2021. Rich men and tax concessions: How certain tax concession are widening the gender and wealth divide. Australian Institute, Canberra.

Guthrie, J. 1998. Application of accrual accounting in the Australian Public Sector – Rhetoric or reality. *Financial Accountability & Management,* 14(1), pp. 1–19.

Gutman, G.M. 2010. Population ageing and apocalyptic demography: Separating fact from fiction. In L.B. Knudsen and A.L. Olsen (eds.), *Our Demographic Future – A Challenge: On the Need for Demographic Analyses* (pp. 11–36). Scandinavian Population Studies 14. Denmark: Aalborg Oest.

Hacker, J.S. 2019. *The Great Risk Shift: The New Economic Insecurity and the Decline of the American Dream* (Second Edition). Oxford: Oxford University Press.

Hamberg, K. 2008. Gender bias in medicine. *Women's Health*, 4(3), pp. 237–243.

Hancock, K., Mitrou, F., Povey, J., Campbell, A. and Zubrick, S.R. 2016. Three-generation education patterns among grandparents, parents and grandchildren: Evidence of grandparent effects from Australia. Lifecourse Centre, University of Queensland. Available at: https://core.ac.uk/download/pdf/43393114.pdf.

Harding, A. and Polette, J., 1995. The price of means-tested transfers: Effective marginal tax rates in Australia in 1994. *Australian Economic Review*, 28(3), pp. 100–106.

Harvey, D. 2007. *A Brief History of Neoliberalism*. Oxford: Oxford University Press.

Harvie, D., Lightfoot, G., Lilley, S. and Weir, K. 2021. Social investment innovation and the 'social turn' of neoliberal finance. *Critical Perspectives on Accounting*, 79. SI: Accounting and Social Impact (Part I), pp. 102248. https://doi.org/10.1016/j.cpa .2020.102248.

Hayek, F.A. 1949. The intellectuals and socialism. *The University of Chicago Law Review*, 16(3), pp. 417–433.

Hemerijck, A. 2015. The quiet paradigm revolution of social investment. *Social Politics: International Studies in Gender, State & Society*, 22(2), pp. 242–256.

Henderson, R. 1975. Poverty in Australia: First main report, April 1975, commission of inquiry into poverty. Canberra: Australian Government Publishing Service, Volumes One and Two and the Outline Report.

Hickel, J., Sullivan, D. and Zoomkawala, H. 2021. Plunder in the post-colonial era: Quantifying drain from the global south through unequal exchange, 1960–2018. *New Political Economy*, 26(6), pp. 1030–1047.

Higgins, W. 1996. The Swedish municipal workers' union a study in the new political unionism. *Economic and Industrial Democracy*, 17(2), pp. 167–197.

Hil, R. 2008. Civil society, public protest and the invasion of Iraq. *Social Alternatives*, 27(1), pp. 29–33.

Hil, R., Pelizzon, A. and Baum, F. 2022. It's time: The re-form of Australian public universities. *Social Alternatives*, 21(1), pp. 3–7.

Hill, E. 2007. Budgeting for work-life balance: The ideology and politics of work and family policy in Australia. *Australian Bulletin of Labour*, 33(2), pp. 226–245.

Hill, E., Cooper, R., Baird, M., Vromen, A. and Probyn, E. 2018. Australian Women's working futures: Are we ready? AWWF Project 2017, University of Sydney.

Hilmer, F. 1993. National competition policy: Report. Australian Government Publishing Service, Canberra.

Hocking, J. 2012. *Gough Whitlam: His Time*. Melbourne: Melbourne University Press.

Hodgson, H. 2011, January. Unscrambling the egg: Reform pathways in the tax transfer system. *Australian Tax Forum*, 26(2), pp. 257–286.

Howard, C. 1999. *The Hidden Welfare State: Tax Expenditures and Social Policy in the United States* (Vol. 171). Princeton: Princeton University Press.

Howe, A. and Healy, J. 2005. Generational justice in aged care policy in Australia and the United Kingdom. *Australasian Journal on Ageing*, 24, pp. S12–S18.

Howe, A. and Spies-Butcher, B. 2022. Integrating the retirement income system and aged care funding in Australia: An aged care Levy as a social insurance option. *Australian Journal of Social Issues*, 57(2), pp. 388–407.

Hudson, R.B. 2014. Contemporary challenges to aging policy. In R.B. Hudson (ed.), *The New Politics of Old Age Policy*. Third edition. Baltimore: Johns Hopkins University.

Humphrys, E. 2018. How labour built neoliberalism: Australia's accord, the labour movement and the neoliberal project. In *How Labour Built Neoliberalism*. Leiden: Brill.

Inglehart, R. 1977. *The Silent Revolution*. Princeton: Princeton University Press.

Inglehart, R. 1990. *Culture Shift in Advanced Industrial Society*. Princeton: Princeton University Press.

Iversen, T. and Wren, A. 1998. Equality, employment, and budgetary restraint: The trilemma of the service economy. *World Politics*, 50(4), pp. 507–546.

Jacques, O. and Noël, A. 2018. The case for welfare state universalism, or the lasting relevance of the paradox of redistribution. *Journal of European Social Policy*, 28(1), pp. 70–85.

Jefferis, C. and Stilwell, F. 2006. Private finance for public infrastructure: The case of Macquarie Bank. *Journal of Australian Political Economy*, (58), pp. 44–61.

Jessop, B. 2015. Neoliberalism, finance-dominated accumulation and enduring austerity: A cultural political economy perspective. In K. Farnsworth and Z. Irving (eds.), *Social Policy in Times of Austerity: Global Economic Crisis and the New Politics of Welfare* (pp. 87–112). Bristol: Bristol University Press.

Jessop, B. 2018. Neoliberalism and workfare: Schumpeterian or Ricardian? In D. Cahill, M. Cooper, M. Konings and D. Primrose (eds.), *The Sage Handbook of Neoliberalism* (pp. 347–358). New York, NY: Sage.

Kadi, J., Vollmer, L. and Stein, S. 2021. Post-neoliberal housing policy? Disentangling recent reforms in New York, Berlin and Vienna. *European Urban and Regional Studies*, 28(4), pp. 353–374.

Kasper, W. 1980. *Australia at the Crossroads: Our Choices to the Year 2000*. Sydney: Harcourt Brace Jovanovich.

Katic, P. and Leigh, A. 2016. Top wealth shares in Australia 1915–2012. *Review of Income and Wealth*, 62(2), pp. 209–222.

Katz, R. and Mair, P. 1995. Changing models of party organization and party democracy: The emergence of the cartel party. *Party Politics*, 1(1), pp. 5–28.Keating, M. 2004. *Who Rules? How Government Retains Control of a Privatised Economy*. Sydney: Federation Press.

Kehoe, J. 2021. NSW Generations Fund needs explanation. *Australian Financial Review*, August 9.

Kelly, P. 2008 [1994]. *The End of Certainty: Power, Politics and Business in Australia*. Sydney: Allen & Unwin.

Kemeny, J. 1977. A political sociology of home ownership in Australia. *Journal of Sociology*, 13(1), pp. 47–52.

Kenny, P. 2005. Australia's capital gains tax discount: More certain, equitable and durable. *Journal of the Australasian Tax Teachers Association*, 1(2), p. 38.

Kingfisher, C. and Goldsmith, M. 2001. Reforming women in the United States and Aotearoa/New Zealand: A comparative ethnography of welfare reform in global context. *American Anthropologist*, 103(3), pp. 714–732.

Kingston, G. and Thorp, S. 2019. Superannuation in Australia: A survey of the literature. *Economic Record*, 95(308), pp. 141–160.

Kirchheimer, O. 1966. The transformation of Western European party systems. In J. La Palombara and M. Weiner (eds.), *Political Parties and Political Development* (pp. 177–200). New Jersey: Princeton University Press.

Kitschelt, H. 1994. *The Transformation of European Social Democracy.* Cambridge: Cambridge University Press.

Klapdor, M. 2014a. Pension indexation: A brief history. Parliamentary Library. Available at: https://www.aph.gov.au/About_Parliament/Parliamentary_Departments/Parliamentary_Library/FlagPost/2014/April/Pension-indexation.

Klapdor, M. 2014b. Changes to support for pensioners and retirees. Parliamentary Library. Available at: https://www.aph.gov.au/about_parliament/parliamentary_departments/parliamentary_library/pubs/rp/budgetreview201415/pensioners.

Klapdor, M. 2022. Social security and family assistance. Parliamentary Library Briefing Book. Available at: https://www.aph.gov.au/About_Parliament/Parliamentary_Departments/Parliamentary_Library/pubs/BriefingBook47p/SocialSecurityFamilyAssistance.

Klein, E. 2021. Unpaid care, welfare conditionality and expropriation. *Gender, Work and Organisation,* 28(4), pp. 1475–1489.

Klein, E. 2023. Towards a reparative welfare state. *New Political Economy,* 28(1), pp. 126–141.

Knotz, C. 2018. A rising workfare state? Unemployment benefit conditionality in 21 OECD countries, 1980–2012. *Journal of International and Comparative Social Policy,* 34(2), pp. 91–108.

Korpi, W. 1989. Power, politics, and state autonomy in the development of social citizenship. *American Sociological Review,* 54, pp. 309–328.

Korpi, W. 2006. Power resources and employer-centered approaches in explanations of welfare states and varieties of capitalism: Protagonists, consenters, and antagonists. *World Politics,* 58(2), pp. 167–206.

Korpi, W. and Palme, J. 1998. The paradox of redistribution and strategies of equality: Welfare state institutions, inequality, and poverty in the Western countries. *American Sociological Review,* pp. 661–687.

Kotlikoff, L. 1992. *Generational Accounting: Knowing Who Pays, and When, for What We Spend.* New York: The Free Press.

KPMG. 2018. *Maranguka Justice Reinvestment Project: Impact Assessment.* Sydney: KPMG.

Krippner, G.R. 2001. The elusive market: Embeddedness and the paradigm of economic sociology. *Theory and Society,* 30(6), pp. 775–810.

La Cava, G. 2019. The labour and capital shares of income in Australia. Reserve Bank of Australia Bulletin.

Lakoff, G. 2014. *The All New Don't Think of an Elephant!: Know Your Values and Frame the Debate.* Vermont: Chelsea Green Publishing.

Lane, W. 2009 [1892]. *The Workingman's Paradise.* Sydney: Sydney University Press.

Latham, M. 1998. Economic policy and the third way. *Australian Economic Review,* 31(4), pp. 384–398.

Lawson, J., Troy, L. and van den Nouwelant, R., 2022. Social housing as infrastructure and the role of mission driven financing. *Housing Studies,* pp. 1–21.

Le Grand, J. 1997. Knights, knaves or pawns? Human behaviour and social policy. *Journal of Social Policy,* 26(2), pp. 149–169.

Le Grand, J. 1991. Quasi-markets and social policy. *The Economic Journal,* 101(408), pp. 1256–1267.

Leeder, S. 1999. *Healthy Medicine: Challenges Facing Australia's Health Services.* Sydney: Allen & Unwin.

Leigh, A. 2006. How do unionists vote? Estimating the causal impact of union membership on voting behaviour from 1966 to 2004. *Australian Journal of Political Science,* 41(4), pp. 537–552.

Lemoine, B. 2017. Measuring and restructuring the state. In D. King and P. Le Gales (eds.), *Reconfiguring European States in Crisis* (pp. 313–330). Oxford: Oxford University Press.

Libich, J. 2015. *Real-World Economic Policy: Insights from Leading Australian Economists.* Southbank: Cengage Learning Australia.

Lilley, S., Harvie, D., Lightfoot, G. and Weir, K. 2020. Using derivative logic to speculate on the future of the social investment market. *Journal of Urban Affairs,* 42(6), pp. 920–936. https://doi.org/10.1080/07352166.2019.1584529.

Lindsay, G. and Norton, A. 1996. The CIS at twenty: Greg Lindsay talks to Andrew Norton. *Policy,* 12(2), pp. 16–21.

Lingel, J., Clark-Parsons, R. and Branciforte, K. 2022. More than handmaids: Nursing, labor activism and feminism. *Gender, Work & Organization,* 29, pp. 1149–1163.

Lipset, S.M. 1981 [1959]. *Political Man: The Social Bases of Politics.* Johns Hopkins University Press.

Macdonald, F. and Charlesworth, S. 2021. Regulating for gender-equitable decent work in social and community services: Bringing the state back in. *Journal of Industrial Relations,* 63(4), pp. 477–500.

Macintyre, C. 1999. From entitlement to obligation in the Australian welfare state. *Australian Journal of Social Issues,* 34(2), pp. 103–118.

Macintyre, S. 2015. *Australia's Boldest Experiment: War and Reconstruction in the 1940s.* Sydney: NewSouth.

Macintyre, S. 2018. Owners and tenants: The commonwealth housing commission and post-war housing, 1943–1949. *Australian Economic History Review,* 58(3), pp. 265–282.

Macintyre, S. 2022. *The Party: The Communist Party of Australia from Heyday to Reckoning.* Sydney: Allen and Unwin.

Maher, S. 2020. Welfare Quarantining in Australia, 2007–2020: A review of the grey literature. Income Management Project, University of Canberra Law School.

Mahony, J.W. 1978. Decisions affecting industrial relations in 1977. *Journal of Industrial Relations,* 20(1), pp. 72–76.

Mair, P. 2023. *Ruling the Void: The Hollowing of Western Democracy.* London: Verso Books.

Manow, P. 2009. Electoral rules, class coalitions and welfare state regimes, or how to explain Esping-Andersen with Stein Rokkan. *Socio-Economic Review,* 7(1), pp. 101–121.

Manwaring, R. 2016. From new labour to Rudd/Gillard–transferring social policy. *Policy Studies,* 37(5), pp. 426–439.

Marginson, S. 1993. *Education and Public Policy in Australia.* Melbourne: Cambridge University Press.

Marginson, S. and Considine, M. 2000. *The Enterprise University: Power, Governance and Reinvention in Australia.* Cambridge: Cambridge University Press.

Markey, R., Rafferty, M., Thornwaite, L., Wright, S. and Angus, C. 2014. The success of representative governance on superannuation boards. A report of the Center for Workplace Futures for The McKell Institute. Sydney, NSW: Centre for Workplace Futures, Macquarie University.

Marmot, M. 2005. Social determinants of health inequalities. *The Lancet*, 365(9464), pp. 1099–1104.

Marriott, L. 2009. The politics of superannuation in Australasia: Saving the New Zealand standard of living. *Australian Journal of Political Science*, 44(3), pp. 477–495.

Marsh, I. 1994. The development and impact of Australia's "think tanks". *Australian Journal of Management*, 19(2), pp. 177–200.

Martinez-Alier, J. 2008. Languages of valuation. *Economic and Political Weekly*, 43(48), pp. 28–32.

Martin, G. and Roberts, S. 2021. Exploring legacies of the baby boomers in the twenty-first century. *The Sociological Review*, 69(4), pp. 727–742.

Mattei, C.E. 2022. *The Capital Order: How Economists Invented Austerity and Paved the Way to Fascism*. Chicago: University of Chicago Press.

McAllister, I. and Makkai, T. 2019. The decline and rise of class voting? From occupation to culture in Australia. *Journal of Sociology*, 55(3), pp. 426–445.

McAuley, I. 2005. Private health insurance: Still muddling through. *Agenda*, 12(2), pp. 159–178.

McCombie, J. 1999. Productivity slowdown. In O'Hara (ed.), *Encyclopedia of Political Economy, L-Z* (pp. 921–924). New York: Routledge.

McDonald, C. and Marston, G. 2005. Workfare as welfare: Governing unemployment in the advanced liberal state. *Critical Social Policy*, 25(3), pp. 374–401.

McKenna, B. 2000. Labour responses to globalization: The Australian experience by Bernard McKenna. *Asia Pacific Business Review*, 7(1), pp. 71–104.

McKenzie, M. 2018. The erosion of minimum wage policy in Australia and labour's shrinking share of total income. *Journal of Australian Political Economy*, (81), pp. 52–77.

McQueen, H. 1983. Higgins and arbitration. In E.L. Wheelwright and Ken Buckley (eds.), *Essays in the Political Economy of Australian Capitalism* (pp. 145–163). Sydney: Australia and New Zealand Book Company, Vol. 5.

Meagher, G. and Goodwin, S. eds. 2015. *Markets, Rights and Power in Australian Social Policy*. Sydney: Sydney University Press.

Meagher, G., Perche, D. and Stebbing, A., 2022. *Designing Social Service Markets: Risk, Regulation and Rent-Seeking*. Canberra: ANU Press.

Melleuish, G. 2004. From the "social laboratory" to the "Australian Settlement". In P. Boreham, G. Stokes and R. Hall (eds.), *The Politics of Australian Society*. Sydney: Pearson.

Mendelson, D. 1999. Devaluation of a constitutional guarantee: The history of section 51(xxiiiA) of the commonwealth constitution. *Melbourne University Law Review*, 23, pp. 308–344.

Mendes, P. 2009. Retrenching or renovating the Australian welfare state: The paradox of the Howard government's neo-liberalism. *International Journal of Social Welfare*, 18(1), pp. 102–110.

Mendes, P. 2019. Top-down paternalism versus bottom-up community development: A case study of compulsory income management programmes in Australia. *The International Journal of Community and Social Development*, 1(1), pp. 42–57.

Mendes, P. 2021. Conditionalising the unemployed: Why have consecutive Australian governments refused to increase the inadequate Newstart Allowance?. *Australian Journal of Social Issues*, 56(1), pp. 42–53.

Miller, P. and Hayward, D. 2017. Social policy 'generosity' at a time of fiscal austerity: The strange case of Australia's National Disability Insurance Scheme. *Critical Social Policy*, 37(1), pp. 128–147.

Mirowski, P. and Plehwe, D. eds. 2015. *The Road from Mont Pèlerin: The Making of the Neoliberal thought Collective, with a New Preface.* Cambridge, MA: Harvard University Press.

Mitchell, D. 1998. Life-course and labour market transitions: Alternatives to breadwinner welfare. In M. Gatens, A. Mackinnon and G. Brennan (eds.), *Gender and Institutions: Welfare, Work and Citizenship.* Cambridge University Press.

Moffitt, R.A. 2003. The negative income tax and the evolution of US welfare policy. *Journal of Economic Perspectives*, 17(3), pp. 119–140.

Montanari, I. 2000. From family wage to marriage subsidy and child benefits: Controversy and consensus in the development of family support. *Journal of European Social Policy*, 10(4), pp. 307–333.

Moody, K. 1987. Reagan, the business agenda and the collapse of labour. *Socialist Register*, 23, pp. 153–176.

Moody, K. 1997. *Workers in a Lean World: Unions in the International Economy.* London: Verso.

Moran, M. 2002. Understanding the regulatory state. *British Journal of Political Science*, 32(2), pp. 391–413.

Morel, N., Touzet, C. and Zemmour, M. 2016. Fiscal welfare and welfare state reform: A research agenda. Sciences Po LIEPP Working Paper [Online]. Available at: https://core.ac.uk/download/pdf/35303565.pdf (Accessed 28 February 2020).

Morel, N., Touzet, C. and Zemmour, M. 2019. From the hidden welfare state to the hidden part of welfare state reform: Analyzing the uses and effects of fiscal welfare in France. *Social Policy & Administration*, 53(1), pp. 34–48.

Mudge, S. 2018. *Leftism Reinvented: Western Parties from Socialism to Neoliberalism.* Cambridge, MA: Harvard University Press.

Muir, K. 2008. *Worth Fighting For: Inside the Your Rights at Work Campaign.* Sydney: UNSW Press.

Navarro, V. 2020. The political economy of the welfare state in developed capitalist countries. In Navarro (ed.), *The Political Economy of Social Inequalities* (pp. 121–169). Routledge.

Neuwelt-Kearns, C. and John, S.S. 2020. *Family Tax Credits: Do Children Get the Support in New Zealand that They Would Get in Australia?.* Auckland: Child Poverty Action Group Incorporated.

New South Wales (NSW) Government. 2022. $20 million boost for Aboriginal Justice initiatives. Media Release. Available at: https://www.nsw.gov.au/enterprise-investment-trade/media-releases/20-million-boost-for-aboriginal-justice-initiatives.

New South Wales Nurses and Midwives Association (NSWNMA). Insist on registered nurses 24/7 in aged care! Available at: https://www.nswnma.asn.au/insist-on-a-registered-nurse-247-in-aged-care/.

Newberry, S. and Brennan, D. 2013. The marketisation of early childhood education and care (ECEC) in Australia: A structured response. *Financial Accountability & Management*, 29(3), pp. 227–245.

Nielson, L. 2010. *Chronology of Superannuation and Retirement Income in Australia.* Department of Parliamentary Services.

Norton, A. 2006. The rise of big government conservatism. *Policy*, 22(4), pp. 15–22.

Norton, A. 2014. *Doubtful Debt: The Rising Cost of Student Loans.* Melbourne: Grattan Institute.

Norton, A. and Cherastidtham, I. 2016. *Help for the Future: Fairer Repayment of Student Debt.* Melbourne: Grattan Institute.

O'Brien, G. 2019. 27 years and counting since Australia's last recession. Canberra: Australian Parliamentary Library Briefing Book, Parliamentary Library Research Publications.

O'Connor, J. 2017 [1973]. *The Fiscal Crisis of the State*. New York: Routledge.

O'Connor, J., Orloff, A. and Shaver, S. 1999. *States, Markets, Families: Gender, Liberalism and Social Policy in Australia, Canada, Great Britain and the United States*. Melbourne: Cambridge University Press.

OECD. 1992. *Historical Statistics 1960–1992*. Paris: OECD.

OECD. 2020. *Social Expenditure Update*. Available at: http://www.oecd.org/social/expenditure.htm (Accessed 22 July 2021).

OECD. 2021. Health spending (indicator). https://doi.org/10.1787/8643de7e-en (Accessed 11 June 2021).

OECD. 2022a. Family benefits public spending (indicator). https://doi.org/10.1787/8e8b3273-en (Accessed 15 July 2022).

OECD. 2022b. Pension spending (indicator). https://doi.org/10.1787/a041f4ef-en (Accessed 15 July 2022).

OECD. 2022c. Social expenditure – Aggregated data. SOCX Database, OECD. Available at: https://stats.oecd.org/Index.aspx?datasetcode=SOCX_AGG.

Offe, C. 2018. *Contradictions of the Welfare State*. New York: Routledge.

O'Keeffe, P. and David, C. 2022. Discursive constructions of consumer choice, performance measurement and the marketisation of disability services and aged care in Australia. *Australian Journal of Social Issues*, 57(4), pp. 938–955.

Ong, R., Pawson, H., Singh, R. and Martin, C. 2020. Demand-side assistance in Australia's rental housing market: Exploring reform options. Final report No. 342, AHURI.

Orloff, A. 1996. Gender in the welfare state. *Annual Review of Sociology*, 22, pp. 51–78.

Osborne, D. and Gaebler, T. 1991. *Reinventing Government*. Reading, MA: Addison/Wesley.

Paisley, F. 2014. An echo of black slavery: Emancipation, forced labour and Australia in 1933. *Australian Historical Studies*, 45(1), pp. 103–125.

Pakulski, J. and Waters, M. 1996. *The Death of Class*. London: Sage.

Palangkaraya, A. and Yong, J. 2005. Effects of recent carrot-and-stick policy initiatives on private health insurance coverage in Australia. *Economic Record*, 81(254), pp. 262–272.

Parham, D. 2002. Microeconomic reforms and the revival in Australia's growth in productivity and living standards. Paper presented to the Conference of Economists, Adelaide, 1 October 2002, Available at: https://www.pc.gov.au/research/supporting/living-standards/mrrag.pdf.

Parham, D. 2004. Sources of Australia's productivity revival. *Economic Record*, 80(249), p. 239.

Parkinson, M. 2021. *A Decade of Drift*. Melbourne: Monash University Publishing.

Parliamentary Budget Office. 2016. Higher education loan programme: Impact on the budget, Report No. 02/2016. Canberra: Commonwealth of Australia.

Pattugalan, K. and Ellis, D. 2010. Australia's marginal tax rates, tax offsets and the Medicare levy. *Economic Round-up*, (4), pp. 1–15.

Peck, J. 2001. *Workfare States*. New York, NY: Guilford Publications.

Peck, J. 2010. Zombie neoliberalism and the ambidextrous state. *Theoretical Criminology*, 14(1), pp. 104–110.

Peck, J. 2012. Economic geography: Island life. *Dialogues in Human Geography*, 2(2), pp. 113–133.

Peck, J., Brenner, N. and Theodore, N. 2018. Actually existing neoliberalism. In *The Sage Handbook of Neoliberalism* (pp. 3–15). London: Sage.

Peck, J. and Theodore, N. 2015. *Fast Policy: Experimental Statecraft at the Thresholds of Neoliberalism*. Minneapolis: University of Minnesota Press.

Peck, J. and Tickell, A. 2002. Neoliberalizing space. *Antipode*, 34(3), pp. 380–404.

Pfeffer, F.T. and Waitkus, N. 2021. The wealth inequality of nations. *American Sociological Review*, 86, pp. 567–602.

Phillips, P.J. 2011. Will self-managed superannuation fund investors survive?. *Australian Economic Review*, 44(1), pp. 51–63.

Pierson, P. 1998. Irresistible forces, immovable objects: Post-industrial welfare states confront permanent austerity. *Journal of European Public Policy*, 5(4), pp. 539–560.

Pierson, P. 2001. Post-industrial pressures on the mature welfare states. In *The New Politics of the Welfare State* (pp. 80–105). Oxford: Oxford University Press.

Pierson, C. 2003. Learning from labor? Welfare policy transfer between Australia and Britain. *Commonwealth & Comparative Politics*, 41(1), pp. 77–100.

Pierson, C. and Castles, F. 2002. Australian antecedents of the third way. *Political Studies*, 50(4), pp. 683–702.

Piketty, T. 2014. *Capital in the Twenty First Century*, trans. A. Goldhammer. Cambridge: Belknap Press.

Piketty, T. 2018. Brahmin left vs merchant right: Rising inequality and the changing structure of political conflict. *WID*. World Working Paper, 7.

Piketty, T. 2020. *Capital and Ideology*. Harvard University Press.

Pocock, B. 2005. Work/care regimes: Institutions, culture and behaviour and the Australian case. *Gender, Work & Organization*, 12(1), pp. 32–49.

Polanyi, K. 1957. The economy as instituted process. In K. Polanyi, C. Arensberg and H. Pearson (eds.), *Trade and Market in the Early Empires: Economies in History and Theory* (pp. 243–269). New York: Free Press.

Polanyi, K. 2001 [1944]. *The Great Transformation: The Political and Economic Origins of Our Times*. Boston: Beacon Press.

Press, F. and Woodrow, C. 2018. Marketisation, elite education and internationalisation in Australian early childhood education and care. In *Elite Education and Internationalisation* (pp. 139–159). Cham: Palgrave Macmillan.

Prime Minister and Cabinet (PM&C) 2023. Draft National Care and Support Economy Strategy 2023. Care and Support Economy Taskforce. Canberra, Australian Government. Available at: https://www.pmc.gov.au/resources/draft-national -strategy-care-and-support-economy

Productivity Commission. 2011. *Disability Care and Support, Overview*. Canberra: Commonwealth Government.

Productivity Commission. 2015. Childcare and early childhood learning productivity commission inquiry report: Overview and recommendations. No 73.

Productivity Commission. 2016. Increasing Australia's future prosperity, discussion paper, November.

Productivity Commission. 2018a. Horizontal fiscal equalisation-draft report, No.88, May.

Productivity Commission. 2018b. Rising inequality: A stocktake of the evidence. Commission Research Paper, Canberra.

Prosser, B. and Leeper, G. 1994. Housing affordability and changes to rent assistance. *Social Security Journal*, June, pp. 40–62.

Psacharopoulos, G. 1994. Returns on investment in education: A global update. *World Development*, 22(9), pp. 1325–1343.

Pusey, M. 1991. *Economic Rationalism in Canberra: A Nation Building State Changes Its Mind.* Cambridge, MA: Cambridge University Press.

Pusey, M. 1993. Reclaiming the middle ground … From new right "economic rationalism". In S. King and P. Lloyd (eds.), *Economic Rationalism: Dead End of Way Forward?* (pp. 12–27). Sydney: Allen & Unwin.

Pusey, M. 2002. *Jurgen Habermas.* Melbourne: Routledge.

Pusey, M. 2003. *The Experience of Middle Australia: The Dark Side of Economic Reform.* Melbourne: Cambridge University Press.

Putnam, R.D. 2000. *Bowling Alone: The Collapse and Revival of American Community.* New York: Simon and Schuster.

Quality Indicators for Learning and Teaching (QILT). 2022. Student experience survey 2021. Tables and figures. International student reasons for choosing to study in Australia (%importance rating, 2021) among undergraduates from all provider types by 21 study areas. Available at: https://www.qilt.edu.au/docs/default-source/default-document-library/2021-ses-report-tables.zip?sfvrsn=55a50ad6_0.

Quiggin, J. 1998. Social democracy and market reform in Australia and New Zealand. *Oxford Review of Economic Policy*, 14(1), pp. 76–95.

Quiggin, J. 2003. The welfare effects of income-contingent financing for higher education. Working Papers in Economics and Econometrics, No. 428, Australian National University.

Quiggin, J. 2006. Stories about productivity. *Australian Bulletin of Labour*, 32(1), pp. 18–26.

Quiggin, J. 2007. The risk society: Social democracy in an uncertain world. Centre for Policy Development. Occasional Paper No.2.

Quiggin, J. 2011. *The Lost Golden Age of Productivity Growth?* (No. 151526). University of Queensland, School of Economics.

Quiggin, J. 2012. The Queensland commission of audit interim report-June 2012: A critical review. *Public Policy*, 7(2), pp. 125–140.

Ramia, G. 2020. *Governing Social Protection in the Long Term: Social Policy and Employment Relations in Australia and New Zealand.* Springer Nature.

Ranald, P. 1995. National competition policy. *Journal of Australian Political Economy*, (36), pp. 1–25.

Ratcliff, S., Sheppard, J. and Pietsch, J. 2020. Voter behaviour. In A. Gauja, M. Sawer, M. Simms (eds.), *Morrison's Miracle: The 2019 Federal Election* (pp. 253–274).Canberra: ANU Press.

Ravlic, T. 2022. Election 2022: Equal pay an objective for labor. *The Mandarin*, May 2. Available at: https://www.themandarin.com.au/187923-election-2022-equal-pay-an-objective-for-labor/.

Rawls, J. 2001. *Justice as Fairness: A Restatement.* Cambridge, MA: Belknap Press.

Rees, S. 1994. Economic rationalism: An ideology of exclusion. *Australian Journal of Social Issues*, 29(2), pp. 171–185.

Reserve Bank of Australia (RBA). 2022. Supporting the economy and financial system in response to COVID-19. RBA website. Available at: https://www.rba.gov.au/covid-19/ (Accessed 13 July).

Reynolds, F., Large, J., Petersen, M., Clark, A., Walsh, K., Fielder, J., Crimmins, F., Tually, S., Sutherland, G., Barbosa, S.K. and Georgopoulos, D. 2018. Retiring into poverty: A national plan for change: Increasing housing security for older women. National Older Women's Housing and Homelessness Working Group.

Riboldi, M. and Hopkins, S. 2019. Community-led justice reinvestment: Rethinking access to justice. *Precedent*, (154), p. 48.

Rollings, N. 1988. British Budgetary Policy 1945–1954: A "Keynesian revolution"? *The Economic History Review*, 41(2), pp. 283–298. https://doi.org/10.2307/2596059.

Ronald, R. 2008. *The Ideology of Homeownership: Homeowner Societies and the Role of Housing.* Basingstoke: Palgrave.

Roy Morgan. 2021. Image of professions survey 2021. Available at: http://www.roymorgan .com/findings/8691-image-of-professions-2021-april-2021-202104260655.

Rush, E. 2006. *Child Care Quality in Australia.* Canberra: Australia Institute.

Ryan, E. 1984. *Two-thirds of a Man: Women & Arbitration in New South Wales, 1902–08.* Sydney, NSW: Hale & Iremonger.

Sano, J. and Williamson, J.B. 2008. Factors affecting union decline in 18 OECD countries and their implications for labor movement reform. *International Journal of Comparative Sociology*, 49(6), pp. 479–500.

Saunders, C. 1994. The Australian experience with constitutional review. *The Australian Quarterly*, 66(3), pp. 49–66.

Saunders, P. 1995. Improving work incentives in a means-tested welfare system: The 1994 Australian social security reforms. *Fiscal Studies*, 16(2), pp. 45–70.

Saunders, C. and Dalziel, P. 2017. Twenty-five years of counting for nothing: Waring's critique of national accounts. *Feminist Economics*, 23(2), pp. 200–218.

Sawer, M. 1993. Reclaiming social liberalism: The women's movement and the state. *Journal of Australian Studies*, 17(37), pp. 1–21.

Sawer, M. 1996. *Femocrats and Ecorats: Women's Policy Machinery in Australia, Canada and New Zealand* (No. 6). UNRISD Occasional Paper.

Sawer, M. 2007. Australia: The fall of the femocrat. In L. Outshoorn and J. Kantola (eds.), *Changing State Feminism* (pp. 20–40). London: Palgrave Macmillan.

Sawer, M. 2015. Does equality have a future? Feminism and social democracy in the era of neoliberalism. In A. Yeatman (ed.), *Feminism, Social Liberalism and Social Democracy in the Neo-Liberal Era* (pp. 24–35). Working Papers in the Human Rights and Public Life Program 1. Sydney: Whitlam Institute.

Sawer, M. 2016. Femocrat. In N. Naples, R. Hoogland, C. Wickramasinghe, W. Maithree, and W.C. Angela (eds.), *The Wiley Blackwell Encyclopedia of Gender and Sexuality Studies* (pp. 187–213). New Jersey: Wiley Blackwell.

Sawer, M. and Radford, G. 2008. *Making Women Count: A History of the Women's Electoral Lobby.* Sydney: UNSW Press.

Sax, S. 1984. *A Strife of Interests.* Sydney: Allen & Unwin.

Schaniel, W. and Neale, W. 2000. Karl Polanyi's forms of integration as ways of mapping. *Journal of Economic Issues*, 34(1), pp. 89–104.

Schumpeter, J.A. 1991. The crisis of the tax state. In R. Swedberg (ed.), *The Economics and Sociology of Capitalism* (pp. 99–140). New Jersey: Princeton University Press.

Schumpeter, J.A. 2003 [1943]. *Capitalism, Socialism and Democracy.* Routledge, e-book.

Scotton, R. 1969. Membership of voluntary health insurance. In J.R. Butler and D.P. Doessel (eds.), *Health Economics: Australian Readings.* Sydney: Australian Professional Publications.

Scotton, R. 1980. Health insurance: Medibank and after. In Cotton and Ferber (eds.), *Public Expenditure and Social Policy in Australia: The First Fraser Years, 1976–8*, vol. 2. Melbourne: Longman Chesire.

Scotton, R. 1993. Medibank: Why, how and wither? In H. Emy, O. Hughes and R. Matthews (eds.), *Whitlam Re-visited: Policy Development, Policies and Outcomes*. Sydney: Pluto Press.

Scotton, R. and Deeble, J. 1968. Compulsory health insurance in Australia. *The Australian Economic Review*, 1, pp. 9–16.

Sharp, R. 1992. The rise and rise of occupational superannuation under labor. *Journal of Australian Political Economy*, (30), pp. 24–41.

Sharp, R. and Broomhill, R. 2002. Budgeting for equality: The Australian experience. *Feminist Economics*, 8(1), pp. 25–47.

Shi, S., Valadkhani, A., Smyth, R. and Vahid, F. 2016. Dating the timeline of house price bubbles in Australian capital cities. *Economic Record*, 92(299), pp. 590–605.

Siedlecky, S. 2005. A short history of the Doctors Reform Society. *New Doctor*, (82), pp. 9–12.

Sinfield, A. 2018. Fiscal welfare. In B. Greve (ed.), *Routledge Handbook of the Welfare State* (pp. 23–33). New York: Routledge.

Smith, J. 2001. Tax expenditures and public health financing in Australia. *The Economic and Labour Relations Review*, 12(2), pp. 239–262.

Smith, J. 2017. Paying for care in Australia's 'wage earners' welfare state': The case of child endowment. In *Tax, Social Policy and Gender: Rethinking Equality and Efficiency* (pp. 161–205). Canberra: ANU E Press.

Smith, M. and Marden, P. 2008. Conservative think tanks and public politics. *Australian Journal of Political Science*, 43(4), pp. 699–717.

Smith, M. and Whitehouse, G. 2020. Wage-setting and gender pay equality in Australia: Advances, retreats and future prospects. *Journal of Industrial Relations*, 62(4), pp. 533–559.

Smyth, P. 1994. *Australian Social Policy: The Keynesian Chapter*. Sydney: University of New South Wales Press.

Spicker, P. 2012. Liberal welfare states. In *The Routledge Handbook of the Welfare State* (pp. 215–223). New York: Routledge.

Spies-Butcher, B. 2014. Markets, universalism and equity: Medicare's dual role in the Australian welfare state. *Journal of Australian Political Economy*, 73, pp. 18–40.

Spies-Butcher, B. 2020a. The temporary welfare state: The political economy of job keeper, job seeker and 'snap back'. *Journal of Australian Political Economy*, 85, pp. 155–163.

Spies-Butcher, B. 2020b. Advancing universalism in neoliberal times? Basic income, workfare and the politics of conditionality. *Critical Sociology*, 46(4–5), pp. 589–603.

Spies-Butcher, B. 2024. Healthcare in Australia: contesting marketized provision. In R. Loeppky, R. Change and D. Primrose (eds.), *The Routledge Handbook of the Political Economy of Health and Healthcare*. New York: Routledge.

Spies-Butcher, B. and Bryant, G. 2018. Accounting for income-contingent loans as a policy hybrid: Politics of discretion and discipline in financialising welfare states. *New Political Economy*, 23(6), pp. 768–785.

Spies-Butcher, B. and Bryant, G. 2024. The history and future of the tax state: Possibilities for a new fiscal politics beyond neoliberalism. *Critical Perspectives on Accounting*. In press. https://doi.org/10.1016/j.cpa.2023.102596.

Spies-Butcher, B. and Stebbing, A. 2019. Mobilising alternative futures: Generational accounting and the fiscal politics of ageing in Australia. *Ageing & Society*, 39(7), pp. 1409–1435.

Spies-Butcher, B., Phillips, B. and Henderson, T. 2020. Between universalism and targeting: Exploring policy pathways for an Australian Basic Income. *The Economic and Labour Relations Review*, 31(4), pp. 502–523.

St John, S. 2006. New Zealand's financial assistance for poor children: Are work incentives the answer?. *European Journal of Social Security*, 8(3), pp. 299–316.

Staines, Z., Marston, G., Bielefeld, S., Humpage, L., Mendes, P. and Peterie, M. 2021. Governing poverty: Compulsory income management and crime in Australia. *Critical Criminology*, 29, pp. 745–761.

Stebbing, A. 2015. The devil's in the detail: The hidden costs of private retirement incomes policy. In G. Meagher and S. Goodwin (eds.), *Markets, Rights and Power in Australian Social Policy* (pp. 115–151). Sydney University Press.

Stebbing, A. and Spies-Butcher, B. 2010. Universal welfare by 'other means'? Social tax expenditures and the Australian dual welfare state. *Journal of Social Policy*, 39(4), pp. 585–606.

Standing, G., 2011. *The Precariat: The New Dangerous Class*. Bloomsbury Academic.

Stebbing, A. and Spies-Butcher, B. 2016. The decline of a homeowning society? Asset-based welfare, retirement and intergenerational equity in Australia. *Housing Studies*, 31(2), pp. 190–207.

Stewart, A., Stanford, J. and Hardy, T. 2022. The wages crisis: Revisited. The Centre for Future Work, Sydney. Available at: https://www.bollettinoadapt.it/wp-content/uploads/2022/05/Wages_Crisis_Revisited_Formatted.pdf.

Stewart, M. 2018. *Personal Income Tax Cuts and the New Child Care Subsidy: Do They Address High Effective Marginal Tax Rates on Women's Work?*. Tax and Transfer Policy Institute, Australian National University.

Stewart, M. and Whiteford, P. 2018. Balancing efficiency and equity in the tax and transfer system. In *Hybrid Public Policy Innovations* (pp. 204–232). Routledge.

Stilwell, F. 1989. Economic rationalism is irrational. *Arena*, 87, pp. 139–145.

Stokes, G. 2004. The 'Australian settlement' and Australian political thought. *Australian Journal of Political Science*, 39(1), pp. 5–22.

Stone, D. 1996. *Capturing the political imagination: Think tanks and the policy process*. Psychology Press.

Streeck, W. 2014. *Buying Time: The Delayed Crisis of Democratic Capitalism*. New York: Verso Books.

Streeck, W. and Schäfer, A. eds. 2013. *Politics in the Age of Austerity*. New Jersey: John Wiley & Sons.

Streeck, W. and Thelen, K. 2005. Introduction: Institutional change in advanced political economies. In *Beyond Continuity: Institutional Change in Advanced Political Economies*. Oxford: Oxford University Press.

Suzuki, T. 2003. The epistemology of macroeconomic reality: The Keynesian Revolution from an accounting point of view. *Accounting, Organizations and Society*, 28(5), pp. 471–517. https://doi.org/10.1016/S0361-3682(01)00061-7.

Sydney Morning Herald (SMH). 2011. What the intervention failed to do. *Sydney Morning Herald*, May 2.

Tattersall, A. 2013. *Power in Coalition: Strategies for Strong Unions and Social Change*. Ithaca: Cornell University Press.

Taylor-Gooby, P. ed. 2004. *New Risks, New Welfare: The Transformation of the European Welfare State*. Oxford: OUP.

Tierney, J. and Cregan, C. 2013. Strategy and structure in a successful organising union: The transformational role of branch secretaries in the Australian Nursing Federation, Victorian Branch, 1989–2009. *Labour History*, 104, pp. 149–168.

Tilley, P. 2021. 1985 reform of the Australian tax system. Tax and Transfer Policy Institute-working paper, 7.

Tilton, T.A. 1990. *The Political Theory of Swedish Social Democracy: Through the Welfare State to Socialism*. USA: Oxford University Press.

Titmuss, R.M. 1965. The role of redistribution in social policy. *Social Security Bulletin*, 28, pp. 14–20.

Thelen, K. 2014. *Varieties of Liberalization and the New Politics of Social Solidarity*. New York, NY: Cambridge University Press.

Thompson, G., Hogan, A. and Rahimi, M. 2019. Private funding in Australian public schools: A problem of equity. *The Australian Educational Researcher*, 46(5), pp. 893–910.

Tobin, J., Pechman, J.A. and Mieszkowski, P.M. 1967. Is a negative income tax practical?. *The Yale Law Journal*, 77(1), pp. 1–27.

Tooze, A. 2021. *Shutdown: How Covid Shook the World's Economy*. New York: Penguin.

Towns, R. 2016. Voting valkyries: The first Australian feminists. *Agora*, 51(3), pp. 4–11.

Treasury. 2010. Intergenerational Report 2010. Australian Government, Canberra.

Treasury. 2012. Distributional analysis of superannuation taxation concessions: A paper to the superannuation roundtable. Australian Government, Canberra. Available online at: http://www.treasury.gov.au/Policy-Topics/SuperannuationAndRetirement/Distributional-analysis-of-superannuation-taxation-concessions.

Treasury. 2022. Statement 5: Expenses and net capital investment. Budget 2022–23. Australian Government, Canberra.

Treasury. 2023. Tax expenditures and insights statement. February 2023. Australian Government, Canberra.

Tronto, J.C. 1993. *Moral Boundaries: A Political Argument for an Ethic of Care*. New York: Routledge.

Tucker, S.B. and Cadora, E. 2003. Justice reinvestment. *IDEAS for an Open Society*, 3(3), pp. 2–5.

Van Gellecum, Y., Baxter, J. and Western, M. 2008. Neoliberalism, gender inequality and the Australian labour market. *Journal of Sociology*, 44(1), pp. 45–63.

Vincent, E. 2023. *Who Care? Life on Welfare in Australia*. Melbourne University Press.

Vinson, T. 2002. *Inquiry into the Provision of Public Education in NSW: Report of the Vinson Inquiry*. Annandale: Pluto Press.

Vromen, A. 2015. Campaign entrepreneurs in online collective action: GetUp! In Australia. *Social Movement Studies*, 14(2), pp. 195–213.

Vromen, A. and Coleman, W. 2013. Online campaigning organizations and storytelling strategies: GetUp! in Australia. *Policy & Internet*, 5(1), pp. 76–100.

Vromen, A., Xenos, M.A. and Loader, B. 2015. Young people, social media and connective action: From organisational maintenance to everyday political talk. *Journal of Youth Studies*, 18(1), pp. 80–100.

Wacquant, L. 2009. *Punishing the Poor: The Neoliberal Government of Social Insecurity*. Politics, history, and culture. Durham: Duke University Press.

Wacquant, L. 2012. Three steps to a historical anthropology of actually existing neoliberalism. *Social Anthropology*, 20(1), pp. 66–79.

Walden, I. 1995. 'That was slavery days': Aboriginal domestic servants in New South Wales in the twentieth century. *Labour History*, (69), pp. 196–209.

Walter, M., Kukutai, T., Carroll, S.R. and Rodriguez-Lonebear, D. 2021. *Indigenous Data Sovereignty and Policy*. New York: Taylor & Francis.

Waring, M. 1999. 'A Women's Reckoning', Counting for Nothing: What Men Value and What Women are Worth. Toronto: University of Toronto Press.

Watson, D. 2003. The rise and rise of public private partnerships: Challenges for public accountability. *Australian Accounting Review*, 13(31), pp. 2–14.

Watts, R. 1980. The origins of the Australian welfare state. *Australian Historical Studies*, 19(75), pp. 175–198.

Weisser, R. 2015. The budget bounce. *Quadrant*, 59(6), pp. 18–20.

Whait, R.B., Lowies, B., Rossini, P., McGreal, S. and Dimovski, B. 2019. The reverse mortgage conundrum: Perspectives of older households in Australia. *Habitat International*, 94, p. 102073.

Whiteford, P. 2013. Australia: Inequality and prosperity and their impacts in a radical welfare state, Crawford School of Public Policy, Australian National University.

Whiteford, P. 2015a. Tales of Robin Hood (part 1): Welfare myths and realities in the United Kingdom and Australia. *Australian Review of Public Affairs*. Available at: http://www.australianreview.net/digest/2015/09/whiteford.html

Whiteford, P. 2015b. Inequality and its socioeconomic impacts. *Australian Economic Review*, 48(1), pp. 83–92.

Whiteford, P. 2017. Trends in income inequality in Australia. *Australian Quarterly*, 88(3), pp. 30–36.

Whiteford, P. and Bradbury, B. 2022. How can more people be on unemployment benefits than before COVID, with fewer unemployed Australians? Here's how. *The Conversation*, April 26. Available at: https://theconversation.com/how-can-more-people-be-on-unemployment-benefits-than-before-covid-with-fewer-unemployed-australians-heres-how-181733.

Whiteford, P., Redmond, G. and Adamson, E. 2011. Middle class welfare in Australia: How has the distribution of cash benefits changed since the 1980s? *Australian Journal of Labour Economics*, 14(2), pp. 81–102.

Whitehouse, E. 2009. Pensions during the crisis: Impact on retirement income systems and policy responses. *The Geneva Papers on Risk and Insurance-Issues and Practice*, 34(4), pp. 536–547.

Williams, F. 2001. In and beyond New Labour: Towards a new political ethics of care. *Critical Social Policy*, 21(4), pp. 467–493.

Wilson, S. 2017. The politics of 'minimum wage' welfare states: The changing significance of the minimum wage in the liberal welfare regime. *Social Policy & Administration*, 51(2), pp. 244–264.

Wilson, S. 2021. *Living Wages and the Welfare State: The Anglo-American Social Model in Transition*. Bristol: Policy Press.

Wilson, S. and Turnbull, N. 2001. Wedge politics and welfare reform in Australia. *Australian Journal of Politics & History*, 47(3), pp. 384–404.

Wilson, S. and Spies-Butcher, B. 2011. When labour makes a difference: Union mobilization and the 2007 federal election in Australia. *British Journal of Industrial Relations*, 49, pp. s306–s331.

Wilson, S., Spies-Butcher, B. and Stebbing, A. 2009. Targets and taxes: Explaining the welfare orientations of the Australian public. *Social Policy & Administration*, 43(5), pp. 508–525.

Wilson, S., Spies-Butcher, B., Stebbing, A. and St John, S. 2013. Wage-Earners' welfare after economic reform: Refurbishing, retrenching or hollowing out social protection in Australia and New Zealand?. *Social Policy & Administration*, 47(6), pp. 623–646.

Wilson, S.R. 1999. Productivity. In O'Hara (ed.), *Encyclopedia of Political Economy, L-Z* (pp. 918–921). New York: Routledge.

Wood, D. and Griffiths, K. 2019. *Generation Gap: Ensuring a Fair Go for Younger Australians.* Melbourne: Grattan Institute.

Woodbury, S.A. 2017. Universal basic income. In *The American Middle Class: An Economic Encyclopedia of Progress and Poverty.* Santa Barbara: ABC-CLIO.

World Bank. 1994. *Averting the Old Age Crisis: Policies to Protect the Old and Promote Growth.* Washington, DC: World Bank.

Wren, A. 2013. *The Political Economy of the Service Transition.* Oxford: Oxford University Press.

Wright, C. 2014. The prices and incomes accord: Its significance, impact and legacy. *Journal of Industrial Relations,* 56(2), pp. 264–272.

Yates, J. and Bradbury, B. 2010. Home ownership as a (crumbling) fourth pillar of social insurance in Australia. *Journal of Housing and the Built Environment,* 25(2), pp. 193–211.

Yates, J. and Yanotti, M. 2016. Australia's 25 years with a deregulated housing finance system: Looking back and looking forward. In Lunde and Whitehead (eds.), *Milestones in European Housing Finance* (pp. 37–53).

Yeatman, A. 2020. *Bureaucrats, Technocrats, Femocrats: Essays on the Contemporary Australian State.* Routledge.

Yoo, K.-Y. and de Serres, A. Tax treatment of private pension savings in OECD countries and the net tax cost per unit of contribution to tax-favoured schemes (October 2004). Available at SSRN: https://ssrn.com/abstract=607185 or http://dx.doi.org/10.2139/ssrn.607185.

Zhang, Y. and Andrew, J. 2014. Financialisation and the conceptual framework. *Critical Perspectives on Accounting,* 25(1), pp. 17–26.

INDEX

www.ingramcontent.com/pod-product-compliance
Lightning Source LLC
Chambersburg PA
CBHW030649270326
41929CB00007B/281